THE COURSE OF GOD'S PROVIDENCE

NORTH AMERICAN RELIGIONS

Series Editors: Tracy Fessenden (Religious Studies, Arizona State University), Laura Levitt (Religious Studies, Temple University), and David Harrington Watt (History, Haverford College)

In recent years a cadre of industrious, imaginative, and theoretically sophisticated scholars of religion have focused their attention on North America. As a result the field is far more subtle, expansive, and interdisciplinary than it was just two decades ago. The North American Religions series builds on this transformative momentum. Books in the series move among the discourses of ethnography, cultural analysis, and historical study to shed new light on a wide range of religious experiences, practices, and institutions. They explore topics such as lived religion, popular religious movements, religion and social power, religion and cultural reproduction, and the relationship between secular and religious institutions and practices. The series focus primarily, but not exclusively, on religion in the United States in the twentieth and twenty-first centuries.

Books in the series:

The Course of God's Providence

Religion, Health, and the Body in Early America

Philippa Koch

NEW YORK UNIVERSITY PRESS

New York

NEW YORK UNIVERSITY PRESS
New York
www.nyupress.org

References to Internet websites (URLs) were accurate at the time of writing. Neither the author nor New York University Press is responsible for URLs that may have expired or changed since the manuscript was prepared.

Library of Congress Cataloging-in-Publication Data
Names: Koch, Philippa, author.
Title: The course of God's providence : religion, health, and the body in early America / Philippa Koch.
Description: New York : New York University Press, [2021] |
Series: North American religions | Includes bibliographical references and index.
Identifiers: LCCN 2020033224 (print) | LCCN 2020033225 (ebook) |
ISBN 9781479806683 (cloth) | ISBN 9781479806720 (ebook) |
ISBN 9781479806744 (ebook other)
Subjects: LCSH: Medicine—Religious aspects—Christianity—History—18th century. | Medicine—United States—History—18th century. | United States—Church history—18th century. | Health—Religious aspects—Christianity—History—18th century.
Classification: LCC BT732.2 .K63 2021 (print) | LCC BT732.2 (ebook) |
DDC 261.5/61097309033—dc23
LC record available at https://lccn.loc.gov/2020033224
LC ebook record available at https://lccn.loc.gov/2020033225

New York University Press books are printed on acid-free paper, and their binding materials are chosen for strength and durability. We strive to use environmentally responsible suppliers and materials to the greatest extent possible in publishing our books.

Manufactured in the United States of America

10 9 8 7 6 5 4 3 2 1

Also available as an ebook

For my parents, Margaret and Gary Koch

CONTENTS

FIGURES

PREFACE

I completed the final revisions for this book under quarantine, prompted by the global pandemic of the coronavirus disease (COVID-19). While I could have done without this confluence of events, I found myself reading with a new perspective, a new empathy.

This book begins with the role of narrative and perspective in sickness writings in order to understand how early Americans—and eighteenth-century Protestants more broadly—perceived the work of God's providence in their past and present illnesses. Their interpretations of God's guidance and direction of human life were varied and changed over the century, but they always sought to find an overarching plot and transcendent meaning in their experiences of suffering. They worked hard to reconsider, to interpret, to narrate, and often to renarrate their stories in light of upheavals, disasters, and pain.

Over the course of writing this book, I revisited whether narrative was the place to start. As I completed this work in the midst of the pandemic, I could not imagine another. The COVID-19 health crisis forced a reaccounting of our lives. Some of us, echoing Susan Sontag, might decry any effort to apply a moral meaning to illness, particularly a meaning that points to a punishing God, a chosen people, or a particular sin.[1] Yet the virus compelled us to confront what lessons could be learned from this experience that we might look back on and apply in the future. Social media became awash with attempts to imagine or to describe a #newnormal; news media offered opinions on how our response will be viewed by future economists, historians, and artists; various archives and libraries urged people to journal and keep records.[2] Most of us are acutely aware of our limited perspective in any effort to rethink, renarrate, reinterpret, or replot our situations and life stories, but we still try.

Religious or not, these efforts map onto or at the very least echo the ways early American Protestants emphasized the role of reflection, repentance, and hope in responding to sickness. Looking back was a chance to recognize the limitations of human perspective and, at the same time, to glimpse the work of God—or, for the more skeptical, the laws of nature—to seek trust and faith, and to hope for a yet uncertain future. Unlike early Americans, however, most Americans today are uncomfortable acknowledging human limitation. We have been shaped by positive thought—popularized most famously by Norman Vincent Peale, a twentieth-century American minister. Peale's best-selling book, *The Power of Positive Thinking* (1952), merged elements of Christianity and New Thought, a movement focused on "healthy-mindedness" with roots in various nineteenth-century American religious communities— from Transcendentalism to Christian Science. Although not without critique, positive thought has proved lasting and is strikingly evident in today's self-help culture and politics. President Donald Trump was a congregant in Peale's Marble Collegiate Church and has been surrounded by Prosperity Gospel preachers steeped in various iterations of positive thought theology as they urge their followers to "name-it-and-claim-it" in their gospel of health and wealth. Even for those Americans who do not participate in the Prosperity Gospel movement—indeed, even for those who do not identify as religious at all—positive thinking is pervasive in our everyday lives in conversations, therapies, politics, and consumerism.[3]

Most Americans have struggled with the effects of COVID-19 and what they reveal in terms of our fundamental human limitations, from inadequate testing capabilities to not having a ready cure or vaccine.[4] We have been stunned by the inadequacies of our economic and health care systems, the weaknesses of which quickly became glaringly obvious.[5] We have been dismayed by the inequities revealed or heightened by COVID-19 and our response: with African Americans and Native Americans disproportionately affected and dying, and grocery store, delivery, and fast-food workers deemed essential and, at the same time, denied hazard pay or benefits.[6] We have been disturbed by the challenges of public ethical reasoning—when we question at what point the number of deaths outweighs the economic damage caused by social distancing, or when caretakers and hospital ethics boards are asked to choose who gets a ventilator, depending on "points" awarded based on factors like life expectancy, quality of life, pregnancy, political office, medical expertise, and more.[7] We have been shocked by religious leaders who flout governmental guidelines, urging followers to gather and worship even as we—and they—saw evidence of how such meetings could result in devastating outbreaks.[8] We have been saddened to see people die and mourn alone.[9]

The modern American can-do spirit has been flummoxed by this epidemic-level confrontation with limitation. This quandary, I came to realize, perfectly illustrates a key argument of this book. We too often assume that early Americans were passive or even "fatalist" in their response to suffering. Resigned to God, the story goes, they simply accepted suffering and awaited death. But early Americans did no better in accepting the limitations imposed by sickness than we. They still tried to write, for example, even with more impediments than we face as we type on our phones with one thumb. They still tried to gather, carefully. They still shared health advice and anecdotes. They still pursued quarantines, cures, and medical advancements. They still sought to care, they still mourned, and they still made meaning. Early American Protestants interpreted their pain in terms of God's providential guidance, but this guidance was more often imagined in terms of a merciful and wise plan than we might expect, given the wrathful punishing God highlighted by some evangelical Christians today—including elected government officials—who claim God is targeting specific communities and "sins."[10] Of course, like us, early Americans could also assign blame: God's judgment over the vanity of the theater was identified as a potential cause of Philadelphia's 1793 yellow fever epidemic, for example, and African American nurses who served during that epidemic were characterized by some as greedy.[11] For the COVID-19 pandemic, in addition to claims of God's judgment, blame has been variously assigned to the Chinese, antiscience evangelicals, Donald Trump, liberal fearmongers, and more.[12]

Like all epidemics, COVID-19 offers an intense reminder of what is actually a constant: the fragility of our bodies and communities, on the one hand, and the way we deal with or interpret our limitations—our mortality—on the other.[13] Because of the successes of modern medicine, many of us have been privileged not to dwell in this constant. Scholars of religion and history, trained to work with our brains and typing fingers, have long loved to explore ideas, epochs, transitions, systems. The virus forced us to type at home, some with children in the background, worried about health, families, and food supplies, and appalled by the vast disparities displayed in pandemic experiences. My hope is that we hold onto this experience moving forward, recognizing that our subjects and their stories likewise were shaped by varied experiences of embodiment—that their theologies, practices, livelihoods, politics, and communal lives were fundamentally shaped by health, sickness, loss, pain, fear, and hope.

Introduction

This is a book about the persistence of religious responses to sickness, medicine, and benevolence in eighteenth-century America and the Atlantic world. It is about the physical realities of suffering and the ways in which Protestants attempted to interpret this suffering, in terms of both God's providence—or direction—over human life and health and the human responsibility and freedom to respond. And it is about the persistence of this providential thought, even at the cusp of modern medicine and in a secularizing world.

As we will see, though many scholars have assumed a turn away from religious understandings of sickness and health during the Enlightenment era, Protestants continued to rely on a religious framework in their responses to suffering and engagements with modern medicine, missions, benevolence, and science. This book offers a counterpoint to those who have presumed that people who embraced a belief in providence would therefore be passive in their response to sickness, perceiving it as God's will. Looking to the practice and embodiment of religious ideas in the eighteenth century, this book shows, instead, how American and European Protestants continued to underscore their faith in God's providence, believing it could and *should* motivate their work in the world.

The book fills a notable gap, as there is much more robust literature on religion and medicine in the nineteenth and twentieth centuries. By focusing on American religion in the eighteenth century, this book shows the continuing salience of a belief in providence, even as modern medicine developed. Indeed, the ways in which the colonial world thought about questions of God's will in sickness and health illuminate the continuing power of Protestant ideas and practices in American society today.

Providence can sound complicated and far removed from everyday life, but early American Christian individuals or communities dealing with sickness and disorder confronted the question of providence on a very immediate level. Where did suffering come from, and what did it mean? Was it sent by God? And, if so, what could humans do to ease pain and promote recovery? How could they live out God's will and intention, and at what point did they risk interfering with God's plan?

These were heady questions, and in the eighteenth century they concerned the foremost philosophers of the age. They were considered and discussed in formal, published treatises. But they were also questions asked in the intimate quarters of the sickroom and in the pastoral and private writings of individuals who suffered pain and loss, and who rejoiced in efforts toward recovery and health.

To understand the place of providential thought in the modern world, we must linger over these personal, intimate, and often tragic accounts of suffering and health. The view of providence forged in response to sickness shaped Protestants' actions and responses to broader social changes, including some of the most important developments of the eighteenth century: transformations in medicine, expanding missionary enterprises, burgeoning reform movements, new ideas of maternity and nature, and a rapidly changing political world.

* * *

Christians have long understood providence to refer to God's oversight and governance of the created order. It is a doctrine that transcends Christian divisions. During the sixteenth-century Protestant Reformation, theologians emphasized anew the role of God's grace in human salvation, and this intensified early modern Protestants' attention to God's providential direction over the details of their individual and social lives. They sought to discern God's hand in human history, in their faith, and in their suffering. To perceive God's providential direction over the chaos of human affairs was to find consolation, meaning, and purpose.[1]

By the eighteenth century, however, Protestants lived in a time of great change in understandings of providence. In the wake of the mechanistic philosophies of Isaac Newton and René Descartes, God came to be seen as more distant, human suffering was seen as a problem to be solved, and humans' ability to interact with and to alter nature and society was viewed more positively. Some people came to limit providence to be more "general" and to think of God as more hands-off—as, famously, a clockmaker who set the world in motion or as a judge who ruled at the end of time. These Enlightenment ideas affected non-Christian views of providence as well, contributing to extensive conversations on God, nature, chance, and, correspondingly, belief and the social order.[2]

Yet even in the midst of this growing emphasis on a more hands-off God and general providence, many Protestants remained committed to a God who was active and involved in the created order—a God of "special" or "particular" providence. This was a God who not only responded to sin with wrath and rewarded repentance with mercy, but also encouraged humans to witness providence through their faithful response to sickness, engagement in medicine, actions to alleviate suffering, and efforts to build God's kingdom through conversion and care. Providence persisted, in part, because it demanded a human response, which, in turn, fostered some of the newest, most forward-looking aspirations of the eighteenth century.

This human responsiveness, engagement, and action in response to sickness and suffering is often missed by scholars of medicine. They tend to ignore eighteenth-century Christian women and men or to dismiss their writings on sickness and medicine as antiscientific, archaically reliant on the spiritual, or fatalist.[3] But these women and men lived in a world where the religious and medical were tightly interwoven. Religious devotion and the pursuit of human knowledge and improvement went hand in hand. Long-standing Christian conceptions of the soul affected how women and men viewed and treated the sick human body, both spiritually and medically, while medicine and health reform became central means for Protestants to pursue missionary goals. The stories of Christian women and men are part of the history of medicine.[4]

To be clear, providence is not the same as predestination, though they are often confused. Both relate to the governance of God over creation, but predestination is a theological doctrine focused specifically on salvation. Doctrines of predestination vary depending on theological tradition, but all connect salvation to God's election rather than human free will. Followers of John Calvin, a Protestant reformer, believe that God has eternally elected some humans for salvation and some for damnation. This election is entirely a matter of God's decree. It is unconditional: once God has decided, neither human will nor effort can affect a person's chance of salvation.[5] Predestination is a critically important doctrine within Calvinist theology and life, shaping views of human nature, the church, and society. Perhaps for that reason it is often conflated with providence, leading scholars mistakenly to perceive providence itself as a particularly Calvinist worldview.

For scholars of religion and medicine of the eighteenth-century Atlantic world, two additional misunderstandings are related to this mistaken identification of providence and Calvinist predestination.[6] First, because studies of early American religion have long focused on New England Puritans—who were theologically Calvinist—many assume that the dominant theology of eighteenth-century America was Calvinism and, therefore, mistakenly associate any early American discussion of providence with Calvinist predestination. In contrast, as historian Alexandra Walsham's detailed study of providentialism in early modern England shows, providential faith was quite widespread, shaping a "collective Protestant consciousness" in an era and place marked by confessional and social divisions. She describes providentialism as "a set of ideological spectacles through which individuals of all social levels and from all positions on the confessional spectrum were apt to view their universe, an invisible prism which helped them to focus the refractory meanings of both petty and perplexing events."[7]

Focusing on providential thought is a way to highlight the unity among the diversity of Christians—particularly among the diverse Protestants—in early America. Even more than early modern England, eighteenth-century America was a religiously diverse place, with Christian communities spanning a wide spectrum of theological commitments. There were non-Christians in early America as well, but most colonists were Christians, and most of these were Protestants. Providence was crucial not only to New England Puritans and their successors, the Congregationalists, but also to Methodists, Presbyterians, and German-speaking Pietist Lutherans, among others. Though few historians study different eighteenth-century Protestant communities together, especially not English- and German-speaking Protestants, Protestants read common works and corresponded, and providence was a part of their conversation.[8]

The second significant misunderstanding caused by identifying providence with Calvinist predestination is that scholars often associate providential faith with fatalism or passivity. Because predestination is a doctrine of salvation in which humans have no ability to change an outcome predetermined by God, some scholars mistakenly assume that faith in providence likewise meant humans were passive in their everyday lives, including in response to sickness and suffering.[9] Nineteenth-century novelists and health reformers played a significant role in creating this illusion about colonial Americans' faith in providence. In Nathaniel Hawthorne's *The Scarlet Letter* (1850), the Reverend Arthur Dimmesdale, Hester Prynne's meek paramour, responded anxiously to her plea to escape: "I have no other thought than to drag on my earthly existence in the sphere where Providence hath placed me."[10] Dimmesdale, with his helpless petition to providence, personified Hawthorne's negative assessment of the Calvinism of his Puritan forebears.

Nineteenth-century health reformers and homeopathic practitioners, meanwhile, presented their approach to health as a shift from the "fatalist" Calvinism of the past to a more active, positive Arminian faith. Arminianism—a theology most often associated with Methodism—distinguished itself from Calvinism by stressing human freedom in the pursuit of salvation.[11] Nineteenth-century health reformers suggested that this Arminian focus on human initiative in salvation paralleled the need for human effort in the pursuit of physical health.[12] But this parallel relies on a false premise; Calvinist predestination does not limit human freedom outside matters of salvation. The image of early Americans resigned passively to disease and suffering is, in many ways, a product of the nineteenth century.[13]

Protestants were active in their response to suffering. In the very effort to understand God's providence in their everyday lives, Protestant men and women were engaged in the significant and active work of interpretation. They sought to comprehend their past and present experiences and actions in terms of God's will and the proper human response. Their involvement in medicine was one example of such a response. Some have suggested that medical activity represented a decline from religious orthodoxy—that it was a sign of secularization—but eighteenth-century Protestants perceived their medical efforts to be a part of God's providential plan for human history.[14]

Protestants did sometimes worry about interfering with God's providence when faced with an innovation. Smallpox inoculation, for example, was a development that sparked intense debate.[15] Yet because the interpretation of providence depended on human reflection on past experiences and outcomes, the concept was flexible. It was possible to fathom that God gave humans reason and resources to improve the world. It had happened before, and with careful discernment, Christians believed they could forge ahead with new ideas and practices, hopeful in God's direction. This approach allowed for Protestants' involvement in some of the major developments of the eighteenth century. The doctrine of providence, like religion itself, was dynamic, responding to changes in the broader society while maintaining its ability to orient believers in times of suffering.[16]

Protestants' interpretation of providence was bound to practices of narrative and reflection. Through shared texts, Protestants both imagined and created a community that taught a certain way of looking back—of retrospecting—on the past and its meaning in terms of their life story and God's superintendence. Retrospection was a crucial tool for contemplating providence. God's will and grace were beyond human reason to know, but Protestants nonetheless thought they could glimpse evidence of God's providence in their lives by reflecting on the past. Looking back on a past sickness offered some clarity about the experience. Protestants could consider their suffering, actions, and the outcome, and—although they could not fully discern God's will—they could begin to fathom God's judgment, mercy, and intent. At the same time, such reflection on the past was a way to contemplate right interpretation and action in the present and future. When faced with sickness and suffering, Protestants tried to discern God's providential direction by considering how their circumstances and current actions might be perceived in retrospect.[17] Retrospection was an activity that occurred, most straightforwardly, in narrative, and narratives became a common and expected way of responding to sickness and suffering. But the habit of retrospectively reflecting on providence also shaped Protestants' actions and decisions in realms apart from writing, including medicine, benevolence, missions, and politics.

This method for contemplating providence and human activity through retrospective narrative is exemplified in a well-known tract by August Hermann Francke. Francke was the founder of a cluster of charitable institutions—including an orphanage, school, and hospital—in Glaucha, later Halle, Germany, in the late seventeenth century. He was part of a larger renewal movement within Protestantism that, within Lutheranism, was known as Pietism. He wrote about this work in a narrative, which was translated into English in 1706 as *An Abstract of the Marvellous Footsteps of Divine Providence*. Francke's story was influential among both German- and English-speaking Protestants throughout the Atlantic world. It was quoted in the private writings of women like Catharina Gronau, a Pietist Salzburger refugee in colonial Georgia, and Sarah Osborn, a Congregationalist and revivalist in Newport, Rhode Island, as well as in published works by ministers like the New England Puritan Cotton Mather and the itinerating Anglican revivalist George Whitefield.[18]

Francke's account is a retrospective reflection on God's providence over his efforts to house, educate, and care for the orphaned and needy—to help the suffering social body. The "footsteps" of Francke's title illuminated how retrospection worked both to confirm God's providence and to further human action on its behalf. Footsteps were, in one sense, the traces left behind. They were visible in retrospect, evidencing God's care to provide and guide in times of need and despair. Even if such care was not immediately obvious in the midst of distress, by looking back and reflecting, Christians found evidence of God's constant superintendence over human affairs. But footsteps could also be followed, pointing to a future direction and course in life. The practice of enumerating God's providences in past events served to foster and strengthen faith moving forward. In a preface to an English translation of Francke's account, the minister Josiah Woodward argued that the narrative revealed "*such a Glorious* Train *of surprizing* Providences" that it was "*enough to* strengthen *a very* weak Faith, *and to* enliven *a Heart almost* dead *in Despondency*." As Francke's account went on to detail, hearts were enlivened to work in the world, to educate, to provide medicine, and to convert sinners.[19]

If we are to understand how eighteenth-century Christians conceived of human freedom in response to suffering and in relation to God, we must avoid nineteenth-century caricatures and return to the voices of eighteenth-century people themselves. They testify that a commitment to providence in interpreting sickness and pain did not demand the rejection of medical treatment or a simple resignation to suffering—at either the individual or social level. Rather, as Francke's account and

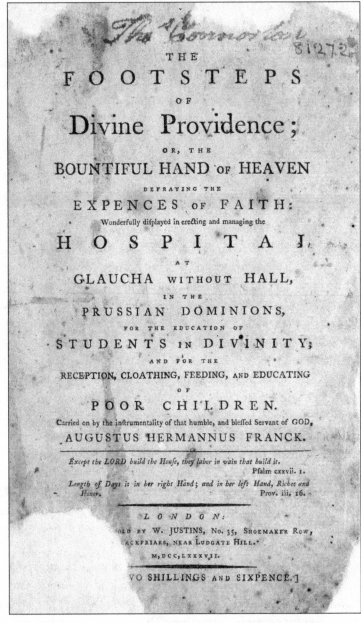

THE

F O O T S T E P S

OF

Divine Providence;

OR, THE

BOUNTIFUL HAND OF HEAVEN

DEFRAYING THE

EXPENCES OF FAITH:

Wonderfully difplayed in erecting and managing the

H O S P I T A L

AT

GLAUCHA WITHOUT HALL,

IN THE

PRUSSIAN DOMINIONS,

FOR THE EDUCATION OF

STUDENTS IN DIVINITY;

AND FOR THE

RECEPTION, CLOATHING, FEEDING, AND EDUCATING

OF

POOR CHILDREN.

Carried on by the inftrumentality of that humble, and bleffed Servant of GOD,

AUGUSTUS HERMANNUS FRANCK.

Except the LORD build the Houfe, they labor in vain that build it.
Pfalm cxxvii. 1.

Length of Days is in her right Hand; and in her left Hand, Riches and Honor.
Prov. iii. 16.

L O N D O N:

OLD BY W. JUSTINS, No. 35, SHOEMAKER ROW,
BLACKFRIARS, NEAR LUDGATE HILL.

M,DCC,LXXXVII.

[TWO SHILLINGS AND SIXPENCE.]

Figure 1.1. Title page of a later English edition of August Hermann Francke's *Segens-volle Fußstapfen*, first published in 1701. Augustus Hermannus Franck, *The Footsteps of Divine Providence* (London: W. Justins, 1787). Wellcome Library, https://wellcomecollection.org/works/su3ek2jv, Public Domain Mark.

its reach and reception attest, providential belief prompted widespread Christian engagement and response.

The unity and activity that providential thought and narration provided to the diverse community of Protestants in the eighteenth-century Atlantic world are significant. While some scholars have recognized the continuing prevalence of providential thought in creating a Protestant consensus—essential to the later construction of American nationalism—they often suggest that this "basic" faith in divine direction was limited: "a kind of lowest-common-denominator Protestantism." The providential thought shared by early American Protestants, however, was far from merely an ingredient in Protestant nationalism and was anything but basic. It was a powerful tool in shaping joint and corresponding Protestant activities, including missions, medicine, benevolence, and—critical for the early republic—the cultivation of maternal ideals. There was a significant consensus surrounding providential thought and practice in Protestant communities. Its power becomes evident when these distinctive communities are brought together, and when we carefully investigate the reach of providence—the idea—into the intimacy of diverse Protestants' lives and practices.[20]

Eighteenth-century Christians lived in a world of words, bodies, and relationships. They were taught to perceive, narrate, and respond to their experiences in terms that stressed God's providence, and they embraced a variety of practices grounded in this providential thought—practices that were central to religious teachings and right belief, familial and communal connection, and missionary and medical endeavors. Their conviction of God's sovereignty and oversight defined how they viewed their bodies and societies, and what they could do to change them. Theirs is not a tidy story of religiously motivated rejection of medicine or secular advancement. It is rather a richly textured story of living in a world of theology, suffering, community, and change.

* * *

Providential faith and Christian activity were joined in the eighteenth century. Protestants who believed in, turned to, and narrated God's providence were not passive; they responded to sickness and suffering by reflecting, writing, engaging medicine, volunteering, and evangelizing. While these activities were shaped by developments in science and political thought, that does not mean they are rightly interpreted as evidence of secularization. Some scholars have seen the eighteenth century as a period of religious decline distinguished by diminished faith in providence. Providence has figured particularly large in narratives of disenchantment, where scholars have argued that Protestants' faith in providence decreased—alongside a decline in magic more generally—in a world marked by increasing faith in human knowledge and capability. I argue, instead, that providential thought persisted in varied, sometimes hidden, and often robust forms in so-called secular developments within human knowledge and action, including medicine and charity.

Recent scholarship has highlighted problematic aspects of key components of secularization theories. Secularization has been defined as a decline in religion in relation to several shifts in the early modern and modern world. One shift is described as "institutional differentiation," that is, the separation of social institutions—including political and economic—from the religious sphere. This kind of secularization occurred in early America when, for example, individual colonies and, later, states developed governments that not only promoted religious toleration but also eventually disestablished religion and repealed religious oaths for holding office. As scholars have shown, however, this differentiation was and is incomplete; there are many ways in which religion—and Protestantism in particular—has continued to shape American political and legal life. Another shift associated with secularization is "deinstitutionalization," which refers to declining membership and participation in religious communities. Deinstitutionalization is also a contested aspect of secularization theses. Membership in religious communities—in terms of both numbers and commitment—is not easy to gauge, and, furthermore, even as some religious communities show declines in membership, other forms of religion and spirituality have been and are flourishing in the United States.[21]

Central for arguments about providence, however, is the final component of secularization theses: "disenchantment." Disenchantment refers to a process of "rationalization," in which "religious categories and interpretations are replaced by scientific ones," and in which religious practice is focused no longer on religious categories but on ethics. This aspect of secularization narratives has had significant staying power, particularly when narrating the shifts in religion, medicine, and benevolence in the

eighteenth century, shifts that seemingly required a corresponding decline in providential thought. Modernity brought with it a seismic rift,
the story goes, and the fault line ran through providence. Rather than
focus on the otherworldly or salvific significance of their experiences,
humans began to focus on this world. They turned to science, reason,
and the mechanical workings of nature and the human body instead of
seeking answers in God's direction. They turned to medical practitioners
instead of pastors. They turned to private charities and reform societies
instead of churches. They sought to work actively to improve human
life—to find "happiness"—instead of to remain passive, to contemplate,
and to please God.[22]

This supposed transformation of providential thought in the eighteenth century has been crucial to the tale of disenchantment and of
the transition to our modern, secular world. Scholars have shown how
in the age of Enlightenment, particularly among Deists, God's providence ceased to be the center around which humans oriented their
actions and became, instead, a more general providence of creation
or final judgment.[23] But there is a problem with this tale. First, there
was no immediate or wholesale paradigm shift from religious to secular, from God's providence to human activity, science, and progress.
As historian Colin Jager has shown, the "familiar modern divisions
between science and religion" developed "gradually and over many
years." And in the seventeenth and eighteenth centuries, "for the great
majority of British intellectuals, science and theology were mutually
informing means of investigating God's world." Many intellectuals presupposed a divinely designed world as they pursued empirical
observations and mechanistic explanations of nature and the human
body. Among eighteenth-century British writers, Jager reveals, a critical consensus of theology and science developed, and it was a consensus that pointed to a continuing role for God, particularly in the realm
of design and creation. These writers would eventually take different
paths, but the modern world they illuminate was always "multiple . . .
an ongoing process of creating and reforming." It was never static.
There was no single paradigm shift.[24]

The second problem with our received tale of declining providential
thought is that it depends exclusively on elite sources and intellectual
debates. When we reach beyond these sources, we further expand our

understanding of providence and the modern world. Narratives of sickness, medicine, and benevolence open the meaning of God's providence to the diverse women and men who applied to, relied on, and struggled with it in their theologies, stories, and everyday lives. Throughout the eighteenth century, the majority of Americans continued to write with constant and central appeals to God's providential direction and the ability of faithful humans to witness this providence in their lives and actions, in belief and doubt, in science and in health. They were part of a consensus; they reveal an ongoing, complicated, and adaptive process, in which providential belief and medical advancements persisted, often side by side, into the modern world.

This more nuanced story challenges stubborn narratives of eighteenth-century secularization and medicine and forces us to consider how a wide variety of Protestants held together new optimism about human reason, science, and benevolence with long-standing Christian commitments to repentance, faith, and salvation. This reassessment is critical as we try to understand better the processes of secularization in our time. As scholars question secularization from multiple angles, they are reimagining "disenchantment" today. There is abundant evidence of people who have maintained—and are maintaining—religious beliefs and practices alongside modern medicine. To comprehend these contemporary manifestations of religious life, some scholars have pointed to a "re-enchantment" in contemporary society.[25] But equally critical is a reexamination of "disenchantment" historically and, in particular, its long-supposed roots in the eighteenth century and the decline of providential thought.

Many early American Protestants were able to accept the new promises and insights of modern medicine and politics within their providential worldview. In fact, many actually relied on providential thought in their pursuit and support of critical social and political visions of the modern world. As we will see, this is evidenced in their embrace of missionary medicine, epidemic responses, and emerging views of maternity. While early Americans adapted their belief in providence in response to new developments in theology, medicine, benevolence, and politics, they also imbued these developments with religious—here providential—meaning.

It is vital that we reconsider the eighteenth century and recognize it as a moment not of decline but instead of persisting and transforming religious belief and practice. This simultaneous persistence and transformation shed light on our own time and our own fraught relationship with modernity and enchantment. We have increasingly realized the failure of modernity's promises to control, alleviate, and end human suffering. Although most of us would never trade our contemporary world for that of the eighteenth century, it is also true that, despite all our progress, humans continue to suffer from incurable diseases, ingrained prejudices, and structural inequalities, among many other problems. Furthermore, many of the ills of modernity—from sickness to social problems—continue to be cast in moral terms. The idea that suffering is a result of sinfulness, moral failing, or weakness is not as distant as we might think. Many Americans still associate some diseases, poverty, and other forms of trauma with "lifestyle" choices, and contemporary self-help culture often doubles down on this continuing tendency. This suffering and prejudice, even as we hear of the progress of our modern world, is why we increasingly see in medical schools and nursing programs a renewed interest in holistic care and curricula that introduce students to ethics, the humanities, and the history of medicine.

Sociologist Martin Riesebrodt saw in the continued reality of suffering an explanation for the universality and persistent relevance of religion, which, he argued, has an ability to explain, deter, and overcome crises: "We cannot surmount the vulnerability and mortality of our bodies; nor will we be able, at any time in the foreseeable future, to exert full control over our natural environment; nor will we succeed in erasing the fact and problematic consequences of differences in power, privileges, and unjust domination." Religions survive, Riesebrodt argued, because they support people in situations of misery and stress and promise a better outcome, either in this life or in salvation.[26]

But what if we were to consider the persistence of religion into modernity not from today's disappointment but, rather, from the viewpoint of the eighteenth century? And not take for granted our retrospective awareness of the failures or unfulfilled promises of modern science, medicine, and politics? In their reactions to sickness and suffering, early

American Protestants give us a different perspective on religion and its responsiveness to stress and suffering in the *midst* of the changes, promises, and challenges of modernity. Living through the transition to the modern world, eighteenth-century Protestants turned to long-standing resources of theology, narrative, and community while engaging and forwarding modern shifts in medicine and politics. Their voices allow us to see how religion remained a central resource not only for those who suffered but also for those actively leading and pursuing the transformations of the modern world. Providential thought and practice were certainly essential tools of consolation, but they must also be recognized as more than a reaction to failure, vulnerability, and loss. They could be powerful resources for action, for claiming an authoritative interpretation, plan, and power in a world of change—and with lasting consequences.

There are many ways in which the themes of sickness, medicine, benevolence, and, above all, providence remain relevant in our contemporary situation. As historian Nicholas Guyatt has shown, providential thought was central to the "invention" of the United States itself, with an enduring legacy for ideas of expansion, mission, and race.[27] In the realms of medicine and health—the focus of the present work—many interlocutors have asked about claims of providential direction today, particularly when people have debilitating disease or injury, or when people die. As historian Kate Bowler has shown, the phrase "everything happens for a reason"—and the corresponding need to explain God's "worthy plan" for human suffering—remains ubiquitous in American society.[28] Are such references to God's providence today, however, the same as in the eighteenth century? Are they simply empty rhetoric—the things people say in response to grief? Do they have the same scriptural and spiritual resonance as in times past? As Bowler illustrates, many of the stock phrases people use to respond to sickness are spoken without attention to their theological coherence or true meaning. In her description of reactions to her stage 4 cancer diagnosis, the response that comes closest to an eighteenth-century Protestant view of providence was, in fact, the one that made no mention of God: the physician who remarks "we're all terminal" and gently encourages her not to "skip to the end." There—in the tension between a forthright acknowledgment of universal mortality and yet also a commitment to a continuing life, story, and future of meaningful activity and purpose—is where a modern view comes close to an early American view of providence.[29]

At the same time, I am reluctant entirely to dismiss contemporary stock phrases like "God is in Control" or "God is using this experience to make you stronger." The inclination to find a narrative and to locate a greater meaning for suffering remains incredibly strong and incredibly appealing to modern American Christians, as Bowler's account itself suggests. As a historian who has spent many hours reading sickness stories from the past, I recognize how intimate sickness narratives are and how their narrative voice, phrasing, and plot are shaped by individual beliefs and contexts that include religious communities, scriptures, ideas, and practices, current medical research, and social and familial traditions. Present or past, if we are to understand how a person views and responds to their body, health, community, and God, we must consider a wide range of deeply personal sources and contexts.

By expanding our narrative of religion and medicine in the eighteenth century and consulting a wider range of sources, a different story of providence and religion in the modern world emerges. We find in early America actively engaged, thoughtful, and anything-but-passive Protestants, with a diversity of experiences and interpretations of God's power and human responsiveness to suffering. Their stories remind us that religion and medicine are not necessarily at odds and that humans are not bound to an unchanging way of seeing or knowing. Faith in providence was a central consolation for those who suffered. It was an important force behind the active engagement of Christians determined to interpret, respond to, and change their world. And, finally, the widespread narrative and vision of providential meaning—even recast into more secular terms like benevolence, design, and nature—persisted and shaped modern visions of medicine, charity, and community.

* * *

This book investigates the uses of providence in several modes, highlighting both its narratival and interpretative power as well as how it was enacted in missions, medicine, and benevolence. In so doing, the book makes the case for how providence was taught, learned, and applied and became a critical and lasting framework for early American Protestants in an age typically seen as central to secularization.

Chapters 1 and 2 look carefully at narrative and how Protestants, on the one hand, were taught in published, pastoral manuals to reflect on sickness and, on the other, pursued this narration in their personal writings. Chapter 1 looks at two pastoral tracts on sickness by the New England Puritan minister Cotton Mather and the German Pietist Lutheran pastor Samuel Urlsperger; both of these tracts were available in the eighteenth-century American colonies. The chapter considers these manuals within the contexts of their creation, in relation to other popular narrative forms of the time, and in terms of contemporary Christian teachings on sickness, original sin, repentance, and salvation. Both manuals offer detailed accounts describing how Christians should interpret and react to sickness. By advocating retrospective reflection on the stories of biblical forebears and on the sufferer's own life, Mather and Urlsperger urged sufferers to think historically about divine purpose and the need for repentance. These manuals offered the sick and their witnesses an active response to sickness, yet they always maintained right teaching by insisting, in the end, on human limitation and God's providence. In the narrative forms they exemplified and encouraged, the manuals provided a means of consolation not only in the trust promised by God's plan, but also in the shared and intimate nature of these theologies and forms of narration.

Chapter 2, then, reads personal—mostly manuscript—accounts of sickness in relationship to this pastoral advice. Individual sufferers and their witnesses adopted the powerful communal norms found in pastoral manuals, emphasizing the themes of repentance and consolation as they narrated a providential meaning to their suffering. Those silenced by pain found an opportunity to voice their experiences through these narrative forms, and they connected to a wider Protestant community through the shared Christian narrative of redemption and salvation. Observers also left accounts of sickness, offering detailed testimonies of both the physical and spiritual condition of the sufferers. Shaped by both Christian martyrological tradition and the medical discourse of the "patient's case," these accounts served to witness God's providential grace in even the most mundane of earthly suffering. While some Christians who faced sickness wrestled with these norms, expressing doubt that reflected the theological changes emerging in the eighteenth century, they nonetheless remained dependent, ultimately, on retrospective language and a plot that stressed God's will and plan.

The book then turns from these foundational narrative and theological practices to look at how Protestants imagined and were inspired by providence as they engaged new scientific, medical, and philosophical ideas in their medical work and missions, visions of benevolence, and understandings of maternity. The focus of the third chapter is three religious communities and their debates over medical intervention—debates that highlight anxieties about medicine and treatment in colonial America and the Atlantic world as well as reactions to the medical materialism and dualism that emerged after Descartes. Within medicine, the body was increasingly viewed as a machine that could be observed, evaluated, and treated based on its physical functions and symptoms. Christians participated in contemporary conversations and debates about medicine, integrating new ideas and treatments within long-standing Christian views of the human body, soul, and knowledge. The Puritan Cotton Mather and the Pietist physician Christian Thilo, for example, insisted on the role of the soul in bodily health, even when contemporary medical theory questioned the soul's importance to the mechanical body. Methodist John Wesley, meanwhile, considered medicine a special providence of God in the natural world, and therefore reacted strongly to the increasingly theoretical medicine that developed after Descartes, which limited the widespread participation in medicine that God had designed. Nonetheless, Wesley, along with Mather and the Pietists, engaged contemporary medical thought and innovation. They understood the vital importance of medical treatment and education for Christian evangelization.

The fourth chapter examines shifting views of God's providence in new forms of benevolence, particularly during the 1793 yellow fever epidemic in Philadelphia. Scholars have argued that the late eighteenth century saw the movement of charity from churches into private sectors alongside a rise in secular social reform. In many ways, the response to the 1793 epidemic confirms such an interpretation: Philadelphians visited, nursed, counseled, and cared for the sick, buried the dead, established committees for the relief of the sick and poor, and created institutions such as hospitals and orphanages. On the one hand, responders—ranging from clergy to citizen volunteers—described their work with recourse to the Enlightenment-era language of innate human sympathy, but, on the other hand, they also imagined the epidemic in terms of providence. God had sent sickness, but God also motivated and provided the means for alleviation and care. When the language and activity of human compassion failed in the most intense suffering, Christians still relied on a narrative of God's direction and mercy.

Throughout the eighteenth century, providence had proven an expansive doctrine that interacted with new medicine and with Enlightenment ideas about human sympathy and compassion. The idea of providence would be adapted and used in various contexts moving into the nineteenth century. As scholars have argued, providence became a crucial component of the concept of nationalism, seen particularly in the idea of God's providential design in the creation and expansion of the United States. This nationalism was, likewise, shaped in significant ways by Protestant missionary endeavors. Missionaries and reformers both at home and abroad, from colonial India to the South Pacific, insisted that their work was God's; this work brought with it the forces of "civilization" and furthered the expansion of European and, eventually, American empire—all in the name of providence. Crucial to the very development of the American nation-state, meanwhile, was the work of enslaved men and women. Many Christians accepted this slavery as a God-ordained means to colonization, evangelization, and economic survival. Even among those who dissented, many nonetheless accepted slavery as an institution approved by earthly rulers, themselves appointed by God.[30]

These are all crucial elements to the story of the concept of providence as it transformed in the early nineteenth century; for this volume, however, the focus is on providence in the realm of religion, sickness, and health. Thus the fifth chapter tracks the complex ways in which providential thought shaped medical debates over the maternal body and maternal knowledge and the implications of this interaction for late eighteenth-century politics and society. Shaped by Protestant ideals of redemptive motherhood—themselves grounded in a long-standing Christian reverence for the Virgin Mary—theologians, medical practitioners, laypeople, and reformers argued over the nature and design of the female body, the appropriateness of human intervention and medical instruments in childbirth, and the correct forms of lactation and infant care. They adapted providential views of faithful and sacrificing motherhood to new mechanistic concepts of design, the investigation of nature, and the improvement of medical practice through training and education. At the same time, however, midwifery manuals and reform literature reveal a persisting providential understanding of what was "natural" in maternity and child care. They wrote an implicitly religious understanding onto what it meant to fulfill maternal design, a meaning that affected views of womanhood in colonial and missionary contexts and that was, in turn, shaped by ideas of class and race. The long Christian association of maternity and redemption proved critical to emerging medical and political claims of right motherhood, informed by "nature" and designed to cultivate virtue, loyalty, and civilization.

These transformations of providence by the end of the eighteenth century are revealing of its extraordinary reach, flexibility, and persistence. Providential thought has a tremendous power to console and motivate humans in times of sickness, suffering, and social upheaval. This same power can also be used to limit debate, to claim right understanding, and—on a very practical level—to control medical discourse and treatments and to define gender, race, class, and political belonging. This does not mean that there is an inherent evil within providential thought. Providence is, ultimately, a human doctrine—a human attempt to understand God and to interpret both the intimate and major events of life in terms of God's sovereignty and human responsibility. While providential language and, in its expansion, appeals to "nature" have, unsurprisingly, been used to secure or defend self-serving human ideas, actions, and institutions, it is also important to recognize how often humans have appealed to providence to "do good" in matters where their own self-interest is not at stake, or is, at the least, more ambiguous.

In sickness, medicine, and reform, faith in God's providence prompted human activity in eighteenth-century America and the Atlantic world. Protestants responded and adapted to Enlightenment-era challenges to traditional Christian conceptions of God, creation, and human agency. A strong commitment to providence and the narrative patterns and activities it evoked remained, always, an enduring feature of early American life into modernity. This commitment was an essential resource for both interpreting and formulating responses to suffering and change and for defining religious life, meaning, and action in a secular age.

1

Wholesome Words

Sickness and Narrative in Protestant Pastoral Manuals

In 1702, the New England Puritan Cotton Mather published *Wholesome Words*, a book on sickness, during a smallpox epidemic in Boston.[1] As the title suggests, Mather perceived words to have a nourishing function in times of sickness. Words were the starting point for narration. And to narrate sickness was a fundamental practice for eighteenth-century Christians, who sought to organize and integrate the physical and spiritual experiences of suffering within their life story. Sickness narratives connected sufferers through familiar ways of speaking about pain, loss, and God's providential plan and mercy.

Ministers wrote about sickness frequently in the eighteenth-century Atlantic world. In an era when pain was a central feature of human existence, a major component of pastoral work was to care for those who suffered and to help interpret that suffering. Unable to be always present, ministers wrote guides for their communities. These guides were prescriptive and theological. They can seem harsh and disciplinary; they often describe a demanding God. Nonetheless, these guides could also console in their commitment to an engaged God and a community of believers. They provided early Americans with an important shared activity, theology, and narrative style for the most common of human experiences: sickness. The influence of these guides—the providential narrative they outlined for human responses to suffering—endured even in an age of enlightenment and increasing skepticism.[2]

Ministerial writings on sickness were not limited to the New England Puritan community from which Mather wrote. Protestants around the Atlantic world participated in widespread renewal movements that promoted the practice of personal writing and witnessing to God's will in human life, including sickness. Mather's *Wholesome Words* exemplifies one perspective of this practice; Samuel Urlsperger, a Pietist Lutheran pastor in Augsburg, offers another. Urlsperger was a well-connected representative of the far-reaching missions of the Pietist movement, including a settlement of Salzburger refugees with Francke Foundations–trained pastors in colonial Georgia, and a member of the Society for the Promotion of Christian Knowledge, the missionary arm of the Church of England. His manual, *Der Kranken Gesundheit und der Sterbenden Leben* (*The Health of the Sick and the Life of the Dying*), appeared on both sides of the Atlantic.[3] Considered in their contexts and alongside the ideas and writings of other leaders of Protestant renewal movements, like the Methodist John Wesley, these sickness manuals reveal central characteristics of Protestant teachings on sickness and models of narrative response.

Ministers wrote about sickness with ample reference to scripture, theology, and personal experiences, but what connected these narratives above all was their dependence on the narrative practice of retrospection and a commitment to God's providence. These two elements went hand in hand. To retrospect is, in its most basic definition, to look back on the past and the course of one's life. For ministers, retrospection was an essential practice for suffering Christians as they plotted their sickness, and it served three key purposes. First, retrospection encouraged the sick to think historically about sin and divine purpose. Second, retrospection helped promote human activity while maintaining Protestant theological orthodoxy on the issue of human works and God's will. Third, and finally, retrospection consoled. It provided a way to respond to painful experiences through a communal practice—a practice that defined meaning and comfort in stories, visions, and hopes of God's providential direction. These pastoral manuals cultivated a practice of providential narration that was pervasive and long lasting, shaping a large community of Protestant writers and witnesses through the religious, social, and medical changes of the eighteenth century.

Plotting Sickness

To imagine providence in terms of human *practice* requires thinking about early American theology as lived and dynamic. Providence was both a teaching encouraged within official pastoral writings and a framework for interpreting the world and human suffering that was shared by individuals across many Protestant communities. Sickness narratives reveal normative teachings on sin, repentance, and salvation, and they highlight narratival expectations within a growing community of writers in the Atlantic world. Yet sickness writings also encouraged a kind of theology on the ground, a theology lived and embodied in the shared and personal experiences of pain and grief.[4] To write about sickness was an active effort to wrestle with God and God's plan, with sin and salvation, and with individual pain and hopes for health. In their careful organization, reflection, and voice—in their retrospection—sickness narratives evince an energetic engagement with ideas about God's providence and its significance in the individual and communal life.

Sickness was a constant presence in early Americans' lives, a stark difference from today, when the vast majority of Americans expect to be healthy—or at least to "feel good"—most of the time. In attempting to capture what it must have been like to live in such close contact with pain, many scholars have interpreted Christian leaders and Christian theologies as almost co-conspirators with the physical experience of suffering that could define, limit, and damage human life. In her study of pain in early America, for example, historian Elaine Forman Crane focused on the prescriptive and disciplinary element of clerical writings on sickness. She argued that these clerical writings fixated on resignation and submission, leaving individuals passive, emotional, and frustrated in their inability to live up to Christian ideals.[5] It is no wonder historical accounts of secularization would expect faith in God's providence to be easily—and gladly—left behind in the hope of medical and scientific advances. But such expectations overlook the fact that narratives are active and powerful tools of meaning making.

Religious leaders sought, through narrative, to control and impose meaning on disease. Scholars of disease and epidemic narratives, influenced by the theoretical work of Michel Foucault, Mary Douglas, and Sander Gilman, have highlighted how such narratives disciplined, marked boundaries, and served larger political and social ends. Epidemic narratives, in particular, exemplify how authorities used stories to direct blame and claim power. Those seeking prestige and influence could write stories of their own courageous and selfless work in response to an epidemic—and, at the same time, buttress their good deeds by highlighting the inaction or corruption of others. This occurred in Renaissance plague narratives that blamed Jews for the spread of pestilential disease, and it occurred when African American nurses during Philadelphia's yellow fever epidemic were depicted as greedily taking advantage of their neighbors in need.[6]

Although less studied than epidemic accounts, day-to-day sickness narratives were also subject to widespread norms that shaped and controlled the meaning of disease and suffering.[7] Contemporary memoirists and scholars of pathography, or sickness writing, have highlighted the ways in which modern humans still encounter expected paradigms for narrating illness. Cancer patients must engage in a "hero's quest," for example, or "battle" their disease into remission. While some question the moralizing potential of such narrative paradigms, most agree on the central role of narrative for people responding to critical illness. The disruption of the physical world demands a recognition of the corresponding alteration of the mental—or spiritual—world of reflection and meaning. Through narrative, the sick person can replot her life's story and trajectory.[8]

Early Americans likewise sought to re-create order in times of suffering and loss, as evidenced in practices ranging from their mourning attire and jewelry to the design of tombstones. Such practices were "attempts to suture the rupture that death created, attempts to restore order to a social body disordered by death, attempts to create lasting memories of parents, children, and spouses, attempts to make meaning and find comfort in the face of calamity."[9] While historians have attended to these material death practices of early Americans, however, their day-to-day sickness writing has generally been overlooked. Scholars of modern pathography, meanwhile, ignore the writings of eighteenth-century Christians. They have not been viewed as participants in the work of narrative reconstruction, work that is often interpreted as a characteristic of a secular era. In their writing, they have been seen, instead, as passive recipients of Christian teachings and authorities, as sufferers who desired only to resign to God's will.[10]

But there is nothing passive about resignation.

To resign to God's providence required, in fact, active effort and a well-established narrative practice. In the eighteenth century, Christians responded to sickness in many ways, including medicine and charity, but narrative was always central. The retrospection that narrative required, the emphasis to look to the past, to replot, and to perceive meaning and right action, was, in fact, crucial to the framing and interpretation of other responses. In their writings on sickness, ministers encouraged suffering Christians first to retrospect: to reflect on past suffering—of not only themselves but also their biblical forebears, like Miriam, Job, and David—as they attempted to discern God's will, their spiritual state, and the long history of the church's journey toward the kingdom of God. This historical work, this perspective, demanded that Protestants place the ultimate outcome of their condition and efforts in God's will. While the language of providence—the complete dependence on God—has, perhaps, caused many scholars to overlook the abundant activity ministers recommended in responses to sickness, including in narrative forms, this activity was, in fact, grounded in narrative and the language of providence.

Pastoral writings on sickness offered an influential framework, or a set of guidelines, for responding to sickness that would be understood, recognized, and shared by the larger community. Advice manuals on any number of topics—from midwifery to letter writing—were widely available in the early modern era, and their pedagogical function was significant; they "nourished a social knowhow and a social imaginary." Protestant sickness manuals were part of this social nourishment. Knowing how to describe and make sense of suffering within a community is an important skill. While it limited individual expression and dissent from norms, it nonetheless also offered connection through a larger "Protestant vernacular tradition." Ministers encouraged sufferers to describe immediate and personal experiences of sickness within the context of Christian scriptures and theology and, at the same time, to reflect and ground the Christian salvation story in individual experience and everyday language.[11] Protestant communities throughout the Atlantic world were taught to look back on their lives, communities, and biblical stories as they plotted a way forward in line with a vision of an overseeing God. They were taught to practice retrospection, and, in so doing, to find God's will, right belief, and communal intimacy in a shared and enduring narration of suffering.

Sickness and Sin, History and Divine Purpose

Cotton Mather published his pastoral manual *Wholesome Words* three times between 1702 and 1721. Each edition appeared during an epidemic in his community of colonial Boston. Mather's immediate and personal encounters with illness and sense of pastoral duty shaped the intent of *Wholesome Words*, which he outlined in the introduction. The tract promised instruction for families both in the present "Epidemical Sickness, *when our* Pastors, *who would fain* Visit all the Sick, *have not Strength*," and in future incidences of disease, for "[the sick] we shall have always with us."[12] Mather's outlined task spoke to the immediate circumstances of epidemic in Boston, the concomitant, overwhelming personal suffering and pastoral obligations, and the fallen human condition of susceptibility to sickness. In pursuing his task, he emphasized repentance and consolation. He modeled Protestant pastoral guidance with a retrospective narrative that worked actively both to emphasize human sinfulness and to discern God's providential will.

Mather relied on painful and evocative images to make his points about human fallenness and divine power. First published during an epidemic of smallpox, a disease with highly visible symptoms, *Wholesome Words* urged readers to meditate on "the Pale, the Swollen, the Wasted, & perhaps the Spotted Faces of the *Sick* in the Family . . . such as our Heavenly Father has been *Spitting* upon: Shall *He Spit in our Faces, and shall we not be ashamed?*" Though modern readers may be appalled by Mather's spitting God, the painful image would have had profound resonance within Mather's community. His words referred to Numbers 12, a scriptural passage about the leprosy of Miriam, the sister of Moses. God had struck Miriam with leprosy because she and her brother Aaron had criticized Moses's choice of a wife and challenged his leadership. Aaron repented their sin, and Moses appealed to God to heal Miriam. God replied, "If her father had but spit in her face, should she not be ashamed seven days?" Miriam had to remove herself from her community, the Israelites, for seven days. The whole community waited for her recovery before they could, together, continue their journey to Canaan.[13]

By opening his account of sickness with a biblical image that would remind his well-versed audience of Miriam's body, "leprous, white as snow," Mather effectively mapped his community's encounters with smallpox and other epidemics onto the biblical narrative of Exodus—a story of the perseverance and hope of a chosen people with whom New England Puritans had long identified.[14] The story of Miriam's illness reminded readers that sickness was not only an individual story but also a story of the entire community, and it was part of a history of God's guidance over sinful humanity that transcended time and space.

For Mather, Miriam's sickness reflected God's righteous and particular judgment on her sins, but more than that, her individual sickness represented the base sinfulness of her wider community and, indeed, all humanity. Mather urged his audience to "acknowledge, that the *Sickness* of any one in the Family" was caused by providence and that "*we all deserve to be Sick*."[15] Constant and inescapable, sickness was a permanent physical mark of human guilt and dependence, not just for a presently suffering individual but for all humanity and for all time.

Mather, like most eighteenth-century Protestants, understood sickness as a product of the Fall. As soon as Adam and Eve disobeyed God and ate the forbidden fruit in the garden, humans became susceptible to sickness. All of human history was shaped by this act, and there was no way of comprehending or describing sickness that could avoid reflection on its long historical association with original sin and God's judgment. No one escaped the Fall and its consequences, including sin and sickness. The human task was not to fixate passively on an individual sufferer's moral depravity, but rather to interpret what individual sickness meant for the larger Christian story and God's providence.[16]

This retrospective and providential connection of sickness to original sin transcended the denominational, temporal, and geographical categories that are often applied to early American religious history.[17] Mather was a Puritan—a renewal movement that emerged from the Church of England in the seventeenth century and that was shaped by Calvinist ideas of divine sovereignty, human depravity, and predestination. In Mather's early eighteenth-century book on medicine, *Angel of Bethesda*, he explained the connection he envisioned between sin and sickness: "*Sin, Sin*, was that which opened the Floodgates for a Flood of *Wretchedness* to rush in upon the world; and *Sickness* is one Instance of *Wretchedness*."[18] Likewise, the Anglican John Wesley, who was instrumental in the development of the Methodist movement in the mid-eighteenth century and an important advocate for Arminianism, also found the beginnings of human sickness in original sin. He wrote so in his own medical manual, the incredibly popular *Primitive Physic*, which he first published in 1747. Wesley's preface, which remained unchanged through each edition into the nineteenth century, included a comprehensive view of the origins of illness in the Fall:

> When man came first out of the hands of the great Creator, clothed in body as well as in soul, with immortality and incorruption, . . . he knew no sin, so he knew no pain, no sickness, weakness, or bodily disorder. . . . And there was nothing without to injure it: Heaven and earth, and all the hosts of them, were mild, benign and friendly to human nature. . . . But since Man rebell'd against the Sovereign of heaven and earth, how entirely is the scene changed! The incorruptible frame hath put on corruption, the immortal has put on mortality. The seeds of weakness and pain, of sickness and death, are now lodged in our inmost substance: whence a thousand disorders continually spring, even without the aid of external violence. . . . The heavens, the earth, and all things contained therein, conspire to punish the rebels against their Creator.[19]

Wesley described a condition in which sickness had become an inherent corruption within the human body *and* a result of the unease with which fallen humans lived in God's creation. Humans' very environment was prepared to crush them, poison them, and sap their strength.

The connection between sickness and sin was a theme not limited to English-language writings on sickness in the Atlantic world. German Pietist theologians and pastors, centered in particular around the Francke Foundations in Halle, likewise saw the origins of sickness in sin. Crucial participants in the larger religious renewal movements of the Atlantic world, Halle Pietists wrote frequently on sickness. Gotthilf August Francke, son of August Hermann Francke and his successor as leader of the Francke Foundations, often discussed sickness and pain in his private correspondence. He saw both as just punishments for all humans, who suffered equally from the consequences of the Fall. Sickness was a symptom of humans' unbelief and a demonstration of their distance from God.[20]

The Augsburg Pietist Samuel Urlsperger, a frequent correspondent of both August and Gotthilf Francke, shared their theological understanding of sickness and its origins in his book, *The Health of the Sick and the Life of the Dying*. This lengthy manual on sickness was first published in 1723 in Stuttgart and appeared in North America by at least 1751, when the Francke Foundations shipped copies of the second edition to the community in Ebenezer, Georgia, led by Halle-trained pastors.[21] In his book, Urlsperger borrowed heavily from other Pietists and Pietist-influenced Lutherans, and he referred readers to *Paradisgärtlein* (*Little Garden of Paradise*), a popular seventeenth-century prayer book by Johann Arndt.[22] The final text was thus deeply shaped by the larger Pietist movement and its understandings of sickness.

In the preface, Urlsperger, like Mather, described that he had been asked to write his book of instruction for the sick and dying as a much-needed pastoral guide. He saw the book as a call to reflection on human sin and to preparation for sickness and death. Such preparation was crucial because "humans unfailingly carry with them *the certain Order that they must die.*" Urlsperger pointed his readers to the prevalent, unavoidable evidence of death. They had witnessed "the corpses lying in the death biers, even if they are covered with many clothes" and had recognized "that the procession will also come to them." Present, physical reminders of inevitable mortality brought "penetrating, indeed heavy, reflections," which spurred preparation for death.[23]

Urlsperger, like Mather, had witnessed suffering and death many times and was convinced that such witnessing should motivate immediate reflection on the universal condition of human sickness and the concomitant need for "heartfelt repentance." The severity of both individual and communal sin was, further, compounded by the greatness of God's promise. The sick must see and repent the depths of human corruption, while admitting the righteousness of God's law and judgment. Through retrospection came acute awareness of the widespread sinfulness that affected all of humanity, generation after generation. Urlsperger thus counseled humility and "Christian patience" in sickness.[24]

Experiences of sickness were opportunities for Christians to reflect on the past and general state of human sinfulness and, from there, to retrospect or imagine their present physical trials and spiritual progress in terms of what these trials might mean in the future and for their salvation.[25] Urlsperger urged the sick to imagine how their story would be told or seen from a point "after death." He asked his readers to think in terms of a "*history*." He wanted sufferers to reflect on the hope that, after death, "one could say of you and me, because so much of our repentance was done and our belief and good conscience were preserved to our end: '*They have blessedly passed away in the Lord*.'"[26] Pietists stressed the role that sickness played in encouraging retrospection on human depravity, divine will, and the need for repentance.

Although emerging from different reformation traditions, Puritans offered a reading of sickness that paralleled that of the Pietists. Puritans had also been taught to find an opportunity to think about history and providence in the fundamental association between sin and suffering. The reformer John Calvin, their chief theological forebear, stressed this reflective approach in his exegesis of the book of Job, a central scripture for the interpretation of sickness within Christianity. As historian Susan Schreiner has explained, for Calvin, Job was about history. To meditate on human suffering in light of sinfulness and divine will was a way to "recommend the works of God in history as well as the study of history as a means for perceiving divine providence." A retrospective look at not only the individual's sins but all humanity's sins provided abundant evidence that all humans deserved to suffer for their pride and corruption—no one escaped the Fall. In Calvin's reading of Job, history and nature offered a "glimpse" and "taste" of God's providence, even if God's actions in history sometimes seemed inscrutable and ambiguous to humans. This history, this foretaste, promised that "the same God who brought the order of creation into existence is powerful and wise enough to govern human events and, on the last day, to bring order out of the present confusion." The past suffering and faith of scriptural paragons like Job ultimately offered the contemporary sufferer "grounds for hope in the present."[27]

Job was an obvious scriptural example for any minister trying to explain the meaning of suffering and divine providence to a troubled community because Job's story highlighted both individual and communal suffering, doubt, and witness. Over the course of his narrative, Job lost his livelihood and family and was, finally, stricken with his own terrible illness, witnessed by his remaining friends. In *Wholesome Words*, Mather focused on the section of Job in which Job's friend Elihu questioned him, his claim to innocence, and his bewilderment at his suffering. This section also served as the epigraph for *Wholesome Words*.

For Mather, Job's interaction with Elihu highlighted both the proper role of those who witness suffering and the appropriate interpretation of sickness and Christian suffering within a larger historical framework. Elihu was the fourth of Job's friends to speak, and his questions were the most pressing. He pointed out that God punished human pride in ways of God's choosing, including through physical pain and suffering: "He is chastened also with pain upon his bed, and the multitude of his bones with strong pain: So that his life abhorreth bread, and his soul dainty meat" (Job 33:19–20). Witnessing sickness was a common task in Mather's community, and he urged readers to experience a companion's suffering and to recognize it, like Elihu, as a testimony to the universal reality of human fallenness and God's overarching power. A witness must "see thy *Sick* Friend Sweating, Hear thy *Sick* Friend Sighing," and consider his own health and be grateful for it, because health was an "an *Unmerited* Favour." Health was an unearned blessing from God, Mather argued. Even in witnessing the suffering of another, one could look back and see that, as Mather had written, "*We all deserve to be Sick.*"[28]

Ministers like Mather and Urlsperger found in retrospection a powerful tool to remind the sick of their past failings as well as the long-lasting and universal legacy of original sin, made visible in the suffering church throughout history. Sickness was thus a pedagogical opportunity for the individual and the community. Far from demanding passivity, suffering was a chance to reflect, to repent, and to witness at the most personal and corporeal level the basic premise of Protestant theology: human faith and dependence on a sovereign God.

Suffering, Repentance, and Right Belief

Sickness narratives made vivid and personal the stakes of Protestant teachings on sin and salvation. Cotton Mather and Samuel Urlsperger both used their narratives to model a correct understanding of repentance, a practice that, within Protestantism, required reflection on sinfulness, an effort to correct and make amends for sinfulness, and, finally, a recognition of humans' innate sinfulness and dependence on God. Repentance was a necessary and expected response to sickness and could, in fact, be a form of consolation. It offered, after all, a framework for action at a time of disorientation. As historian Ronald Rittgers has argued, repentance "accorded to the Christian a measure of spiritual agency that it denied to the sinful human being."[29]

Protestant ministers nonetheless had to ensure that they did not encourage an attitude of too much human freedom; Protestants abhorred the idea that humans could earn their salvation through repentance and good works—a teaching they ascribed to Catholicism. Mather and Urlsperger had to balance, then, a need for human responsiveness to suffering with an insistence on God's providence. This balance was found in retrospection and repentance. Christians must try to understand their past sins and the meaning of their present suffering, to repent, and, all the while, to acknowledge that they and their efforts remained subject to God's will and mercy. Retrospection provided the narrative structure necessary to maintain theological orthodoxy while encouraging human response. To look back always reveals past missteps, misunderstandings, and misperceptions. Retrospection—like repentance itself—demands human activity while insisting on human limitation.

Writing on sickness was a spiritual discipline. Mather invited his readers to retrospect on their lives in the hope that they might find grounds for repentance and consolation in the activity—as well as faith in the recognition of their dependence on God. As historian W. Clark Gilpin has argued, Puritans were to "discern a plot and coherence to life" that "was not a look backward merely from the present situation. It was a look backward over the whole journey of life from an imagined end point."[30] To consider life from the point of death—to imagine how current actions might look from the moment of judgment—provided narrative structure and meaning, and it was not an uncommon practice. When the Puritan Jonathan Edwards preached a funeral sermon in 1734 encouraging young people to consider their "shocking" and "vain" life should they die in their youth, he went so far as describing such a perspective from a coffin.[31] A century later, in a tribute to his aunt Mary Moody Emerson, nineteenth-century author Ralph Waldo Emerson wrote that "for years she had her bed made in the form of a coffin" and, like Saladin, made and wore her shroud as a gown. Her anticipation of death was a sign of her faith and dependence on God in her day-to-day life.[32]

For Mather and Urlsperger, retrospection and repentance were a matter of both consoling practice and theological orthodoxy. They revealed human limitation and God's grace. Scholars have nonetheless often overlooked or dismissed the practical and theological importance of repentance for eighteenth-century Protestants in times of sickness. During the 1721 epidemic in which the third edition of *Wholesome Words* appeared, Mather was involved in a controversy over smallpox inoculation, and most scholarship on Mather, sickness, and medicine—including beyond the 1721 episode—has focused on his role in this debate. Mather's promotion of inoculation and the public resistance he encountered have led scholars to argue about the decline of Puritan orthodoxy in early eighteenth-century New England, the rising influence of physicians as a profession separate from ministers, and the attempts of Puritan clergy to reassert orthodoxy, power, and ministerial authority against the forces of enlightenment.[33]

Without a sufficient understanding of the work of sickness narratives or Puritans' theology and context, it is easy for a modern reader to find the call for repentance in times of sickness off-putting—a harsh and authoritarian move that seems to take advantage of the sick and vulnerable in the name of orthodoxy. Repentance was a central and early theme of *Wholesome Words*. Mather certainly cared about his clerical authority in the community, but that is an insufficient interpretation, overlooking the retrospective language, scriptural and theological resources, and conceptions of power represented within the text itself.[34] Mather considered himself and all humans to suffer from original sin and to be at the mercy of one ultimate power—God. He found immense comfort in this power as well as in the human work of repentance that responded to it. He sought to showcase the experience of God's power over humanity throughout history, not just in his own time and local community, but also in the time and wider community of biblical forebears, and in the future, anticipated salvation.

Mather's tract began with this emphasis on God's power throughout history. He highlighted the depths of humans' fall from God's grace by repeated reference to biblical stories in which God sent sickness, plague, and death as punishment for human faithlessness and pride. The tract referred to the plague begun after the punishment of Korah—when the people murmured against Moses—which was relieved upon atonement, although only after fourteen thousand died (Numbers 16:46). The tract cited another biblical plague that killed seventy thousand, this occasioned by David's ambition and pride in conducting a census of Israel

(1 Chronicles 21:16). God's punishments could also be more limited and directed at a single individual or family. Mather highlighted the story of the Lord striking the son of David and the widow of Uriah the Hittite, in response to David's unjust killing of Uriah (2 Samuel 12:15). The tract also pointed to Job, an upstanding, faithful man, whose losses and sufferings were well known.[35]

Mather did not, however, leave his readers with these devastating punishments, but he offered a vision of God's providence and grace that might inspire human response and repentance. In the second part of *Wholesome Words*, he turned increasingly to passages from Psalms and the New Testament in order to focus on faith and the promise of salvation and resurrection. Citing Psalms and the Epistle of James, Mather described the spiritual rewards given to those Christians who worked faithfully on behalf of the sick. This work involved exhorting, praying, and providing charity, even in the face of physical harm and contagion. Faithfully pursued charity was a Christian duty, and those who followed this mandate were scripturally promised God's transcendent care and protection in their own sickness. Mather exclaimed that "*The Prayer of Faith shall save the Sick*" (James 5:16). He reminded his readers of the ancient Christians in Alexandria, who remained and cared for those suffering from the "Pestilence" when all "the *Heathens* ran away from their dearest Relations, under the dread of the Infection." Mather urged readers to extend their charity not only locally but also abroad and to reflect on the "Wonderful Encouragement" found in Psalm 41:1–3: "*Blessed is he that Considers the Poor, the Lord will Deliver him in time of Trouble; the Lord will Preserve him, and Keep him Alive, and he shall be Blessed upon the earth; The Lord will strengthen him upon the bed of Languishing; Thou wilt make all his Bed in his Sickness.*" Mather lingered on the transcendent medicinal power of this scriptural promise: "Every Syllable is a Cordial, beyond the Richest *Elixir* in the World!" He elaborated by referring his readers to Psalm 91, which proclaimed trust in God's promise to serve as a "refuge" to the faithful: "There shall no evil befall thee, neither shall any plague come nigh thy dwelling" (Psalm 91:9–10).[36]

A "Cordial" in Mather's time was a heart stimulant; God's promise of deliverance and preservation was intended not merely to ease pain but also to spur human responsiveness through repentance. Likewise, Mather's "*Elixir*" was not simply a medical tincture but, in its alchemical connotation, a substance that could transform a base metal into gold. By dwelling in God's promise, Mather suggested, and by faithfully following God's commands, one might truly be strengthened for service and sanctified. This was an extraordinary consolation, but it nonetheless rested on the reflection and repentance demanded by the punishments and wrath of God featured in the first part of the tract. Mather reminded the reader that true repentance was preceded by reflection on sinfulness—the "*Moral Cause*" of sickness. Only then could repentance be followed by faith in the "*Blood of Jesus Christ the Son of God, which Cleanseth from all Sin.*" The sick must first "*Know the Plague of thy own Heart*" (1 Kings 8:38) and mourn and lament the time lost to sin. The rewards for this retrospection were, however, compelling. The promise of salvation and resurrection offered in scripture, Mather explained, would succeed this period of trial with a consolation beyond all earthly medicines.[37]

Mather turned often to the material world and physical experiences as he sought to convey the Christian path to repentance, faith, and resurrection. Beyond medicinal cordials and God's spit, Mather also mingled physical language of healing, movement, and the senses with spiritual ideas of salvation. "*Fly*" unto the refuge of Christ, Mather encouraged his readers; "*Look*" to God "and *be saved!*" (Psalm 142:5; Isaiah 45:22). To die in faith, he wrote, "will be *the Salvation of the Soul.*" For Mather, the New Testament epistles reflected on Old Testament exemplars like Abel, Noah, Abraham, and Sarah who had "*Dy'd in Faith.*" Although they had not yet "received the promises," they were "persuaded of them, and embraced them" (Hebrews 11:13). Mather seamlessly joined a physical verb like "embrace" with the spiritual promise of salvation.[38] His theology depended not only on suffering and repentance but also on this full experience of embodiment, retrospection, physical transformation, and divine promise.

Mather relied on a community of biblical exemplars to further his corporeally grounded spirituality of suffering and salvation. He crowded his tract with figures like Job, David, Miriam, and Moses, who grappled with their sinfulness and distance from God, repented of pride and disobedience, recognized their dependence on God, and flew to God with faith. These well-known figures demonstrated the crucial steps a human could take in reacting to sickness and brought readers to the end of Mather's tract. After repentance came grace, hope, and the resurrection, which were the central consolations of the Christian's spiritual journey. While these consoling themes were the focus of the tract's second half and ending, Mather did not omit them from the beginning, as seen in the verses he selected for the epigraph to *Wholesome Words*. There, his readers were reminded that the sufferer would in the end be delivered "from going down to the pit," and "his flesh shall be fresher than a child's" and he "shall see [God's] face with joy" (Job 33:24–26).[39]

This pivot to deliverance, joy, and renewal is a crucial part of Mather's writings on sickness, and—as the epigraph—it foregrounds the entire tract. While the first part of the tract emphasized physical corruption, original sin, and repentance, it must be read with an eye to the Puritans' theology of faith and salvation and their practice of retrospective narration. With their gaze on the biblical sufferers who went before, readers always had a peripheral view of the absolute need to trust in God's providence as well as the resulting benefits. Persevering through trials with faith and repentance, biblical exemplars were ultimately healed and achieved deliverance. Their ends reflected God's providential guidance and care.

Like Mather, Urlsperger also crafted an account of sickness that emphasized repentance and the consolation readers could find in responding to sickness through the practice of retrospection. Urlsperger's book on sickness has not been the subject of the same scholarly scrutiny that Mather's writings have faced, but Pietists have been accused—like Puritans—of an excessive authoritarianism and demand for individual piety and discipline, with broader implications for questions of social control and the rise of the nation-state.[40] Urlsperger's work has long been regarded as representative of Pietist teachings, but his manual did face critique in his own time. Most readers, including those in colonial Georgia, where the second edition of his manual was received in 1751, did not know of the concerns surrounding the book's earliest printing in 1723.[41] Nonetheless, the controversy that emerged after the first publication of *The Health of the Sick* reveals the careful theological work Urlsperger's narrative did both to respond to various levels of Lutheran and civic leadership and their concerns over his theological orthodoxy and to serve as a tool of consolation for the sick and suffering Christian.

In his manual, Urlsperger promoted retrospection and repentance in response to sickness, much like Mather had in *Wholesome Words*.

But soon after the book's publication, Urlsperger faced a large group of critics, who claimed that he offered too much potential for human freedom in repentance, rather than insisting on human dependence on God. There were social elements that contributed to these critiques of Urlsperger; he himself acknowledged party divisions within the governing Evangelical Ministerium and concerns over his status as a recently arrived leader in the Augsburg community. Nonetheless, the debate played out over issues of theology.[42]

From 1723 to 1725 the accusations against Urlsperger took many forms, but at their core was always a question of whether his sickness writings correctly reflected Lutheran doctrine. Soon after the book's appearance in Augsburg in 1723, Urlsperger corresponded with his mentor August Hermann Francke regarding the Ministerium's suggested changes to his text. The Ministerium's recommendations reveal a deep concern that the manual taught a version of works righteousness—or that Urlsperger himself was even a crypto-Catholic. Where Urlsperger wrote "there is no doubt in the kingdom of God," for example, the Ministerium had commented that, while true, Urlsperger should be cautious with such statements. The consequences of this idea could lead to superstition, the Ministerium wrote, as the "history of the papacy sufficiently demonstrates." In another place, the Ministerium emphasized the need for the text to explain that repentance—the response to sickness—"is not enough by humans themselves, but rather by Christ."[43]

Martin Luther, the sixteenth-century reformer and spiritual forebear of Lutherans (and the Pietist renewal movement), had insisted on the bondage of the human will. Corrupted by original sin, humans could do nothing to earn their salvation, Luther wrote; it ultimately rested in God's power: "God has taken my salvation out of my hands and into his, making it depend on his choice and not mine, and has promised to save me, not by my own work or exertion but by his grace and mercy."[44] The Ministerium in Augsburg questioned Urlsperger's commitment to this core Lutheran doctrine.

Despite Urlsperger's engaged response to the Ministerium's suggestions, the debate continued over his orthodoxy and the potential works righteousness of his sickness writings. In 1725, much aggrieved, he wrote to Francke that he had been labeled with "7 impure spirits," including "Novatianist, Pietist, Quakerish, Calvinist, Papist, Anabaptist, and Syncretist." The accusations against Urlsperger, more specifically, included incorrect scriptural exegesis, an incorrect understanding of the Augsburg Confession, and an incorrect understanding of angels. He was forced to answer questions on baptism, separatism, and "inspirational Donatism."[45] Urlsperger's critics in the Ministerium had chosen these labels with intention; within early Christianity, Novatianism and Donatism were deemed heresies, movements that church leaders had seen as too focused on rigorous purity in the aftermath of persecutions. By linking these early Christian movements to more recent communities formed in the context of reform and renewal—including Pietism—and with "Papist" Catholics, Urlsperger's critics within the Ministerium cautioned against his seeming promotion of works righteousness. His advocation of an active repentance in responding to sickness was dangerous; it skirted close to human freedom rather than dependence on God.

Pietists have long been characterized as breaking with Luther on the issues of human freedom and repentance, and scholars have debated the precision of such an assessment. Historian Alexander Pyrges has argued that "the elements from Martin Luther's *simul iustus et peccator* [simultaneously righteous and a sinner] were, in a way, uncoupled by the Pietists and resituated in a sequence, so that the Christian was no longer a sinner and righteous at the same time but rather, in principle, one after the other."[46] In their everyday practice of teaching and comforting parishioners, however, Lutheran pastors had long "preached, exhorted, instructed, and consoled as if Christians had some necessary role to play in remaining on the road to heaven, though certainly not in entering upon this road in the first place." Protestant consolation literature encouraged humans' effort, historian Ronald Rittgers has argued, even if the literature also showed "them how they could not possibly fulfill these expectations on their own; God had to do so in them via the Word and the Spirit."[47] Urlsperger's sickness manual—including his discussion of repentance—developed within this tradition of consolation literature.

In *The Health of the Sick*, Urlsperger worked diligently to encourage readers to action while always defending Lutheran teachings of God's overarching will and providential plan. His success in this effort depended on a joining of retrospective narration with the theological premise of the divine order of salvation (*Heilsordnung*), that is, first repentance, then belief. This order, based on the biblical text, "Repent and believe in the Gospel!" (Mark 1:15), was a command from Jesus in the New Testament and central to Urlsperger's work. The "entire book," he wrote, was "a divine trumpet call of repentance and faith," focused on spiritual steadfastness in the time of trial. The goal was to wake up individual sinners and direct them to the right path, beginning with repentance. With proper preparation and attention to this divinely ordained order, humans could "overcome" sickness and suffering with faith in Christ "and, with the last and general trumpet sound, may arise to eternal life."[48]

Like Mather, Urlsperger promoted retrospection during sickness in order to draw attention to, on the one hand, the consolation of God's promise of salvation and, on the other, the active response this consolation required in terms of both repentance and faith. Both Mather and Urlsperger pivoted between repentance and God's promise to the faithful in times of sickness and trial, even citing similar scripture (particularly Psalm 91) as evidence of God's promise. Unlike the Puritans, however, the Pietists did not emphasize a retrospective understanding of sickness as suffered by the wider community of the church throughout Christian history. Rather, Pietists stressed a retrospective interpretation that focused on the individual sinner and his or her progress in the "divine order of salvation."[49]

It may be this focus on the individual that opened Urlsperger to the critiques of works righteousness, and yet, like Mather, he turned to retrospection to maintain an insistence on God's providence. Mather had pointed to passages filled with biblical exemplars of suffering, sickness, and redemption—figures like Miriam and Job—who, for Calvinists, shared in the full and unified Christian salvation history and whose actions and lives could be understood retrospectively in terms of God's oversight. Urlsperger, meanwhile, urged individual sinners to follow the proper order of salvation as found in Jesus's command to "Repent and believe in the Gospel!" (Mark 1:15). In exegeting this command, Urlsperger relied on retrospection. For him, Jesus's command to repent and then believe was the central reminder to Christians that the promise of salvation was "not enough": "it was not enough to say: the door to heaven is opened; it was not enough to proclaim the kingdom of God comes nigh." But before Urlsperger could begin with the task of repentance— the first step in the order of salvation—and turn to the Old Testament prophets, he made his readers see the significance of repentance with retrospective clarity. He did this by establishing, first, the promise of salvation. Without that promise, Urlsperger knew, Christians—and not only those suffering from disease and epidemics—could be weighed down by the immensity of the task of repentance. Christians found knowledge and strength to continue in their present struggle when they knew that their repentance was ordained by God's providence and grace, and when they recognized the significance of repentance for their future salvation. In framing this retrospective perspective, Urlsperger in fact followed his central refrain: Jesus's command—"Repent and believe in the Gospel!"—demanded repentance but simultaneously assumed knowledge of the promise of the Gospel.[50]

Then, and only then—despite the label of "works righteousness" he faced—Urlsperger turned backward to repentance. He insisted that Christians could not focus solely on God's offer of salvation; they must still repent past sins. The order of salvation "had to be followed." Only by following the order of salvation could the faithful Christian "come through the opened door into heaven and enter into the kingdom of God." The spiritual and physical trials of repentance could not be avoided by anyone "who wants to have part in God and his kingdom here and there."[51]

For Urlsperger, the New Testament promised the fulfillment of the Old Testament prophecies and the coming of the kingdom of God. While it would be appealing simply to believe the promise and avoid the difficult work of repentance, God had ordained otherwise. Urlsperger emphasized this by focusing on repentance first, after his brief acknowledgment of God's promise. Christ wanted you to "change and transform your sin," he wrote, and then believe in him "who is offered to you in the Gospel."[52] This meant meditating on the Old Testament prophets. Urlsperger selected passages from Joel, Jeremiah, and Isaiah, which made clear the need for Christians' full commitment to repentance of their past sins: "turn yourselves to me with your entire heart" (Joel 2:12), "'turn again, you backsliding Israel!' says the Lord, 'so I will not distort my countenance against you'" (Jeremiah 3:12), and "wash, purify yourselves, put your evil essence from my eyes" (Isaiah 1:16).[53]

Urlsperger set Christians to the arduous and constant tasks of turning, washing, and purifying themselves. Here he opened himself to the critique of his Augsburg colleagues, and, indeed, it might seem counter to Lutheran theological understandings of the bondage of the will to place so much emphasis on individual effort in repentance and transformation. Urlsperger was always careful, however, to stress the simultaneity of the Christian condition—at once sinner and righteous—through constant retrospection. While he focused on the human effort of repentance, the future promise of God's grace was always there, always anticipated. Fulfilling the prophets' past calls to repent depended, ultimately, on Christians' recognition of their limitation and belief in God's future mercy: "surrender," Urlsperger wrote, "to God through his grace."[54]

Perceiving that the order of salvation involved simultaneous repentance and belief allowed readers to move both backward and forward with Urlsperger as he discussed the theological meaning of physical suffering. In the tract's section on pestilential epidemics (*pestilenzialischen Seuchen*), Urlsperger argued that sickness—and the order of salvation that it brought into clarity—was a gift. If used correctly, it focused sufferers not only on the general sins of humankind but also on their individual dependence on God for redemption. He offered an explicit scriptural example that evocatively illustrated both the order of salvation and the faithful Christian response to the worst disease and suffering: referring to 1 Samuel 3, Urlsperger wrote that if it was decreed that "you and everyone in your house would have to die, answer '*He is the Lord; He does what pleases him!*'" In this commitment to providence, Urlsperger found a model of the Christian practices of repentance and faith in the face of prophesied mortality. These practices were essential for Christians who sought to overcome the natural fears and questions that accompanied sickness and who found in sickness an opportunity to focus on their salvation. When praying for community and neighbors, readers should not think first of their physical survival, "of the avoidance or lifting of the plague," but should rather dwell on "the gift of repentance." The sick should be exhorted "to murmur not against the Lord and his laws, but rather against their own sins."[55] They should trust in God's providential promise; then reflect on its meaning, the depths of their sins, and the effective and purposeful use of the opportunity pestilential sickness provided for repentance.

God's providence was found in recognizing that the order of salvation was a "*gift of God*" and that this was true even in the most difficult, repentance-inducing suffering. For Urlsperger, the order of salvation was to be seen as "an *encouragement*"; indeed, "the entire book rests on such order as its *cornerstone*."[56] Although the order of salvation came with great requirements and difficulties, it also gave Christians a clear and essential roadmap for their journey in faith and active response to sickness. Mather had also sought to give his audience a narrative that would support them through present suffering and the difficult work of repentance to which they were called. He did this by focusing not on the order of salvation but instead on biblical exemplars, whom the audience already knew would ultimately be saved. Thus, as in Urlsperger's writing, God's promise and the challenge of repentance always stood side by side.

Both Mather and Urlsperger structured their work with community in mind. Both assumed that repentance would find its fruition only with trust in God's promise and the retrospective perspective and reflection made possible by this promise. These ministers offered a balance that Protestants sought: the consolation that could be found through both the activity of repentance and the trust in divine oversight. Through narrative, Protestant communities actively reckoned with personal and emotional experiences of present suffering, and these intimate narratives ultimately gave them a lens to God's transcendent power and mercy throughout time. Christians could repent past failings and hope in the future clarity of God's providence; they could remember that epidemics and death were but part of a longer Christian story.

Sickness and Narrative, Community and Intimacy

Ministers like Mather and Urlsperger wrote on sickness not only from the demands of pastoral care with attention to theological orthodoxy but also from the personal experience of suffering and loss. They sought order and the need to balance right belief, but their writings were also shaped by intimate and emotional relationships and experiences within a community. They did not simply seek passive acceptance of their authority, church doctrine, or even of God's providence; they were convinced that an active response to sickness would bring consolation through connection to community. Christian narrative responses to sickness were intimate and emotional acts; these acts were shaped by social expectations as well as by the experiences of each individual in unique relationship with family, community, and God. Mather and Urlsperger modeled this narrative response to sickness; they enacted meaning by seeking God's providence at the nexus of practice, community, and theology.[57]

Mather wrote his first version of *Wholesome Words* at a time of deep suffering and loss within his family. In 1702, a smallpox epidemic was spreading through Boston, infecting several of his children, while his first wife, Abigail, was in the final stages of an unknown illness, possibly breast cancer. In a journal entry, he wrote that he had printed *Wholesome Words* as a "Sheet" of pastoral advice at his own expense, divided his "Flock" into three parts, and tasked three men with its circulation. He offered the sheet in his stead, as he could not constantly attend the sick because of his duty to "the sick in my own Family." The second edition, published in 1713, likewise appeared at a time of profound loss in Mather's household: a measles epidemic took his second wife, Elizabeth, their newborn twins, a two-year-old daughter, and a maidservant. In suffering, Mather looked to his community and the promise of consolation; he practiced a narrative of repentance and retrospection, seeking God's providence.[58]

While Mather's authority and discourse within his community were important, his narrative must also be read in this context of his own pain. His writing was a deeply personal act that both reflected and promoted Protestant norms. His position as a "relational subject" reveals a complex view of subjectivity and power—a view that accounts for how subjectivity and power can be "internalized, enacted, and transformed" within society and its configurations. Mather's pastoral guidance on sickness—like Urlsperger's—details a practice not only of power but also of individual experience and relationship. The ministers both demanded and, in turn, depended on community and right relationship with God.[59]

Mather lived these challenges of community and theology within his own home. Early in 1702, before the smallpox epidemic that prompted *Wholesome Words*, his wife Abigail began showing signs of sickness. On May 25, she had a miscarriage in the fourth or fifth month of her pregnancy. This loss marked a period of worsening health for Abigail, and in early June she was momentarily thought to have died before staging a remarkable recovery. Abigail's health again worsened, however, and the Mathers consulted a variety of medical advice, including pursuing a curative Abigail learned of in a vision. At the same time, Cotton prayed fervently for God's mercy and grace, continually repenting his sins and failures.[60]

As he counseled his own community, so Mather also sought a retrospective perspective on this personal trial and a spirit of resignation to God's providence. In his journal he acknowledged that Abigail had repeatedly been spared by God following their fervent prayers. In late August, however, Mather paused to write that he might have been "too hasty and sudden" in interpreting his wife's periods of comfortable health as a blessing from God. Mather's emotional attachment to the woman he described as "my dearest Creature" and "*Desire of my Eyes*" (Ezekiel 24:15) had made Mather "shortsighted" in his faith in God's plan and knowledge: "The Lord may have marvelous Blessings in store for me, and my poor Family, beyond anything that I can at present imagine, or would, indeed be willing to imagine. In those Things may my Prayer and Hope have a glorious Accomplishment, and the Holy One must not be limited unto the Sense which my Folly and Fondness, would putt upon the Expectations which He has given me." Mather knew not to limit God to his human perspective and creaturely love; he knew his wife was dying and he needed to prepare. He did so by reflecting on divine love—"*an everlasting Love*"—that pardoned human sins through its own intimate sacrifice, the loss of "*the Son of thy Love*."[61]

After Abigail died on December 1, Mather decided to publish her funeral sermon, alongside the sermons for their five previously deceased children, in a compilation titled *Meat Out of the Eater. Or, Funeral-Discourses Occasioned by the Death of Several Relatives. Work Accommodated unto the Service of All That Are in Any Affliction; but Very Particularly Such as Are Afflicted with the Loss of Their Consorts or Children.* Mather's grief was profound; in his preface to the section of the book on Abigail, he wrote of a mother sleeping with her children in a tomb, after "the saddest Funeral that ever he saw." He hoped his writing would be a consolation to others.[62]

The title of Mather's sermon collection was taken from Judges 14:14: "Out of the eater came meate, and out of the strong came sweetness," a riddle from the story of Samson. After a lion had attacked Samson, he ripped it in two and later found within the carcass a beehive with honey. He offered the riddle as a wager to a group of Philistines, who coerced his new bride to reveal the answer. Furious, Samson slaughtered another group of Philistines. Left alone, he remarried a second Philistine woman, Delilah, who betrayed him, leaving him blind and imprisoned; yet Samson finally triumphed over the Philistines.[63] Although this is a disturbing and bloody story, Christians have long found the lion to be a type of Christ, and as historian Adrian Chastain Weimer has argued, for Puritans the text took on an explicitly providential significance: "The Geneva Bible commentary emphasized God's providential purposes, calling attention to the 'secret worke of the Lord' in Samson's delivery of Israel from Philistine rule." The phrase "meat out of the eater" became a frequent "stand-in for the inversion of hardship into blessing," a theme evidenced most notably in the popular devotional reader *Meat Out of the Eater* (1670) by Puritan Michael Wigglesworth.[64]

Like generations of Puritans, Mather sought to invert the suffering and losses of his community into blessings. In his sermon dedicated to Abigail's life, he relied on the scriptural story of Ezekiel, whose wife, "*the desire of his eyes*," was taken suddenly by God as a sign to his many enemies within the community. Mather wrote that he did not mean to compare his own life to that of Ezekiel, an important prophet. Rather, the suffering of a great servant like Ezekiel was a reminder of all humanity's inescapable condition of original sin. As in the case of Miriam's leprous suffering, the "affliction upon [one] Family . . . is but a sign of a greater Confusion to come upon the Publick." Indeed, in Mather's Boston, the suffering was widespread: "Tis a Season, wherein Desireable Relatives are taken away, from very many of our Neighbours. Many Eyes are Weeping, because the Desire of those Eyes is taken away." For Mather, the epidemic was a time to reflect on God's hand in sending disease, the "Little Time that you have to be together," and how to "Improve this Little Time, to the best Advantage for Eternity." Mather did not understate the challenges of loss; he dwelt on the physical transformations of mortality that reveal the folly of human perceptions: "When we see Beauty turn'd into Ashes, Loveliness become Loathsomeness, the Greatest Charms become a prey to Worms, and the Desire of our Eyes become the Horror of our Eyes." Yet, for Mather, this inversion of beauty into the grotesque was where faith was born. Only in such loss did one truly resign in dependence on God, the "Eternal *Potter*," who was both righteous and comforter.[65]

As bleak as Mather's suffering was, he did find comfort in "the Hand of God," which, though it took his loved ones, also left a "very rich Anodyne and Cordial unto us to think unto whom and what He has taken them." In life, Mather and his family had encouraged one another in faith; therefore he trusted that "the God, who has taken them away, has then Taken them to Himself," to "where all Tears are wiped from their Eyes." With the anodyne and cordial of their memories, Mather and his community could look forward, moreover, to a future reunion of their Christian community: "when we meet them again in the Heavenly World, there will doubtless be some Rapturous Expressions of Gladness agreeable to the Heavenly State, upon the meeting of such as have been Instrumental to bring each other unto it." Mather longed for the consolation that his current sufferings would be transformed by a future perspective; as his wife's last words proclaimed, "HEAV'N, HEAV'N WILL MAKE AMENDS FOR ALL."[66]

The promise of a future salvation and reunion was thus a major concern of Mather's personal experience at the time *Wholesome Words* first appeared, and this promise shaped his text. While the tract (as it appears in surviving later editions) stressed repentance and God's judgment, particularly in its early sections, future consolation was an ever-present theme, a theme that required the practice of providential thought. Mather relied on biblical forebears—part of the larger community of the faithful—whom readers knew would ultimately be saved. These biblical figures and stories should not be read as mere examples for Mather's Puritan audience. For Calvinists, the church of the elect in the Bible was part of the single unified church that spanned history.[67] The sins, repentance, and faith of these Christian forebears could be understood retrospectively as part of the universal and superhistorical salvation narrative of the true church. Mather called individuals to see themselves—as he saw himself and his family—in this communal narrative of repentance and deliverance.

In *Wholesome Words*, Mather's words bridged earthly and heavenly time and community. They turned to time past, through biblical exemplars, in order to connect suffering and faith as the illuminating manifestations of God's providence and grace. Mather stressed this communal and transcendent nature of narrative with the inclusion of a speech, which he recommended could be read aloud to sufferers as a final consolation. The speech emphasized the promise of resurrection by addressing the deepest human fears concerning the body, soul, and time after death. It cited Christ's sacrifice for humankind and encouraged the sick and dying to die with the trusting and Christlike faith of the martyrs, especially the first Christian martyr Stephen. The speech concluded with a rhythmic series of injunctions to be read to the dying: "*Dy*, Perswaded, that thy *Soul* shall never *Dy*. Fully Believe, the *Immortality of the Soul*; *Departing hence*, think, *I am going to the Immortals*. *Dy*, Perswaded that thy *Body* shall after *Death* return to *Life*. Strongly Believe, *The Resurrection of the Body*, when thy *Mind* is taking a Farewel of thy Weakned *Body*. *Dy*, Perwaded of the Heavenly Blessedness, which is *Reserved in the Heavens* for the Righteous." If the faith of the sick person was not strong enough to confront the encroaching breach from the earthly body and time, Mather cautioned, the speaker should urge him or her to look to the past and to believe in the future. The dying should have faith in Christ who had triumphed over death and believe that God will watch over the orphans left behind. In the end, the goal was "*Peace*."[68]

With faith in the promise of resurrection and salvation, Mather brought his tract to the culminating solace of Christian theology: the salvation, resurrection, and reunion of the entire Christian community, including children. He urged his audience to reflect on the paragons of Old Testament trust, who had faith in "a better country, that is, an heavenly" (Hebrews 11:16), even though they lived before Christ and the early Christian martyrs. Unlike these Old Testament figures, Mather's community knew the story of the resurrection and of the martyrs who faithfully followed, and this knowledge was a paramount advantage for his parishioners in their own suffering and in their witness of the suffering of others. What followed death, after all—and which Mather knew so well—was the grief of the family and community, and such was particularly the case in the death of children. Mather counseled "the *Profoundest Resignation*" in this instance. He cited the scriptural examples of Abraham, who was ready to give up his son Isaac according to God's command, and Rachel and David, who refused comfort on the death of their children (Genesis 22:12, Jeremiah 31:15, 2 Samuel 18:33). "*Lamentations* are not *Amiss*," Mather wrote. "We must not be Stocks and Stones." But the parent must "*not Sorrow as others, that have no Hope*" (1 Thessalonians 4:13).[69]

In the end, as above, Mather began another rhythmic repetition of consolation: "*Why make ye this Ado?*" a phrase that he wrote and repeated four times as he brought his tract to a close. The question came from Mark 5:39, a passage in which Jesus, after healing one woman from the plague, also brought the synagogue ruler's daughter back to life. Mather elaborated on the question "Are not the Dead gone only a Little before, and shall not you Quickly follow them?"[70] With a long retrospective glance—through the Old and New Testaments, the martyrs and the plague victims, the despairing and the trusting—Mather wrote a Christian story of sickness and made a case for repentance and faith in God. It was a story that relied on both community and the providential promise of the ultimate consolations of future salvation, resurrection, and reunion.

Like Mather, Urlsperger wrote his text from communal and personal experiences of sickness. Although there are fewer sources on Urlsperger's intimate experience of sickness, his text nonetheless highlights how sickness narratives reflected not only authoritative norms but also popular and relational writing practices of the broader Protestant community.[71] The very structure of Urlsperger's narrative, for example, demonstrates an underlying theological commitment or practice of reading that grew out of the larger Protestant community of readers and witnesses. This practice of reading is apparent in how Urlsperger expected readers to be able and willing to move back and forth in confronting the order of salvation (repentance then belief), an "order" that was not in fact sequential or orderly.

Eighteenth-century Protestant readers were well trained in this reading practice by popular writings of their time, including conversion narratives. Readers knew the theological story of sin, redemption, and salvation. They also knew the struggles and setbacks that constantly affected the Christian faithful. John Bunyan's *Pilgrim's Progress*, an incredibly popular text in both English and translation, was a classic model of constant forward movement and repeated falling back. Overall, the pilgrim Christian is on a journey of progress toward the promise of salvation, but he faces numerous challenges, he loses his way, he must relearn lessons he already knew, and he is willing, always, to do this because of his hope for the future, his recognition of past failings, and his faith in God's providence. In this way, Protestants wrote narratives that constantly linked "memory and expectation."[72] In an era of proliferating print culture, with much of the new writings emphasizing the authority of individual experience, Protestants both privileged the unique Christian life and subsumed it into the larger story of God's providential direction. Sickness writings—like spiritual autobiographies—were to weave together intimate individual experiences with communal expectations.[73]

Urlsperger's audience thus expected his manual on sickness to offer a framework for individual response within communal theology and narrative norms. He tightly bound sickness to Protestant notions of sin; disease, epidemic, and pain were ever-present and repeatable realities for all Christians. In this way, intimate bodily health and sufferings, in their constancy and repetition, could be bound to the simultaneous and cyclical sensations of assurance and anxiety expected of an individual Christian working toward salvation. These cyclical sensations, made familiar in popular conversion narratives, are often identified within Puritan piety but are also found within Pietism.[74] Urlsperger's narrative asked readers to move back and forth between, on the one hand, the "memory" of past sins, sicknesses, and evidences of God's promise and providence and, on the other, the "expectation"—or hope—for salvation and for clarity over the meaning and significance of suffering. In this way, Urlsperger structured his sickness narrative after a conversion narrative: for an individual but always with the spiritual emphases and practices of his community in mind.

Urlsperger's own experiences of sickness evidence his personal engagement in this narrative practice of pursuing God's providence. When his wife was dangerously ill in 1718, Urlsperger wrote to August Hermann Francke, detailing the eruption of a white rash all over her body. "Between fear and hope," Urlsperger wrote, he turned to God, who tested them, and he asked God to be their strength, to lift up their souls, and to refresh the body. Urlsperger continued, reflecting that "such struggles of suffering and belief" allow God to be rightly revealed and known as "our only ground."[75]

God's sovereignty was a major theme of Urlsperger's work, providing not only a course of action for the suffering but also a familiar consolation—a consolation that required not only the acknowledgment of humans' limited perspective but also their complete dependence on God. He highlighted this consolation perhaps best in his section on epidemics in *The Health of the Sick*, where he created a hypothetical dialogue that envisioned a loving, fatherly, providential God. In describing epidemics, Urlsperger wrote that God sends them, but that God also protects—as a father cares for suffering children and as a physician heals the sick. With this love and care in sight, Urlsperger anticipated the questions, doubts, and anxieties of the sick with responses that offered comforting references to God's faithfulness, dependability, and strength. To the reader's potential fear of being "entirely helpless and forsaken," Urlsperger provided, "is one abandoned, then, who sits under the umbrella of the highest and remains under the shade of the all-powerful?" To the common and unnerving concern of insanity or delirium in final illness, Urlsperger wrote, "God beholds the heart, not the external senses." To anxieties over the speed of decline—"Oh! if only it didn't go so quickly"—Urlsperger exhorted that, with proper preparation, a quick ending meant only that "you are so much earlier in heaven."[76]

Urlsperger's hypothetical dialogue then turned to the most troublesome, intimate fears concerning death: the community left behind and the final condition of the individual, physical body. He again pointed readers to God's providence. In responding to concerns over dependent family and children who survived, he wrote that they would be cared for "according to the will of God . . . he cares for all." Humans were not in command, Urlsperger reminded readers. Rather "God sits in the regiment and leads everything well." One difficult objection focused on the individual body and resurrection: "What will happen with my poor corpse?" This was particularly worrisome to those who feared they would not be properly buried during the mass deaths of a plague and the corresponding social breakdown. God did not care, Urlsperger wrote, "whether or not your body was under the Earth, as long as it happened according to God's will. . . . Why do you worry about the future? Care for your soul. The external house is already watched over by the universal architect."[77] While Urlsperger did not emphasize future familial reunion, as did Mather, he told a story of God's providential and fatherly care over the entire Christian community. The consolations offered by God's promise were numerous and extended to the physical, created world. They were concrete reminders of the rewards of individual preparation and repentance.

Urlsperger urged his readers to think of this providence and, in so doing, to look to the past for evidence that would buttress their faith

Figure 1.1. Plate introducing Part I of Samuel Urlsperger's *The Health of the Sick and the Life of the Dying*. The text reads, "Nach deiner cúr mein Arzt ich gülffe, / Bey dir allein steht meine hülffe" (I plead for your cure, my physician, / My help stands with you alone). Samuel Urlsperger, *Der Kranken Gesundheit und der Sterbenden Leben* (Stuttgart: Müller, 1723). Bayerische Staatsbibliothek München, Asc. 5516 k, p. 25, urn:nbn:de:bvb:12-bsb10270065-1. Reprinted with permission.

and perseverance in sickness. "You should believe," Urlsperger wrote, "that God, in the middle of his wrath, thinks to his mercy; and that he proves such with many words and examples."[78] The section on plagues did not list any specific biblical examples of consolation in the midst of loss and grief, as Mather had done with his repeated reference to Mark 5:39 ("Why make ye this ado?").[79] Rather, the section left readers to re-flect individually and retrospectively on "words and examples" through which God had shown providential care and signs of past, present, and future mercy—be it in biblical forebears or in their own lives.

Although sources on Urlsperger's personal experiences with suffering are limited, there is evidence of the pastoral transmission of his teach-ings on sickness in Ebenezer, Georgia, among the small community of Salzburger refugees whom Urlsperger helped to sponsor and who re-ceived a shipment of the second edition of his book. It is likely the com-munity's ministers also had—or had read—the first edition. In the fall of 1750, Ebenezer Pastor Johann Martin Boltzius recorded a parishio-ner's interpretation of a recent epidemic of "Rothe Friesel," which in two months killed more than a dozen children in the small community.[80] Boltzius himself lost two children. After the funeral of the second, a pa-rishioner named Brandner told Boltzius that he "considers it significant that God began his chastisements" in the pastors' houses. Brandner then connected the present 1750 epidemic and Boltzius's loss of children with an event from seven years previously, when an epidemic killed many of the cattle in the community, striking first the house of another Ebenezer pastor, Israel Christian Gronau. When the previous epidemic began in a pastor's home, the community was astonished and had questioned what such a beginning meant in terms of God's providence. On that occa-sion, the pastor Gronau responded by reading to the community from 1 Peter 4:17–19: "For the time is come that judgment must begin at the house of God: and if it first begin at us, what shall the end be of them that obey not the gospel of God? And if the righteous scarcely be saved, where shall the ungodly and the sinner appear? Wherefore let them that suffer according to the will of God commit the keeping of their souls to him in well doing, as unto a faithful Creator." Brandner's recognition of a "parallel" between the two epidemics saddened the grief-stricken Boltzius. Yet he was also deeply moved by the parishioner's recollection of Gronau's impromptu lesson. He wrote, "From it I see how our dear parishioners profit in a Christian way from the things that occur among us."[81] The parishioner encountered disease, looked back to a previous moment of suffering and its lesson, and reflected anew on a scriptural passage that highlighted the universal corruption of original sin, warned unrepentant sinners, and encouraged faith in God's providence.

Reminded of the past and hopeful in the future, Boltzius found comfort in Brandner's narrative of the present epidemic. His journal entry recorded a moment of transmission—it evidences that the practice of retrospection and the appeal to God's providence were important components of sickness narratives, shared in intimate community between both clergy and laity. It is difficult to know with certainty how Urlsperger's and Mather's tracts were read and interpreted in the Puritan and Pietist communities of eighteenth-century New England and Georgia, or the specific ways in which they shaped deeply personal narratives of disease. Evidence like Boltzius's journal entry, however, suggests that the themes that appeared in pastoral manuals reflected and infused descriptions of disease in the wider community.

* * *

Writing about sickness in the eighteenth century was a chance to practice providential thought. Ministers modeled a narrative form that gave believers an opportunity to respond to sickness—to seek God's will in their suffering, to repent and perceive God's promise, and to find consolation both in this promise and in their place in Christian history and among intimate community. Narrative was crucial to responding to sickness, to right Christian belief, and to community. Through retrospection, the sick could replot their lives and their relationships—to God and to their community—and in so doing they could live Christian theological principles of repentance and hope in connection with family, community, and forebears.

These accounts reflected powerful communal norms and expectations, as many scholars have observed. Nonetheless, sickness manuals—and the patterns and forms they advocated—were also established in and reflected the emotional experience of the sickroom and the lives of the writers and readers. These narratives were at once intimate and disciplinary; they consoled as they controlled. Protestants placed enormous value on the individual account of the Christian life, in part because each individual account affirmed anew the experiences and truths of the past and the continuing extent of God's providence over both the individual life and the wider Christian community. The community depended on widespread participation in this conviction. That does not minimize, however, the significant consolation individual accounts offered in times of sickness, providing both sufferer and witnesses with an activity and connection. Sickness stories brought together the "extraordinary and the ordinary, the normative and the transcendent."[82] At once deeply personal and theological, these accounts both provided and demanded a practice: to retrospect, to repent, to find providence—and, in so doing, to find order, community, and hope.

The theology and language of sickness articulated in Mather's and Urlsperger's manuals were appropriated in personal illness narratives of the eighteenth century. Understandings of disease are socially created and, as some scholars have argued, can ostracize those who are sick and suffering. But the work of applying or finding meaning in sickness can also reflect the agency of individuals struggling to interpret suffering.[83] When confronted with pain, eighteenth-century Protestants employed the language with which they and their audience were familiar. They wrote stories that explained their individual difficulties and circumstances and that addressed their most fervent theological questions and spiritual concerns. But, always, they used the tool of retrospection and appealed to God's providence. Providence suffused writings on illness at this time, appearing not only in published pastoral tracts but also in the published and unpublished letters, journals, and memoirs of men and women around the Atlantic world.

2

Writing Sickness, Witnessing Providence

Letters, Journals, and Memoirs of the Atlantic World

In two letters from January and March 1776, Eli Forbes described his wife Molly's final sickness and death to her father, Ebenezer Parkman of Westborough, Massachusetts. The previous December, shortly after moving to Gloucester, Molly Forbes had developed a cough, a burning sensation in her stomach, and pain in her breast. She found a hard spot under her nipple. Treatment with a plaster uncovered an ulcer, but she was convinced that it was not as bad as a previous ulcer she had suffered. Eli Forbes did his own examination and saw worrisome signs of spreading hardness in the back of her breast and the glands under her arm. He decided not to tell Molly his worst suspicions. The doctors treated the ulcer with plasters until a discharge appeared, offering some relief; but the case became dangerous, and Molly Forbes realized she would die.

Thereafter, Eli Forbes's account alternated between a passionate description of his own despair and a beautiful narrative of his wife's final days. He described her "free" conversation and prayers for sanctification, her gradual assurance of God's care, and her final transformation from a mortal to a spiritual state—a narrative that, in the end, transformed Eli's despair as well. According to Eli, Molly requested no further prayers for her life but asked, rather, "tht I may be enabld to honour God by my dying behavor." She "continued in a most Heavenly Frame and when she saw me dissolved in Tears and my Heart ready to bust she said, Dont weep so, you have more Reason to Rejoyce I shall leave you but have still in God." In her final moments, Eli wrote, "I went to put my Face to hers . . . but she put me from her as having done with all Mortals without a Sigh without a groan or a struggle she breathd out her Soul before nine." Distraught, Eli Forbes nonetheless was eventually able to write that Molly's "Death was in short as comfortable as Death can be—and She dyed as [I] wish to Dye."[1]

Eli Forbes recorded his wife's sickness and death with painstaking detail. His account served as a detailed testimony to his community of his wife's physical experiences and salvation story—and his own. As Protestant pastoral manuals had urged, he used the experience of corporeal pain and loss to act, to reflect on his wife's and his own spiritual state, and to find consolation in God's direction. Through narration, Forbes offered an account for those absent; he included everything his contemporaries would expect. He described with direct, precise observation the physical and spiritual state of the sufferer, he ordered the events into a familiar narrative, and, finally, he confirmed God's mercy even in the midst of suffering and doubt.

In witnessing Molly Forbes's sickness and death, Eli Forbes told a common if generally overlooked story in the history of medicine and religion. Historians of early modern medicine often focus on epidemics, which offer plentiful and evocative sources of past diseases, medical interventions, and social divisions. Yet, like Molly Forbes, most early Americans' experience of pain and suffering was defined by nonepidemic disease.[2] Sickness was nonetheless still a communal experience, meant to be witnessed and shared both immediately and in writing, and, as Eli Forbes's account attests, this witnessing and narrating was a deeply religious and social act. Scholars in the medical humanities have highlighted the important role narrative can play by allowing sufferers to connect the often isolating, individual experience of disease to broader communal paradigms. But this scholarship discounts early modern sickness narratives and focuses on contemporary accounts, relying on an old-fashioned yet still persistent dichotomy between the "religious" views of the past and the "scientific" world of now. Pathography, one scholar argues, is a modern genre, "appropriate to a more materialistic culture where the physical replaces the spiritual as a central concern, where the physician replaces the clergyman as the agent in the healing process."[3] Such claims rest in the common story of a radical break from the past—a secular transformation—and are deeply problematic. As Eli Forbes's account demonstrates, spiritual concerns were significant for eighteenth-century sufferers, but so were the material and physical realities of suffering and healing. Eighteenth-century Americans wrote about sickness in spiritual *and* physical terms; and their language, fears, and hopes were rooted in the dual experiences of spiritual forsakenness and physical pain.

To write about sickness was to witness God's providence in the individual life—in all its spiritual and bodily detail—while inhabiting a narrative form familiar to the wider Protestant community. From New England Congregationalists to German Pietists in colonial Georgia, this narrative form proved appealing and pervasive in the eighteenth-century Atlantic world notwithstanding the challenges presented by pain itself, by medical advances, and by increasing skepticism. Sickness and pain could be silencing for some sufferers, affecting the very ability to write, but narratives were often finished by others, demonstrating the immense social importance of such sickness accounts as confirmation of God's providence in the life of the individual sufferer and of the community. As the Enlightenment-era emphasis on firsthand observation and the medical "case" emerged, sickness narratives merged this focus on recording physical and medical details with preexisting Protestant patterns of martyrological witness to God's grace in the individual life and death. And, finally, by the end of the eighteenth century, changing ideas about heaven, God, and predestination caused some authors to chafe against the parameters and norms of Protestant theology—particularly the concept of an inscrutable and punishing God, on the one hand, and a predestination that limited human freedom, on the other. Yet in writing sickness, skeptical authors still remained fundamentally tied to a retrospective narrative of human suffering and redemption as a witness to God's providential grace.

Detailing Sickness, Overcoming Silence

When confronted with physical suffering, eighteenth-century Protestants placed urgent importance on the act of writing as a means to interpret, comprehend, and communicate their pain. Even in the face of increasing silence, with limitations on their ability to communicate, writing remained crucial. It allowed sufferers to enunciate their pain and apprehension and to narrate and maintain their identity and relationships. Through narrative, they articulated and eased both spiritual and physical anxieties by connecting to their community. Protestants did this by following the narrative patterns encouraged by their pastoral leaders and accepted and expected by their community. They looked back on their life, seeking and interpreting God's providential direction and care in sickness and health and considering their own actions and spiritual state as they discerned meaning in their pain and loss. Writing and sharing stories captured an individual's narrative from spiritual disorientation and physical silence, making it a story of the community and a story of God's providence.[4]

Eighteenth-century Protestants were familiar with narrating their experiences in relation to community norms. Conversion narratives were a widely read genre, in which authors were expected to follow a well-worn pattern. A template for writing both is incredibly useful and can be confining. Yet Protestants had often used such templates as "a creative means of literary self-discovery," as historian Bruce Hindmarsh has shown. Conversion and sickness alike were narrative opportunities for individuals to interpret and relate their unique experience of God's grace in familiar, communal terms. The collection of unique individual experiences with common narrative features, at the same time, confirmed God's providential direction over both the individual and the community.[5]

Unlike conversion, however, sickness could be a very mundane event, even if it was at times life defining. On any given day, the effects of sickness could frustrate an individual's plans or profession. Because of its persistent and universal character, sickness was thus a never-ceasing opportunity for individuals and communities to reflect and locate their day-to-day life within a narration of providence. On the evening of June 28, 1774, for example, the Methodist itinerant Francis Asbury took up his journal and recorded a frustrating day of sickness and limited speech. A crowd of people had attended public worship that day, but Asbury was unable to preach more than a "few words of exhortation." Asbury later narrated his silence before the eager audience as Satan's way of tempting him "to murmuring and discontent." Writing allowed Asbury to reflect and to interpret his sickness and limitation. He prayed for resignation to God's will while questioning why, as a servant of God, he suffered silence during worship. He found guidance in scripture, recording the passage, "*If I be without chastisement, then am I a bastard and not a son.*"[6] Through writing and scriptural reflection, Asbury worked to interpret his quotidian physical suffering and silence as marks of his spiritual chosenness and God's providence.

When Asbury overcame his silence through writing, his account became another piece of the many writings shared among communities of like-minded faithful throughout the Atlantic world. In Asbury's case, his journals were published in the United States beginning in 1789 with the first publication of the *Arminian Magazine* of the Methodist Episcopal Church in the United States. Methodist readers, publishers thought, would profit from Asbury's writing and witness of God's providential ways; they would be able to apply such a narrative to their own unique experiences.[7] This interpretive work demanded active engagement in the practice of not only writing but also reading, rereading, and sharing writings for spiritual comfort and retrospective clarity.

As Asbury's account reveals, there was often a hybridity between private reflection and public sharing at this time. Sharing the minutiae of physical setbacks and challenges was essential to the larger stories of conversion, revival, mission, and—above all—God's oversight in the Protestant Atlantic world. Accounts of conversion and of sickness were often passed around both informally, as journals and letters were reread and moved between friends and community members, or more formally, as manuscript or published volumes or as features in religious magazines. This widespread practice of Protestant print and correspondence culture extended beyond English-speaking Protestant communities and into German Pietism, where the correspondence and journals of missionaries and their communities were edited, published, and shared throughout the Atlantic world and beyond—Pietist mission sites reached from North America to Tranquebar (today Tharangambadi) on the eastern coast of India. Within revivalist and missionary communities, ministers' journals, like Asbury's, focused on everyday details and community life, but they were also written with full knowledge and anticipation that they would be published and distributed to a large audience of religious sympathizers and possible benefactors. Such was the case, as well, with the journals of well-known English itinerant ministers George Whitefield and John Wesley. These accounts, at once private and public, were essential to the Protestant renewal movements that defined eighteenth-century Christianity; readers were "edified" and inspired by accounts of the challenges and perseverance of diverse Protestant communities, all showcasing God's providential power and reach.[8]

Writings did not need to be formally published—like Asbury's—to be shared. The 1750s memoir of Sarah Pierpont, which was compiled from her journals and "published" as a manuscript volume by her minister Ebenezer Parkman, reflects the private and public nature of a lay individual's account of God's providence over her day-to-day experiences and sicknesses. Pierpont called her diary the "Minutes of the Breathing of God's Spirit on Her Heart." A Congregationalist from New Haven, she "began early to observe the Motions & Influence of the Holy Spirit on Her Inner-Man" and kept a journal "of Her Experiences or soul Exercises." For Pierpont—or, at least, for her editor Parkman—narrative provided an opportunity to record those experiences into a treasury for the future, for moments when "she could hardly belive [*sic*] herself to be a Christian." She could look to previous times, and when "the Evidence broke out, with such irresistable brightnes, & Glory . . . she could no longer Doubt."[9]

For Christians like Pierpont, the practice of writing tracked the moments of God's work in their lives. Such a record could be reread during future struggles and a former spiritual state reflected upon. For Parkman, editing and sharing Pierpont's account after her final sickness and death was an act of preservation. The book was, first, "To be a universal Example to all Christians In (all most) all Times, Cases, & Conditons [*sic*]. Secondly that it be read, & considerd, with a serious Mind; even as a soul, looking into Eternity; and to the awful Tribunal, of a just, & Holy Judge; where we must all shortly appear, to give an account of all things done in the Body, whether Good, or Evil." Meanwhile, Pierpont's triumphant spirit "(that once Experienced those Things in the Flesh)" looked on, "going along with you, as you read," and praying that "[you] fight the good Fight of Faith, as to lay hold an Eternal Life." Pierpont's manuscript memoir, as edited and introduced by Parkman and shared among her community, demonstrated an intimacy and community that transcended time and place, and that recorded a voice lost to the material world.[10]

The centrality of writing to Protestant spiritual practice and community is perhaps best demonstrated by sickness sources that lamented an *inability* to write or a profound limitation on writing. When eighteenth-century sufferers attempted to write despite sickness and disease, the act attached them to a larger community and allowed them to find some voice and control in suffering. The resulting narratives also provided a record upon which Protestant authors and audiences could later look back, when they feared, like Pierpont, they might suffer uncertainty or unbelief. An inability to write, then, not only was a significant sign of physical deterioration, but also could leave the sick and their loved ones or witnesses feeling unanchored and adrift.[11]

It is not hard to find evidence of the silencing effects of illness in eighteenth-century sources. Archives offer evidence in abundance. In a collection from 1790s Virginia, for example, periodic sickness disrupted the attractive, regular, and error-free script in John Hargrave's letters to his employer, Henry Banks, a land speculator in Philadelphia. Hargrave always apologized for any silence or irregularity, and his apologies remind us of the physical requirements of writing in the eighteenth century. During a sickness in September 1797, for example, Hargrave wrote, "You will meet with some difficulty reading this letter, for I am obliged to write as I lay on my pillow."[12] In October 1798, Hargrave suffered from what may have been yellow fever and, again, explained his illness in terms of his near inability to write: "But I can assure you that I am at this time scarsly able to hold a Pen, for I have been immensely unwell for a considerable time." By December he was worse, writing, "I am scarsly able to set up having on me a voilent [sic] Yellow Jaundice, which makes my skin and eyes precisely the Colour of Saffron and Gives me fevers. As soon as I am able to say much I will write you a long letter."[13] Hargrave, in ways, measured his escalating health issues in terms of his ability to sit up, hold a pen, and write.

In citing the limitations sickness placed on their ability to write, authors revealed the importance they placed on the activity of narrating sickness. Writing allowed them to witness the providential meaning they found in their suffering. In 1744, for example, Gotthilf Francke, the director of the Francke Foundations in Halle, Germany, wrote to Pietist Lutheran missionaries in Georgia. Francke's wife had died a year previously, and since that time, Francke wrote, he had suffered emotionally as well as physically. During Lent he was attacked by a painful rash all over his body, which prevented him from preaching and other work. Although the illness had eventually eased, Francke could still "not write much" without "always renewing my pain." Francke wrote despite the pain, however, and also because of the pain: "I have wanted to report this only to continue unshaken your revival in intercession for me. God alone helps me and us all through this valley of sorrow."[14] Francke's words evinced a difficult mixture of physical and emotional distress, but through that distress he sought to emphasize God's help. This help could be manifested physically (as seen in the illness's diminution and the accompanying ability to write again) as well as spiritually, which he could testify through writing.

In May 1754, Francke's correspondent in Ebenezer, Georgia, the pastor Johann Boltzius, suffered from a difficult eye ailment that caused great discomfort and taxed his remaining eye and his ability to read and write. He wrote a supervisor in London that he would no longer be able to "keep an official journal [or] write according to my duty and heartfelt desire." Boltzius was nonetheless necessitated periodically to take up journal keeping and letter-writing duties, but he rarely failed to mention the pain in his eye and the difficulty of the task. He grew weary but continued to write of not only his own hardships but also those of his community's members, and, like Francke, he never ceased to narrate these trials as gifts of God.[15]

Boltzius viewed his suffering and that of the community providentially. It was sent by God to strengthen faith, and writing was a practice that allowed him to confirm this view. Narrative offered a break from the pain that figured so large in his temporal existence and provided a retrospective voice in which he could find a different perspective on time and human limitations. He wrote joyfully of God's sustenance for Christians in this life and the feast that awaited the entire Christian community in heaven, after persevering through all of God's chastisements on earth.[16]

Limitations were a powerful reminder of a human's dependence on God's providence. Not only ministers felt stress at the physical impediments to writing that often accompanied sickness and pain. Sarah Pierpont, the New Haven Congregationalist, was dismayed by how sickness caused major pauses in her journal keeping, but she persisted—hoping her sickness and narrative would have providential significance for both herself and her community. According to Ebenezer Parkman, her editor, Pierpont's journal "was Interupted, by many avocations, & Changes of Life: but Especially by Bodily Disorders, Illnesses, Sicknesses, & Confinements to Her chamber, & often to her Bed." Even when Pierpont did manage to write, she remained affected and narrated her pain in terms of spiritual trial and separation from the written word. On July 25, 1742, she awoke "very Dull & stupid this morning in Spiritual Things no life in Reading or Secret Prayer." Her physical inability to read weighed heavy on her. She described her pain in terms of her hope for a future spiritual blessing:

> O Lord pitty me_ My earthly Tabernacle is often shaking and now seems to be very Tottering O that my inner Part may grow Strong Blessed savior come in by thy Spirit and put all Things in Order in my Disordered Soul O that when ever I shall be calld to quit this House of Clay I may quietly yea Joyfully sleep in the Arms of Jesus And whilst thou art embraceing me in the Arms of thy Love Let me take thee Dear Lord in the Arms of Faith then I can say Now let thy Handmaid Depart in Peace.

Pierpont prayed for God's guidance and imagined a future state of spiritual health from which she could look back and see her life as "a shining Example" to her neighbors. She knew she could "not live such a Life of my Selfe"—that is, through her own power—any more than she could "create a world," but God could "effect it" through "Grace & Power."[17] Pierpont denied her own power to create, through her actions and words, a model Christian life. She distanced herself from the work of creation, work that the literary scholar Elaine Scarry cites as an important component of the language that emerges after pain.[18] For Pierpont, creation was God's work. She could not on her own turn her pain into redemption, nor could she achieve a post-suffering position of spiritual meaning and purpose. Relying on the providential stress of Protestant sickness narratives, nonetheless, Pierpont could write about her sickness, imagine its spiritual fruits, and witness God's grace.

Sarah Osborn, who was, like Pierpont, a New England Congregationalist, also struggled to write due to illness, especially at the end of her life. She suffered for much of her life from pain in her hands and diminishing eyesight; by 1770, Osborn wrote her friend Mary Fish Noyes that her pain hindered her ability to write. Reflecting on Osborn's increasingly infrequent writings, historian Catherine Brekus has written how troubled Osborn was by the silence caused by her pain: "The desire to write still burned 'like a fire' in her heart, but because of her poor eyesight and physical weakness she rarely picked up her pen. Hungry to express herself, she sometimes asked friends to write letters for her or composed poems in her head. But one of the greatest joys of her life had been lost. Each day she had to reconcile herself to silence."[19]

Osborn had long used narrative to navigate and enunciate her physical suffering, which suggests how difficult this inability to write might have been for her. Silences like Osborn's, however, "are not likely to be an emptiness," as historian Greg Dening observed. Through writing, Osborn had long interpreted her suffering in terms of God's providence and ensured herself of a record that would, after the passage of time, offer a valuable retrospective perspective. On July 28, 1753, for example, Osborn wrote of how she awoke with a "sick headache, much out of order every way, and my spirits sunk exceedingly." She was downcast by her physical symptoms and acknowledged that "Satan or unbelief took the advantage of my indisposition," causing her to despair over troubles with her work. But Osborn did not give in. Her long-standing practice of writing allowed her to imagine providential guidance even in the midst of troubles. She wrote, "I reward the trial that I may see the hand of Providence providing and over-riding all things well for me, as faith tells me it will." As if to prove the point, she returned to this entry seven years later, on April 15, 1760, and wrote in the margin, "Time has shown me how needless these cares and fears were, for hitherto the Lord has helped me." Osborn ended her original passage with a prayer for forgiveness and renewed trust in God's "providential care."[20] One can imagine that, even when resigned to silence in her writing, Osborn continued to interpret her suffering as a witness to God's providence.

When it came to the final days and moments of illness, narratives were almost always the responsibility of able-bodied (and able-minded) witnesses. Some account of the state of the body and the soul at death was expected among eighteenth-century Protestants.[21] As in Eli Forbes's letters to his father-in-law, these accounts offered important last observations on an individual's spiritual state as well as more general thoughts on decline, suffering, and the meaning of these experiences.

Sarah Pierpont could not write during her final illness, and her only witness, her attendant, died soon after. Pierpont's editor, Ebenezer Parkman, lamented this fact, but he presumed to fill in the lacking details, writing that Pierpont's final illness "was the most bright & glorious Part of all her Life." According to Parkman, Pierpont "might well be enrolled among the Ancient divine Heroes" and the "sacred Catalogue of Christian Worthies" found in Hebrews 11. Through her faithfulness, she brought forth great spiritual fruits and hope for salvation. Parkman went so far as to narrate Pierpont's ultimate salvation: "at length an Entrance was administered unto her abundantly into the Kingdom of our Lord & Saviour Jesus Christ."[22]

Pierpont's final sickness narrative was not her own. It witnessed God's providence through biblical citations, but it lacked the details and vividness of her earlier retrospective descriptions of her pain and her efforts to enunciate that pain. Such personal details were a crucial part of these narratives—they demonstrated God's providence on a personal and local level and allowed readers to imagine the surprising ways in which God's plan might work out in their own bodies and spiritual lives.

Observers of suffering and pain often wrote accounts of sickness; what was unusual about Parkman's description of Pierpont was his complete lack of a firsthand account as he composed her narrative. Nonetheless, Parkman could not complete Pierpont's memoir without a description of Pierpont's final end and spiritual state. These accounts were crucial for eighteenth-century Protestants; any reader of Pierpont's memoir would expect such a narrative conclusion and find it lacking without.[23]

We cannot surmise how a contemporary reader would have felt about the indirect and impersonal description of Pierpont's final illness, but perhaps they found Parkman's words tenable because they followed narratival norms and were based on his earlier selections from Pierpont's journal. Parkman described Pierpont's occasional "Frame" of "ruminating" on "Divine Providences[,] Past experiences & the present temper of her Mind," in which she sometimes "chids her selfe." He then quoted an example of Pierpont's self-chiding: "'O my unbelieving Heart! Lord helpe me to believe still to trust in thy kind Providence &c which I have abundantly experienced throwout my whole Life. Lord 'tis base Ingratitude in me to mistrust, I that have had such Things shown me such great Things done me." Throughout her life, Pierpont sought to trust in the "kind Providence" of which she saw evidence whenever she reread her diary. She hoped that this providence would lead her through each—yet unknown—stage of her life, even to salvation.[24]

Above all, Pierpont's memoir is a striking reminder that sickness narratives, no matter how personal, operated always between the personal story and the narrative themes expected by a wider community. Eighteenth-century Protestants wrote carefully about sickness; they often described their suffering in intense detail and in spite of physical limitations. They conveyed the brokenness caused by pain and their efforts to enunciate that pain, and they articulated spiritual experiences. This challenging work was always oriented toward the end of highlighting God's providence over the entire community of Christian faithful. Sufferers—and, sometimes, their scribes—sought consolation in each distinct story of physical distress and a new witness to God's direction over sickness and its spiritual dividends in the Christian's life.

Witness to Suffering and Death

Observers of suffering and death played an essential role in bearing testimony for those not present, including both absent contemporaries and an imagined posterity. Such testimony was shaped by a desire for details—physical and spiritual—and for a discussion that reflected on the providential significance of the suffering. Emerging from both an Enlightenment-era focus on the medical "case" and the Christian tradition of martyrology, testimonies stressed firsthand observation, precise dating or organization, and meticulous evidence, all of which would allow audiences vividly to imagine sufferers, their patient and faithful endurance of physical pain, and, correspondingly, their spiritual state and hope for salvation. The dual empirical and martyrological characteristics of witness accounts spanned the entire eighteenth century and were common to diverse Protestant communities, from New England Calvinists to Georgia Pietists. In narrating sickness and death in terms of God's providence, writers needed both physical and spiritual evidence and careful interpretation.

Narratives of sickness and death were expected; they and letters requesting them appear frequently in eighteenth-century archival collections. Witnesses left detailed accounts of sickness for loved ones, for communities, and—sometimes—for themselves in letters, journals, and memoirs. In a study of eighteenth-century correspondence, historian Bruce Redford has argued that a central characteristic of letter writing is that it presumes absence. In a way, letter writers are magicians, who work to sustain "the illusion of physical presence."[25] Though not all witness accounts of sickness came in the form of letters, Redford's insight is nonetheless useful for understanding a fundamental aspect of sickness narratives. The central moment of sickness had to be recorded painstakingly. The point was to create that illusion of presence—to make the audience feel the immediacy of a physically and spiritually tense situation.

In their effort to create this illusion of presence—to provide a detailed testimony—witness accounts of sickness and death were shaped by both medicine and martyrology. Medical epistemology of the era privileged empiricism and a detailed narration of the patient's symptoms. But this careful observation of suffering was also rooted in martyr accounts. The Greek word for witness is "martyr," a term that developed within Christianity to mean one who bears witness to his or her faith in God's will and mercy, even unto death. Although "martyrdom" is associated with death at the hand of persecutors, there is a long tradition within Christianity that the holy suffering and death of the martyr could and should be emulated in even the most ordinary sickness and death. This tradition developed with and from the *Ars moriendi*, or the "Art of Dying," a set of medieval texts that described the temptations and struggles Christians would meet and need to overcome on their deathbed in the final struggle between God and the devil over their soul. To suffer and die well—patiently and without fear—was to bear witness to one's Christian faith and to God's mercy.[26] As in martyr accounts, witness accounts of sickness could, in turn, inspire observers and audiences in their own Christian journeys.

When witnesses included individual details of suffering and faith, they ensured both that the sufferer was real and recognizable to the intended audience and that the account reflected God's providence. Eli Forbes, whose account of his wife Molly opened this chapter, had taken seriously the task of witnessing and narrating his wife's sickness and death for her absent father. Forbes wrote his father-in-law a detailed account the day after Molly died. When his father-in-law did not immediately respond, Forbes wrote a second account, even more detailed than the first. The careful dating and organization of the second letter suggest his effort to perform adequately as witness to his wife's sickness and death: both to maintain his control of the narrative and to display his firm mnemonic grasp on the essentials that would accurately convey his wife's symptoms and make the story real for her father. These essentials included both the physical manifestations and treatments of sickness—the coughs, lumps, plasters, and discharge—and the several affirmations of Molly Forbes's strong faith. He emphasized his father-in-law's role in this faith, writing that his wife urged him to thank her father "for his pious Care of her Youth, tell him (So she) those impressions made on my mind by the grace of God thru his pious care offerd me the greatest Support in Death." Writing letters required the fashioning of "a distinctive world at once internally consistent, vital, and self-supporting."[27] By offering details of his wife's suffering and faith, Eli Forbes told his wife's personal story in a way both he and her father would find familiar and complete. Such details upheld Molly Forbes's life as a true and suffering example of faith and God's mercy.

In addition to offering recognizable details, witnesses also often stressed and explained the exemplary and inspiring suffering and martyr-like faith of their loved ones. In 1745, Catharina Gronau, a Salzburger living in Ebenezer, Georgia, wrote of her deceased husband to his absent family and benefactors in Europe. She reported the active medical interventions to save her husband, a missionary, who suffered intensely and eventually became bedridden.[28] He remained, nonetheless, "always content and at peace with his savior." Gronau witnessed her husband's final sickness and death as a testimony to true Christian faith. She described his efforts to bring souls to Christ while he was still able to work, and this work continued in the last six weeks of his life, although he was confined to his bed. Though he "suffered much in body," Gronau wrote, "his heart was always content and at peace with his savior." She stressed God's providence over her husband's life and death. The physician and other caretakers did everything in their power to treat him, yet "the wonderful God had decided to fetch him home, and so he did, and since God decides and does nothing but what is useful and blessed to his children, so we may much less criticize his ways; rather we must—although with bowed hearts and weeping eyes—say: the Lord has given, the Lord has taken away, the name of the Lord be praised."[29] Gronau interpreted her husband's sickness and death by remembering the clarity his suffering gave him in his calling on earth and by citing a text from Job, a reminder of God's faithfulness to humanity throughout history.

In a letter to Samuel Urlsperger, Ebenezer's sponsor in Augsburg, Catharina Gronau remembered her husband's faith as she contemplated her own. She echoed the consoling language of the verse with which she began her letter: "If I sink down into a powerlessness / Then he lifts my soul out again / The balsam of life flows into it." The verse came from a hymn based on Psalm 23 ("The Lord is my shepherd"), a psalm that evokes images of spiritual guidance and physical care, even through periods of darkness. Gronau ascribed to God great power over the recent events in her life. With the death of her husband, she had lost a "spiritual guidepost," yet his faith at death further bore witness to a God who soothed her grief and taught her to follow "in his footsteps." Gronau's witness of her husband's sickness and death transformed her present observation into a testimony for distant relatives, confirming her husband's life and death witness to God's plan and grace.[30]

Ministers played an important role in ascertaining and detailing the physical and spiritual state of sufferers and in interpreting these details in terms of God's providential guidance over the wider community. Many accounts of sickness and death were recorded by pastors, whose presence was expected at the bedside of the sick and dying. In October 1741, Pietist minister Johann Martin Boltzius recorded a difficult fever that had swept through his community of Ebenezer, Georgia. The account appeared as part of a general summary that he submitted to his supervisors in London and Halle, which he expected would be published and distributed to a large audience of Protestant sympathizers. In his account, Boltzius explained his recording of the widespread sickness in light of a scriptural passage—Tobit 12:8: "One should conceal the secrets of a king; but it is honorable to make public and praise God's works."[31]

For Boltzius, narrating sickness in his community was a biblically mandated part of his pastoral duty; sickness was part of an important update regarding the new community's precarious survival and anxieties over it. His circle of correspondents expected his report, and he found writing an uplifting spiritual exercise. Boltzius described the circumstances of sickness as a "cross," which, he reflected, had been God's "wonderful way" of bringing several community members to conversion and others to repentance—or at least to awareness "of their carnal and obstinate minds."[32] The act of writing allowed Boltzius to look back on the physical trials of the year and not despair but rather see, in the end, spiritual benefits for the social body.[33] His narrative—per Tobit—publicly praised God's work.

Sickness in a community could dominate small-town pastors' daily journal entries, and they often used the occasion to retrospect on the spiritual state of their community and their own household. In the challenging work of caring for the sick, they sought and described God's direction. This was the case in the journal of John Ballantine, a midcentury pastor in Westfield, Massachusetts. In the early part of his ministry, Ballantine kept his journal on pages interleaved in an almanac. The format left very little room for detailed entries; Ballantine briefly recorded his pastoral work and, at the end of the year, a summary of major events in his community, including baptisms, admittance to church, deaths, and marriages. The short journal entries generally included remarks on sermon texts, visitors, and occasional strange occurrences, such as an earthquake. In periods of sickness, however, the entries became crowded with Ballantine's duties and movement. In a twenty-day period in July 1743, for example, Ballantine made at least sixteen visits to different families with illness, recorded fourteen prayer requests for the sick, and attended three funerals in addition to preaching four regular sermons, one of which required travel to the neighboring town of Blandford, where the population suffered from worms. These difficult twenty days were the most intense of a four-month period of "putrid fever" in Ballantine's small community, during which he recorded at least twenty-five cases of the illness and seven resulting deaths.[34]

Ballantine reflected on the sicknesses and deaths of his community, finding, as in martyr accounts, spiritual admonitions and inspiration in the suffering he witnessed. In his early journal, such reflections were limited by space: he gave thanks for deliverance and prayed that "God would sanctify the sore strokes of his providence of late." Beginning in 1759, however, Ballantine began keeping a larger-format journal, which provided more room for such reflections. When reflecting on the sickness and death of an enslaved eleven-year-old named Cesar, for example, who suffered "great distress and pain" from "Consumption and Dropsy," Ballantine recorded a testimony to God's providence for both the youth and the enslavers in his community. The young, he wrote, needed to prepare; Cesar's early death was a reminder that one never knew when sickness might strike. Masters, meanwhile, "must take care of the souls of their Servants as well as their bodies." Cesar's death was an opportunity to reflect on the sins of the wider community and to find comfort

WRITING SICKNESS, WITNESSING PROVIDENCE | 71

in God's providence. Alluding to the bad weather at Cesar's funeral, Ballantine wrote, "In the grave secure from storms . . . the weary are at rest and servants are free from their Masters. Death levels all, the lowest are equal to the highest."[35]

The Protestant narrative of redemption and providence infused Ballantine's pastoral and personal recordings as his journal continued, over the next few months, to pivot between medical details of community members' sicknesses and deaths and his private and spiritual reflections on sickness within his own family. His children became sick with first the measles and then a fever between May and September 1759. He prayed for recovery and thanked God, again, for previous recoveries. Between these sicknesses within his own family, Ballantine reflected on the recent death of Abigail Fowler, a fifty-five-year-old woman. He described her patience in distress and her exemplary Christianity, and trusted—despite the loss felt by her friends—that she "gains by death." Ballantine echoed this attitude when the whooping cough appeared throughout the town in August and his infant Lydia became ill. He wrote that he desired to resign his children and himself to God's providential direction, praying that "the Lord spare her and make her a blessing, fit her and us for his Sovereign will."[36]

During this time of sickness, Ballantine witnessed his faith in God's providence with two retrospective entries. The first marked the anniversary of the death of his son Winthrop; he prayed that the death "be kept in remembrance and have a suitable influence." The second appeared on the occasion of Ballantine's birthday. He reflected, "I have lived 43 years in this world. Do I live so as becomes one that has had so much time and so many advantages to know my duty, how have I spent this time, have I spent it for God, my great Master, whom I am on so many accounts obliged to serve, how great has been God's patience towards me. I am nearer my end, am I nearer to God, nearer to heaven? May I work while it is yet day, for the night cometh when no man can work."[37] Ballantine's journals attended keenly to the passing of life, the suffering of those around him, and the constant threat of sickness and death. He recognized the importance of preparation, and he used his journals not only to reflect on the physical and spiritual examples he found in his community and family but also to witness God's patience with his own faith and preparation.

Having faith and hope through the end of sickness and life was crucial for eighteenth-century Protestants, who, as the martyrological tradition exemplified, interpreted such evidence as a sign of God's mercy and grace. Such faith and hope could inspire and console family left behind. The importance of this final faith was, perhaps, most evident in sickness accounts where the sufferer lost the ability to speak or sank into delirium. Observers, in these cases, turned to memories of the deceased's either general state of Christian faithfulness or last moments of cognition. For example, the Reverend Thaddeus Maccarty was prevented from hearing his wife Mary Maccarty's dying words in 1784 because pain impaired her speech. He penned a touching memoir for his daughters, emphasizing his wife's previous state of cognition and strong faith, as well as his conviction of her salvation and hope for their future reunion:

> She lov'd the Day, the House, the Worship & Ordinances of God. She prized her Bible, and was wont to say, that that was one of the last things she should ever part with. She read it much, with the Annotations, was well acquainted with the Contents of it, and it had its practical Influence with her. She was very careful in her Preparations for the holy Communion, spent much time in reading, meditation & Prayer. Prayer was her delight & daily Practice. She declared that she always came from the Sacrament, rejoicing. And the last time she attended (a few Weeks before she died) she told one of her Daughters, when she came home, that God had met her at the Ordinance and blessed her, and that her Saviour bid her welcome to his Table. And we entertain the hope that she has gone to sit down at the marriage-supper of the Lamb in the upper World.

Mary Maccarty's life left an example of trust in God's providence for her family: to "be followers of her, so far as she followed Christ, and have the unspeakable happiness & Joy of meeting her in the blessed World above, where there will be no more painful Separation." Such trust echoed a martyr's unspeakable consolation in Christian faith—a hope in the Christian's final triumph over suffering.[38]

Maccarty's trusting narration of his wife's death echoed the providential interpretation of suffering that he had outlined in a 1779 sermon, which stressed the importance of retrospection for interpreting the suffering and loss that characterized the fallen human condition.

Maccarty's sermon followed the story of Job, encouraging those who were suffering to remember that there would be a future perspective from which they could look back and find an order and a meaning to the events that caused so much pain. Maccarty wrote of the inevitability of pain and grief for all humans: "Bodily sickness & Pain, Bereavements of near friends & Relations &c., these are among the Evils, w[hich]. they are called to meet wth. These naturally produce Grief & Sorrow of heart. It can't be otherwise, as they have not & cannot put off human nature." He concluded, however, with great hope that they "are for the most part succeeded with Joy." Job exemplified this. Though "things may look dark & gloomy in the Course of God's Providence," the Christian knew of the "various Instances wherein God blessed [Job]." In both his personal writings and sermon, Maccarty stressed that, just as night turned to day, suffering turned to joy. Humans' perspective of God's providence was limited and incomplete, yet stories of great faith—like those of the martyrs—offered hope to Christian believers, hope Maccarty himself grasped in the death of his wife.[39]

Like Maccarty, minister Justus Forward relied on narrative and hope in providence as he struggled to interpret the death of a loved one whose capacity to speak at the end was marred by physical suffering. Forward's account is painstaking in its detailed description of his father's physical and mental decline. In a journal entry from 1766, he narrated his father's last waking moments, during which he shouted deliriously about robbers burning his house, intent on murdering the family. After his father's death, Forward decided to add a note to the end of the previous month's careful journal entries. He emphasized that during that month—before the delirium of the deathbed—his father had "a good Hope of himself" and "was sensible of the dreadfulness of being deceived, but upon the best Judgment he could make, tho't it would be well with him." Forward remarked that he had committed his father's good account of his spiritual state to writing at that point, when his "Reason was . . . intire."[40] Forward also mapped his father's final place of rest, in the midst of family members who had gone before and who had been noted for their faith. He found great comfort in this community of saints in which his father's body rested; and, though he suffered great sadness and even nightmares in the immediate aftermath of the loss, he thanked God that his father "left us exceeding good ground to think he was prepared for Death &

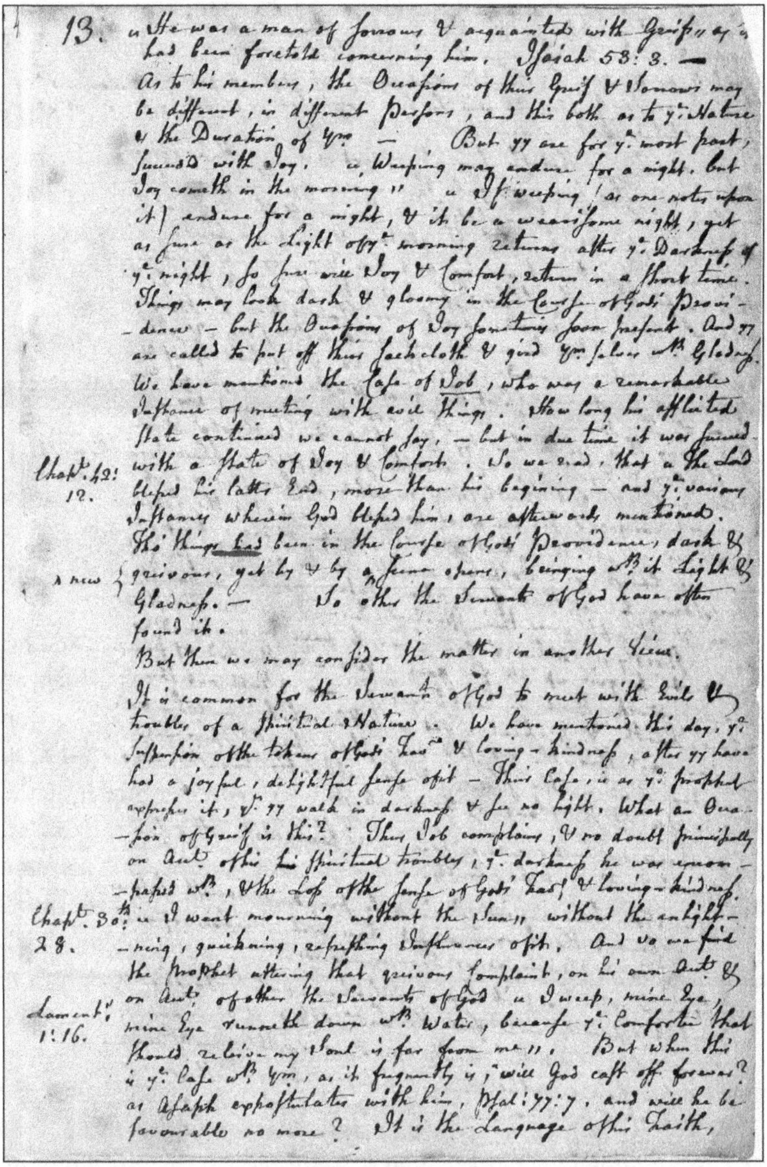

13. "He was a man of Sorrows & acquainted with Grief," as it had been foretold concerning him. Isaiah 53: 3. — As to his members, the Occasions of their Grief & Sorrows may be different, in different Persons, and this both as to ye Nature & the Duration of ym — But they are for ye most part, succeeded with Joy. "Weeping may endure for a night, but Joy cometh in the morning" "If weeping (as one notes upon it) endure for a night, & it be a wearisome night, yet as sure as the light of ye morning returns after ye Darkness of ye night, so sure will Joy & Comfort, return in a short time. Things may look dark & gloomy in the Course of God's Provi-dence — but the Occasions of Joy sometimes soon present. And they are called to put off their sackcloth & gird ym selves wth Gladness. We have mentioned the Case of Job, who was a remarkable Instance of meeting with evil things. How long his afflicted state continued we cannot say, — but in due time it was succeeded with a state of Joy & Comfort. So we read, that "the Lord blessed his latter End, more than his begining — and ye various Instances wherein God blessed him, are afterwards mentioned.

Chapt. 42: 12.

Tho' things had been in the Course of God's Providence, dark & greivous, yet by & by a new scene opens, bringing wth it Light & Gladness. — So other the Servants of God have often found it.

But then we may consider the matter in another View.

It is common for the Servants of God to meet with Evils & troubles of a spiritual Nature. We have mentioned this day, ye Suspension of the tokens of God's Love & loving-kindness, after they have had a joyful, delightful sense of it — This Case, is as ye prophet expresses it, ye they walk in darkness & see no light. What an Occa-sion of Grief is this? Thus Job complains, & no doubt principally on Acct of his spiritual troubles, ye darkness he was encom-passed wth, & the Loss of the sense of God's Love & loving-kindness. "I went mourning without the Sun," without the enlight-ening, quickening, refreshing Influences of it.

Chapt. 30th 28.

And so we find the prophet uttering that greivous Complaint, on his own Acct & on Acct of other the Servants of God "I weep, mine Eye, mine Eye runneth down wth Water, because ye Comforter that should relieve my Soul is far from me". But when this is ye Case wth ym, as it frequently is; will God cast off forever? as Asaph expostulates with him, Psal: 77:7. and will he be favourable no more? It is the Language of his Faith,

Lament. 1:16.

Figure 2.1. Page from Thaddeus Maccarty's manuscript sermon on Psalm 30:4. Twelve lines from the top, Maccarty wrote, "Tho' things had been in the Course of God's Providence, dark & greivous, yet by & by a new scene opens, bringing wth it Light & Gladness." Thaddeus Maccarty, Sermon, 26 November 1779. Maccarty Family Papers, 1742–1863, American Antiquarian Society. Photograph courtesy of the American Antiquarian Society.

that it ~~will be~~ is well with him."[41] Forward's editorial change of the verb
from future to present tense suggests his concern to record his firm conviction that his father had died in faith and with a hope of salvation. For
witnesses like Forward and Maccarty, turning to memories—alongside
the contemporary details—allowed them to piece together a narrative of
Christian hope and God's mercy even when the most desirable evidence
of salvation—based on cognition in the final moments—was unavailable
in the confused and frightening life's end.

Witnesses to sickness and death often found hope in God's providence by describing their loved one's suffering and medical disappoint-
ments in terms of Christian faith and the healing power of Christ, as
found in scripture. In 1750, German minister Johann Boltzius wrote to
Gotthilf Francke regarding his wife Gertraud Boltzius, who had been
suffering for fourteen years from complications resulting from the birth
of their first child. Boltzius began the letter by thanking Francke for a
shipment of medicine, but the most important medicine for treating his
wife was missing. He continued, recording what seems to be a mixture
of both his own and his wife's interpretation of this lack of medicine and
of her physical and emotional suffering. Regarding the missing medicine, he wrote,

> But she also has seen in it the hand of the Lord and awaited his help
> through the remaining blessed remedies, according to his merciful will;
> whereby, however, it is said: My hour is not yet come; indeed, also: do not
> be afraid, only believe; through which sweet words the Lord has power-
> fully raised especially my heart that is often anguished on her behalf. She
> rests with her great pain and long suffering through faith completely in
> her Savior, which rest is disturbed only from time to time through severe
> inward assaults [*Anfechtungen*], in which, however, our kind Savior does
> not test beyond ability, but rather after the thunderstorm allows the sun
> to shine again, and also makes her soul elect in the furnace of misery
> [*Elend*]. She very sincerely yearns to be soon with her Savior.[42]

The letter presented Gertraud Boltzius's suffering—both the physical
pain caused by lack of a needed medicine and the concomitant spiritual
torments—as sent by God as tests that prepared her for salvation. The
two biblical passages embedded in the text ("My hour is not yet come"

and "do not be afraid, only believe") were both from the Gospels. Both, intriguingly, came from scenes involving women, and both appeared shortly before Jesus performed a miracle. Using these passages, Boltzius connected his wife's long sickness to biblical stories of faith and salvation, thus narrating his wife's physical suffering with hope of future healing through faith in Christ—whether accomplished physically in this life or spiritually in the next.

Scripture was an invaluable resource for witnesses to sickness, even those distant or absent, who confronted the limitations of human life and perspective and wished to stress God's providence. Mary Fleming, a woman in Williamsburg, Virginia, found consolation in scripture when writing to her convalescing uncle Charles Fleming of the Seventh Virginia Regiment in 1777. Charles Fleming had just recovered from smallpox, which he contracted through inoculation. Mary Fleming gave thanks for the woman named "Robinson" who nursed her uncle, and urged her uncle to care for his health so she would "not be depriv'd of all that's dear." She had recently lost her brother, and when she felt overwhelmed by her own perspective on sickness and suffering, she imagined how her deceased brother—whom her uncle had been with at the time of death—would wonder at her mortal, "short-sighted" grief. To her uncle, she wrote,

> I thought of your situation at the time of his Death, and believe me I suffer'd more for the surviver, than for Him whom I trust is supremely blest and out of the reach of those distresses we mortals soon are subject to, & no doubt looks down with pity and compassion on those he has left behind him, & wonders how they can be so short-sighted as to grieve for those who enjoy the blessings prepar'd for them who [crossed out word] die in the Lord: they enjoy that Happiness which no tongue can tell, no pen describe, nor has it enter'd into the Heart of Man to conceive [page blotted].[43]

Ending with a reference to 1 Corinthians, Fleming questioned the ability of the human pen to fathom God's providential grace, yet she attempted to describe it by appealing to an imagined perspective through the eyes of her lost—and presumed saved—brother.

In the narration of sickness and death, witnesses recorded the persevering faith of the sufferer and themselves, and, correspondingly, God's mercy. These accounts were shared throughout eighteenth-century America among diverse Protestant communities. Observing and writing sickness and death created a testimony for the witness, their community, and their posterity. Protestants found meaning in intense suffering by narrating it with material details and evidence such that their audiences could imagine an individual's final sickness and death. Without fail, loved ones and ministers connected the mundane physical suffering of the medical case to spiritual themes of redemption and salvation that the wider community would understand. These themes included the exemplary death of martyrs, who died with hope in their salvation—the ultimate witness to God's providence over earthly life.

Change, Doubt, and Persistence

Toward the end of the eighteenth century, changing theological understandings of heaven, God, and predestination began to emerge in the context of the Enlightenment. Long celebrated as a place of unchanging glory, heaven began to be imagined as a place where progress and change might occur. And this shift, in turn, shaped Protestants' views of the end of life. At the same time, many Protestants developed an increasingly benevolent image of God. In a world where human happiness, choice, and freedom were increasingly prized, some grew wary of theological outlooks that emphasized God's wrath and predestination.[44] New ideas about heaven, God, and human agency altered specific features of sickness writings, but the providential and retrospective narration of redemption nonetheless remained the organizing premise of interpretations of suffering and death.

At the beginning of the eighteenth century, Protestants perceived heaven as it had long been seen: "as a place of rest and eternal contemplation." This idea of stasis had been crucial to the spiritual practice of retrospection, through which Protestants imagined an "end point" for gazing back on their life and spiritual journey. Yet over the course of the eighteenth century, as historian Catherine Brekus has argued, evangelical Christians developed a new vision of heaven, influenced by contemporary philosophical attitudes that saw change and progress as good. Evangelicals increasingly "hoped that [heaven] would be filled with progress, activity, knowledge, and friendship—heaven as a more perfect earth."[45] Even with this changing understanding, however, Christians continued to interpret the time leading up to death as an important opportunity to look back, repent, and prepare, and they continued to find consolation as they narrated their trials and active endeavors in response.

Between 1788 and 1792, Jeremy Belknap, a New Hampshire Congregationalist minister, and Ebenezer Hazard, a New York publisher, corresponded regarding the illnesses and deaths of their sons. Belknap's eighteen-year-old son became very ill in December 1788, and Hazard wrote Belknap several times through the sickness, praying that the "dispensation of Providence" might provide strength. He also encouraged Belknap to accept God's providential will and to adopt a retrospective perspective. Though "Divine rebukes" might be difficult, Hazard wrote, "they are proofs of a Father's love. They should lead us nearer to him; and, if they do, the time will come when even the remembrance of them will be sweet." Hazard maintained a traditional view of God's providence in human suffering: in the immediacy of loss, Belknap's afflictions were grievous, but such suffering could strengthen faith. With time and perspective, Hazard wrote, Belknap would remember his experience and pain with hope.

When Hazard's newborn son died a few years later, in 1792, Belknap condoled with his friend by merging the familiar language of God's providential care with a vision of heaven as a place of transformation. Belknap grieved that Hazard lost the "great satisfaction" of watching his child grow, along with the pleasure and assurance of his child's hope for salvation that such witnessing would have afforded. But Belknap also imagined a parent's proud perspective on his child's life in heaven, positing that Hazard's son would have an opportunity to grow and progress there: "He is safely lodged in that apartment of the universe which is destined to receive infant humanity, and preserve it from the contagion of the present state, that it may be introduced with greater advantage into a more exalted sphere, and that its faculties may expand and improve by the most rapid degrees in a superior world."[46] Belknap had lost his own son after a long and debilitating illness, and perhaps he found comfort in imagining, on behalf of his friend, the possibility of the safe and continued growth of a child in heaven. It was a way to retain an imagined retrospective view of the lost child's life and development and to find some hope in a spiritual maturation, progression, and salvation that would occur in the next world. Such a view offered providential consolation in the loss of a young child, whose promise, though unfulfilled on earth, would be fully unveiled in heaven.

Not all illness narratives were infused with unmitigated certainty and faith in God's providential care. Shaped by contemporary discussions of theodicy, American Protestants were increasingly concerned with how to reconcile suffering in the world with an image of God as good. While some Christian thinkers addressed theodicy by limiting God's intervention in the created order and relegating God's actions, instead, to creation or the eschaton, those who wrote about sickness generally maintained a strong conviction of God's active presence in their lives and pain.[47] When they expressed doubt or questions over the righteousness of God's actions in sending sickness, they nonetheless remained committed to a retrospective framework that confirmed God's providence in their own and others' suffering.

John Ballantine, the minister in Westfield, Massachusetts, faced many sicknesses in his congregation and within his home, and he recorded them in his journal with resolute faith in God's goodness in sending them—except one. On August 13, 1760, Ballantine took up his pen and questioned God's ways: "My child is dangerously sick, she is greatly distressed. Righteous art thou O Lord, yet let me plead with thee. I have sinned and done wickedly, but these sheep, what have they done. I can easily reconcile my afflictions to the divine perfections. That one who knows not the difference between good and evil and is not capable of getting good from affliction is thus distressed, is hard to be accounted for." While Ballantine admitted the righteousness of God's judgment in sending sickness to an adult like himself, he stumbled to account for his daughter's suffering or the use toward which such suffering could possibly be directed. He ignored even his own journal entries from the previous year, when his family encountered the dangers of measles, fever, and childbirth, and when he variously called on God to "fit her and us for his Sovereign will" and to "spare him and make him a blessing[.] [M]ay the Lord who revived him from the measles, recover him from the fever, that will be another obligation to devote him to Thee." Over the course of many previous diary entries, Ballantine had perfected the retrospective analysis of illness, the perspective it provided on God's design for humans, and the corresponding faith and trust such design encouraged.[48]

Yet despite the doubt conveyed in his plaintive exclamation of August 1760, Ballantine in fact retained a providentially and retrospectively inflected sickness narrative, as evidenced in the scriptural citations he embedded in the journal entry. "Righteous art thou O Lord, yet let me plead with thee" came from Jeremiah 12:1, a passage that followed the story of God's judgment against the people of Israel for worshipping other gods; and "I have sinned and done wickedly, but these sheep, what have they done" was from 2 Samuel 24:17, David's response to the plague that God sent in response to his presumption to conduct a census. Ballantine's choice of these passages is fascinating. Before questioning God's justness in afflicting his daughter, Ballantine chose to frame his question with the words of the prophet Jeremiah and the king David—as if he buttressed his right to plead with God by pointing to scriptural exemplars of faith who had also done so. These citations demonstrate how Ballantine couched his query within his commitment to a providential understanding of tribulation: God's righteousness and direction were assumed, because they were established in the past as illustrated throughout the Hebrew Bible. Ballantine's question over the rightness of his daughter's suffering may have been influenced by new ideas of human and divine goodness, but his narrative framing relied, ultimately, on a long tradition of humans who acknowledged—and yet were occasionally distraught over—God's hidden ways.

Those who witnessed sickness in their lives and writings were often moved by grief and perplexity to question God's providential design. Their accounts demonstrate that it was not always straightforward to narrate suffering and loss in terms of God's plan and mercy. As outlined by Mather's *Wholesome Words*, grief over the death of a loved one was understood as a natural human response, but it should be accompanied by a certain resignation to God's providential plan.[49] Sometimes, though, grief could almost overwhelm sickness narratives, creating holes of doubt and despair. Writers nonetheless always returned to—indeed, clung to—the providential emphasis of Protestant sickness writing.

Eli Forbes's letters regarding his wife Molly's sickness and death exemplify the extent to which grief could upset normal narrative patterns. In writing his father-in-law, Eli Forbes sought accurately to witness his wife's death, but he also conveyed his tangled emotions of horror and despair: "O my Father! my Father!—God, a Sovereign God who has said be still—has taken away from me my dear Partner,—my *Molly* whom I loved most tenderly—I know that it is God, a holy a wise God, a good and gracious God that has done it- and yet O Sir it cuts my soul thro, and thro." Eli Forbes described his emotions variously: his "passions" were unbalanced, his heart was made to "bleed afresh," the situation placed him "under such a cloud," the circumstance "has brake me al to pieces [sic]," and he was "in a great measure unfit for any Business but tht of weeping."[50]

Eli Forbes recognized in his wife's death a model for his own and, after several letters, was eventually able to write that "God has in his Wise and sovereign Providence seen fit to call home your dear child and my dearest *Molly*." He recorded her feeling of assurance, her perspective on her past, and her faith in God's providence, but in quoting her words he made clear that they were her sentiments: "She prayed me to imbrace the first opportunity to acquaint her Father of her Death and thank him for his pious Care of her Youth, tell him (So she:) those impressions made on my mind by the grace of God thru his pious care offerd me the greatest Support in Death."[51] Forbes knew the narrative pattern with which his letter should conform—his dear wife had dictated it in her last words—and it infused aspects of his account of her death, but he struggled to assume it fully as his own.

Forbes finally adopted a providential narrative of his wife's sickness and death in a letter written three months after her death, on March 14, 1776. He had at last heard from his father-in-law and appears to have found some consolation in this letter. After being in "so dark, so painful a Spot," he had found "Comfort and Light and cant but rejoice in tribulation. O may I have grace to conduct with Christian meekness and Prudence under this Rod." He still struggled with his loss, however, writing, "I loved her intirely it may be too much. She is gone but not lost therefore I love her still, and I believe she loves me, with what kind, I don't know. My affection is not lost, it is immortal, I love her *Name*, her *Dust*, her immortal *part*." Forbes nonetheless attempted to check these outpourings of grief and to use the language of trust in God's providence that he well knew. Thus, even while he despaired that "all the world is a Blank to me," he concluded, "may God point out the Path and dispose and enable me to walk in it."[52]

A providential narrative of suffering was not easily overtaken in the eighteenth century—not by grief, a new conception of heaven, a more benevolent image of God, or, finally, a rejection of the theological doctrine of predestination. In 1807 Samuel West, the Congregationalist-turned-Unitarian pastor of the Hollis Street Church in Boston, wrote a memoir that speaks eloquently to the power of providential themes in Protestant sickness narratives. Born in 1737, West had grown up in a Calvinist family in Rochester, Massachusetts. His father, Thomas West, was a Congregationalist minister. At some point, West chose to break with the theology of his upbringing and to reject the notion of God as a partial and "austere parent," who only "designed to rescue a Small part [of humanity] from sin and misery." West found such a representation of God as "dishonorary to the Great God and distructive of that peace and consolation [for] which Christianity was evidently designed." God was a "kind and impartial parent," West wrote, and salvation "belongs to us." It rested not on God's predestination but on human effort and will.[53]

West rejected predestination, but he held fast to the notion of God's providential guidance over human life—even in very active and particular ways—and this conviction was evidenced most strongly in his discussions of sickness and death. In February 1776, West's daughter Priscilla became ill with the throat distemper while staying with her grandparents. West's wife was expecting a child at the time, and although West was able to visit his sick daughter, circumstances pulled him painfully in different directions. Priscilla died and was buried soon after; West was left to comprehend the loss. Writing many years later, he stressed God's providence: God "who sees the end from the beginning" took children from the world "to preserve them and their friends from more painful events which He [God] alone could foresee." In retrospect, West could confirm that God always "consults our interest and happiness and it is both our duty and interest to acquiesce in his decisions and to say in the language of our divine Saviour and perfect example 'Father thy will be done.'"[54]

West looked back with a perspective that confirmed God's providence and power, and he merged this perspective with an interpretation of sanctification that required human work and effort. Reflecting on his loss after his daughter's funeral, West wrote that he sought "to improve the event by illustrating the example [of] David on the death of a child." Mather had also cited David's grief over his son's death in *Wholesome Words*. For Mather, David was an example that grief was natural for parents who had lost a child, but David (and—to note Mather's other example—Rachel) also served as a caution for Christians who refused the comfort accorded to people of faith. Echoing Mather, West reminded himself that he had a concrete example of God's comfort for the faithful in the midst of judgment: the birth of his son Benjamin shortly after Priscilla's death. West saw in the birth "nothing more perfectly wise and good than the measures of his [God's] Government." Such reflection on God's providence, West wrote, opened humans to happiness: "It would reconcile us to the most painful events and enable us to enjoy peace amid all the uncertainties and doubtful expectations with which we are here surrounded."[55] Remembering occurrences that confirmed God's good government girded faith during the trials of sickness and loss.

Ministers might exhort sufferers to patience and to submission to "the allotments of Providence," but West did not believe that religion could ever make humans find in pain "a state of enjoyment." Humans could never be "reconciled" to pain, West wrote, and "all the Philosophy and all the Religion in the world cannot convert pain to pleasure nor make us think that we are perfectly at our ease while we feel ourselves tortured in every joint."[56] He might have been responding here to teachings of the New Divinity movement—a reassertion of Calvinism among the followers of Jonathan Edwards, such as Samuel Hopkins—which taught that pain and suffering were good and could lead to a state of happiness found only in belief.[57] West rejected such an idea, but he remained committed to a traditional understanding of providence that relied on a retrospective perspective. When pain subsided, he wrote, "time and reflection will reconcile us to our situation."[58]

West argued passionately for human freedom, but he confined that freedom within strict limits over which God maintained an extraordinary power. "Man is indeed a moral and therefore a free agent," West wrote. He "bears the image of his Maker," and thus possesses power over his actions and morality. The sphere of humans' "agency," however, was severely curtailed. They were "completely dependent . . . even in that narrow sphere, on the universal agent, who fills, upholds and governs all!" Humans should fulfill their free agency "with propriety" and "according to the dictates of Conscience." The reward, thereof, was God's acceptance and human happiness.[59]

Thus West acknowledged human freedom in a limited way and framed God's power in general terms of creation and salvation, but he nonetheless also left considerable room for God's "particular Providence." He cited Alexander Pope's observation that "the World is governed not by partial but general laws," but West modified Pope's assessment. He wrote, "It ought to be remembered that the great Author of the Universe is intimately present at every instant of time with every particle of this grand machine, and that the operation of its laws is nothing more than the agency of the first cause, who can with infinite ease either increase or diminish their force for the accomplishment of his own particular purpose, and that without any appearance of miracle in the case." West was undoubtedly influenced by intellectual strands that posited God as first cause, but he did not relinquish his conviction of God's active engagement with and responsiveness to faithful Christians. West's father had favored interpreting his experiences in terms of "divine interposition," and, indeed, West saw "no absurdity in admitting it." Scriptures confirmed it, and it offered a great motivation for prayer and faith in the lives of Christian believers.[60]

West remained bound to the doctrine of providence, and it, along with a strong retrospective voice, shaped each page of his memoir, from the beginning to the end, and in the most profound moments of sickness, pain, and grief. Early on, West commented, "I am on a retrospect of my life thoroughly convinced of the truth of the following observation That Man is the child of Providence." For West, this recollection shaped his reflections throughout, even his reflections on the writing of the memoir itself. Illness repeatedly hindered his writing, and he occasionally decided to end his memoir, only to begin again when he had recovered.[61] After one close call with death, West reflected, "I gratefully adore that divine goodness which has thus rescued me from the hand of death, and rendered me capable of so much enjoyment as I now find, especially in writing these memoirs. I have recorded the acts of the loving kindness of my God, and I pray it may be useful to those very few of my friends who may think it worth their time and trouble to read them; that they may be excited to repose confidence in God and his all governing Providence as the only way to secure present peace and future happiness."[62] West perceived a spiritual practice in his retrospective recording of the events of his life; in so doing, he witnessed God's providence throughout his life and found faith in his future state.

Although West's emphasis on human freedom could have considerably weakened his commitment to providential thought, his reflection on sickness and death shaped how he wrote about his life and forged the final meaning he took from suffering. As in the writings of Ballantine and Forbes, doubts and uncertainties could overwhelm observers of sickness and pain, but their narratives returned always to God's providence. Their community expected this emphasis; looking back, seeking, and narrating the evidence of God's providential direction and human faith were central tasks for individual sufferers and their observers. These tasks provided a framework and voice in the midst of pain and loss.

* * *

Personal narratives of sickness shared the central themes of faith and consolation found in more formal, published pastoral manuals. Sickness and fear of sickness were constants in the eighteenth century, and pastoral manuals like those of Cotton Mather and Samuel Urlsperger recognized the effects disease and suffering could have within their communities. They offered messages of repentance, consolation, and faith to their readers by stressing God's providential care and by reminding sufferers that time and patience would bring a different perspective to pain and grief. Some scholars consider such published pastoral narratives as instruments of control, as opportunities for hammering orthodoxy or dogma on the sick without pity, and as speaking only of God's will while avoiding practical treatment advice. But such interpretations, which see narratives of disease as, in short, encouraging human passivity in the face of suffering, miss the point.

Narrative was an opportunity for activity in the face of sickness. Writing allowed sufferers to break free from the silencing effects of pain, to describe and make sense of their suffering, and to connect to their community through shared language and ideas. Through letters, journals, and memoirs, sufferers and observers recorded details of sickness for themselves, absent loved ones, and community members. These details reveal, on the one hand, the influence of emerging scientific and medical discourse that emphasized firsthand observation. On the other hand, the details and interpretation of faithful suffering and death also witnessed, as in martyrologies, God's providence; the minutiae of sickness and pain grounded and confirmed those seeking God's grace in everyday life, in community, and in final sickness and death. In both cases, the repetition and accounting of these details offered an activity and consolation in a time of turmoil. Although shifting Enlightenment-era ideas of human nature, the afterlife, and God challenged the providential commitment of some eighteenth-century authors, they could not, in the end, avoid it. Reflecting retrospectively on pain, death, and loss, writers remained committed to providence. It was a deep-seated and compelling theme for comprehending the challenges of human life, connecting the suffering faithful, and witnessing God's direction and mercy.

3

Experience and the Soul in Eighteenth-Century Medicine

In April 1748, in a small community in colonial Georgia, missionary pastor Johann Boltzius wrote a despairing letter to his supervisor Gotthilf Francke in Germany. A strange condition had appeared in Boltzius's community of Ebenezer: people—mostly children—were eating raw corn and rice, dirt, ashes, and clay. Nothing could turn them from their appetite for these things; even sugar and honey could not compete. Parents, distressed by their powerlessness, could barely stand to look on as their children became bedridden, feverish, and unwilling and seemingly unable to eat anything of nutritional value. Boltzius interpreted the condition and its spread as a trial sent by God, whom he called on for aid. He also asked Francke to send advice from the physicians associated with the charitable Francke Foundations and the medical university in Halle.[1]

Christian Thilo, the local missionary physician in Ebenezer, reported his own observations of the peculiar distemper in a letter to Francke. Thilo described an eight-year-old girl whose strange eating habits had eventually led her to eat tobacco stalks. He could find no medicine that worked; the girl would eat nothing else. She died, and Thilo feared the younger brother, who had learned her habits, would soon follow her to the grave.[2]

In September, Francke responded to Boltzius with the advice of a physician named Johann Juncker, who had been one of Thilo's medical instructors at the university in Halle. According to Juncker, the described disease was not unknown, but called pica. Pica was not a corruption of the body but rather the sign of a corrupted appetite or desire. Because the corruption had to do with desire, medicine was unnecessary. Instead, treatment should involve a bit of trickery: giving the patient the dirt—or whatever she most desired—secretly mixed with an unpleasant-tasting tincture of bitter apple or ox gall. This treatment would cure the disordered desire of the patient, particularly, Juncker added, in the case of children.[3]

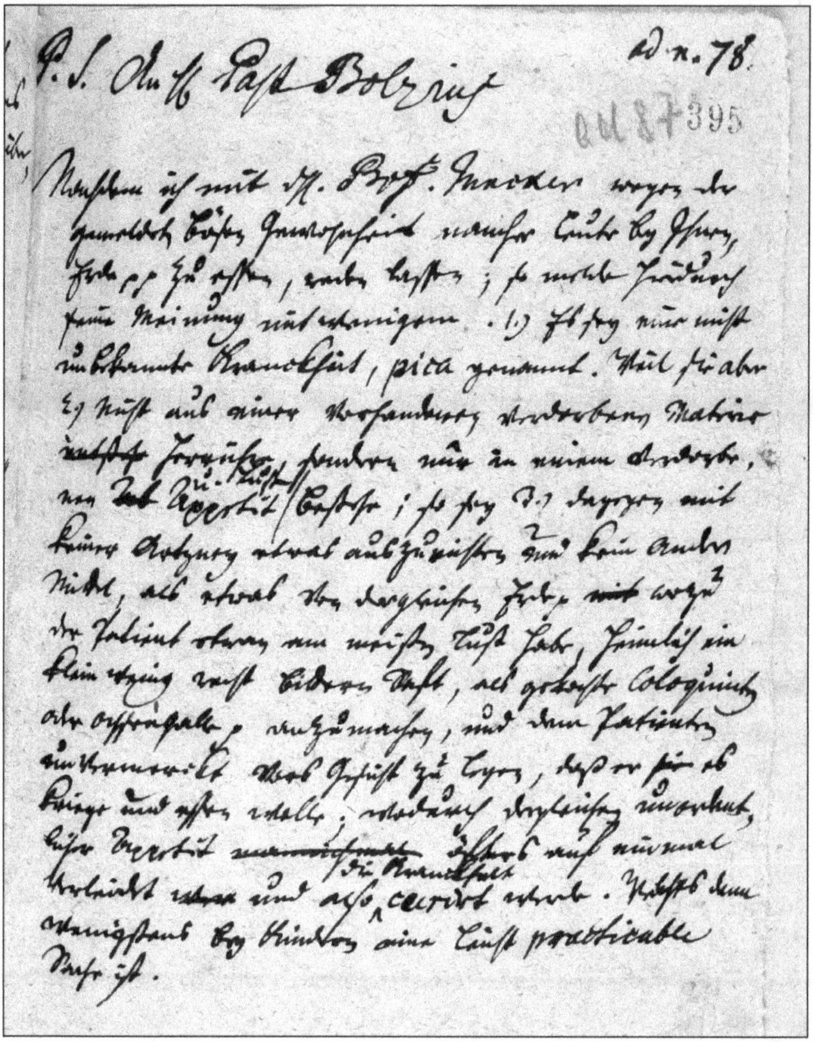

Figure 3.1. Postscript containing the physician Johann Juncker's advice on the treatment of pica in Ebenezer, Georgia. Although the letter is mostly written in Kurrentschrift, an older form of German cursive, the word "pica" is spelled out in Latinate letters, as was often the custom for writing medical terms at this time. It can be found in the fifth line down. Gotthilf August Francke to Johann Martin Boltzius, 9 September 1748. Missionsarchiv der Franckeschen Stiftungen 5A11: 87. Photograph courtesy of the Francke Foundations, Halle (Saale).

Two years later, in 1750, Boltzius was still reporting cases of pica in his journal, suggesting that Juncker's remedy was never received, was disregarded, or was ineffective. Boltzius tried bribing children, going to their school and offering rewards to those who did not eat the dirt, charcoal, or raw rice. The children could not control their appetites when they were alone, however, and he remained frustrated. He wrote that he had circulated an article on a cure, which he had found in a London magazine and translated into German for his community.[4]

The Ebenezer community's encounter with pica is a story of the intersection of religion and medicine in the Atlantic world. For eighteenth-century Christians, the created order, including the individual body, served as a symbol of the spiritual world. Disorder in the physical world meant something was spiritually amiss; it drew attention to the soul of the sufferer—or to the spiritual state of the suffering community—and called for close observation in order to discern God's will. In the case of pica in Ebenezer, not only clergy but also trained medical practitioners made their diagnosis and treatment in terms consistent with a long-standing Christian conception of a corrupted will causing bodily disorder. They echoed the conflict described in Paul's letter to the Romans: "I can will what is right, but I cannot do it. For I do not do the good I want, but the evil I do not want is what I do."[5] The human body, vitiated by the effects of original sin, was prone to sickness. Sickness thus demanded reflection on the state of the individual soul. It required repentance and dependence on God's grace.

Sickness was a problem not only for the individual body but also for the social body. As the pica episode demonstrates, both the minister and physicians were committed to combatting illness within the community. In so doing, they relied on an empirical approach to medicine that involved detailed observation, wide reading, and hands-on treatment.

Alongside their theological and narrative practices, eighteenth-century Protestants were also inspired by their widespread engagement with the natural world around them, including the medical theories, debates, and transformations of their time. Coupled with their faith in providence, this engagement often came in the form of mission. As Protestants rapidly expanded their evangelistic reach both locally and across the globe, many conceived of the world as a place given by God to explore and further human knowledge, while at the same time expanding and improving God's kingdom. Although some scholars might dismiss ministerial and mission-ary participation in medicine as nonscientific—or as a sign of religious decline or secularization—the historical record shows a fervent religious concern with the contemporary medical world. Protestants saw medicine and medical knowledge as divinely given and were convinced that caring for the sick offered an opportunity to do God's work in the world. Medi-cine was a chance to rid both the individual and the social body of physi-cal and spiritual corruption. Successful ministry and missions demanded direct involvement in the material world. They required communities to balance an attention to the human soul and salvation with the more earthy concerns of human curiosity, physical need, and communal survival.

Eighteenth-century Protestants lived radical lives as they pursued an impulse to evangelize, or to "do good," and as they experimented with medicine in conversation both with leading theorists and on their own terms. The Puritan Cotton Mather in colonial Boston, the Pietist Johann Boltzius in Ebenezer, Georgia, and the Methodist John Wesley in Eng-land (and beyond) participated in emerging arguments over the soul's role in bodily health, used new medical theories and treatment, relied on empirical approaches, turned to enslaved persons and women for medical knowledge, and participated in medical print culture. From de-bates over smallpox inoculation in Boston and concerns over the use of Peruvian bark in the treatment of malaria in Georgia to anxieties over a developing and at times abstruse medical orthodoxy, Protestants joined actively in a larger medical world undergoing key changes. They worked within multiple networks of knowledge, perceiving God's wisdom throughout the natural and human world and hoping to use this knowl-edge to pursue the providential call to build Christian community.[6]

Protestants, Early Modern Medicine, and Mission

Eighteenth-century Protestants engaged in a medical world that was both changing and diverse. New, mechanistic approaches to medicine had developed that challenged long-standing Christian understandings of healing. The soul's role in maintaining health came under dispute, as did the accessibility of medicine itself, as new medical orthodoxies often required extensive training and expertise. Christians participated widely in these developments and debates.

Protestants' attention to the role of the soul in bodily health had corresponded well to the holistic approach to medicine characteristic of empiricism in the early modern era. Empiricism, which had roots in the scientific method of Francis Bacon, depended on the firsthand observation of patients long emphasized within humoralism. Humoral medicine itself was grounded in the work of the ancient Greek physician Hippocrates and his second-century transmitter Galen. It divided the body into four humors (yellow bile, black bile, phlegm, and blood) and stressed the balance of these humors in the maintenance of health. This balance could be observed and promoted through diet and exercise as well as through treatments, like bloodletting or blistering, that drew out an excess of the humor perceived to be creating an imbalance and corresponding physical ailments. For example, fevers were often understood to indicate an excess of blood, and therefore a recommended treatment could require the removal of blood through bloodletting or cupping. Connected to the humors were the passions (choleric, melancholic, phlegmatic, and sanguine), which over time were variously related to the nerves or emotions. Someone with an oversupply of black bile, for example, might be melancholic. Humoralism thus provided the crucial groundwork for a holistic approach to healing with attention to both physical and interior health.[7] This concept, merged with empiricism, appealed to early modern Protestants, concerned with healing the individual, both body and soul.

This happy confluence of medicine and theology had allowed for the importance of the soul in body and health, but it was challenged by the development of mechanism in the seventeenth and eighteenth centuries. Following René Descartes and, later, Isaac Newton, the body increasingly came to be seen as fully observable and like a machine—a machine that could be opened and fixed mechanically, with attention to unique individual parts, studied and treated by a highly trained expert. The role of the soul was called into question in some circles, but mechanists were far from establishing a new secular medical orthodoxy. Rather, mechanism, as it emerged alongside a burgeoning and expansive medical print culture, was but one part of a transformed medical world characterized by a wide variety of ideas, practices, and even "orthodoxies" in approaches to education and treatment. The empirically oriented physician Thomas Sydenham, for example, remained popular on both sides of the Atlantic, and many nonacademic medical practitioners also flourished at this time, although often criticized as "quacks." Increasingly attentive to the varieties of medical education, practice, and knowledge in the eighteenth century, historians of medicine now analyze these varieties as part of a continuum rather than as a simplistic dichotomy of "orthodox" and "fringe."[8] The emergence of modern medicine does not follow an easy, linear trajectory.

Despite recent attention to this diversity and the importance of cultural and social context in unraveling the complex history of eighteenth-century medicine, scholars continue to overlook the role of religion. The medical participation of many eighteenth-century men and women—including trained medical practitioners, clergy, and laity—remained motivated by an understanding of God's providential gifts of medicine and knowledge, a commitment to the soul's role in human health, and a belief in God's call to evangelize, which included helping and healing those in need. Some medical historians have dismissed religious involvement in medicine in this era as nonscientific, or, indeed as antiscientific.[9] Other scholars have offered simplistic or theologically uninformed assessments, arguing that participation in medicine was a symptom of secularization or decline from Calvinist orthodoxy.[10]

Studies of religion and medicine often amplify this oversimplification, mistakenly connecting Protestant medical intervention to Arminian theology, as developed by John Wesley and the Methodist denomination. Wesley was an eighteenth-century Anglican minister whose renewal movement, emerging first at Oxford, led to Methodism, one of the most rapidly expanding denominations of the early American republic. Wesley was a proponent of Arminianism, a theology that responded to the Calvinist theology of predestination by emphasizing individual Christians' responsibility to work toward their own salvation. In studies of the nineteenth century, scholars have seen a parallel between, on the one hand, the Arminian principle of individual discipline and striving toward holiness and, on the other hand, the emerging medical literature that promoted self-medication and individual regimen in the pursuit of health. But scholars have uncritically read the eighteenth century through the nineteenth, applying to the former alien paradigms of Arminian rejection of providence and of Calvinist aversion to medical intervention. Such a conclusion overlooks both the strongly providential cast of Wesley's medical writings and Calvinist medical engagement. It mistakenly assumes that an Arminian assertion of agency in salvation precluded the discernment of divine direction in earthly events, and that a Calvinist commitment to predestination—the belief that humans have no agency in earning salvation—entailed a rejection of activity to better "earthly" existence.[11]

Eighteenth-century Protestants from diverse backgrounds, including Calvinists, Lutherans, and Arminians, actively participated in the emerging medical debates and treatments of the era. This participation was motivated by their commitment to God's providence. Puritan minister Cotton Mather interpreted the physical efficacy of smallpox inoculation in terms of its effect on the animal soul, created by God to serve as a mediator between God and the human body. He also saw the promotion of inoculation in Boston as a divinely designed opportunity for Christians to "do good." Pietist pastor Johann Boltzius in Ebenezer, Georgia, meanwhile, became frustrated with his community's university-trained physician, whose obsession with the soul and spirit-led medical treatment hindered the interventions Boltzius saw as vital to the community's survival and evangelistic goals. He increasingly turned, instead, to his own observations, reading, and women's medical knowledge. John Wesley's popular medical manual, *Primitive Physic*, finally, relied on a traditional providential understanding of the human, fallen in both soul and body. Wesley's manual stressed the divine origins of empirical and accessible medical knowledge and its missionary potential.

These communities exemplify the theological and geographical diversity within eighteenth-century transatlantic Protestantism, while also illustrating a trajectory of Christian engagement with medical knowledge and practice that began long before Wesley's "enlightened" Arminianism. Indeed, these communities show how, despite theological differences, Christian medical participation of the eighteenth century was both grounded in the scientific and theoretical conversations of the time and motivated by a shared conception of God's providence. Providential belief was not antithetical to medical activity. Rather, it shaped all aspects of Protestants' medical involvement. Protestants interpreted the human body and soul as integrally connected parts of God's providential creation. They believed medical knowledge and medicine were part of this created order, inviting humans to act as God's intermediaries in the work of healing. And they perceived in this work a significant opportunity to build God's kingdom.

Cotton Mather: Managing Body and Soul, Devising Public Good

When a smallpox epidemic threatened Boston in 1721, Cotton Mather had a plan. After living through several previous smallpox epidemics, Mather had learned of a possible treatment that would stall the disease and save hundreds of lives, particularly the lives of those most vulnerable to the nonendemic smallpox cycles of New England: previously unexposed children. Along with other prominent Boston clergy and the physician Zabdiel Boylston, Mather promoted a new procedure called inoculation. Mather had learned about inoculation both from Onesimus, a man he enslaved, who described the use of the procedure in West Africa, and from a report in the Royal Society's *Philosophical Transactions* by Emanuele Timoni, who witnessed the procedure in Turkey. Inoculation worked by taking live virus from the pustule of someone sick with smallpox and implanting it into incisions cut in the arms of a healthy person. The patient would generally develop a less virulent form of smallpox, which he or she usually survived with less suffering and scarring than in the normal form. The procedure stirred great controversy.[12]

Mather's involvement in smallpox inoculation has been a central focus of scholarship on religion and medicine in eighteenth-century America. Scholars have characterized Mather as an important early American medical thinker—indeed, even a "first." They have debated his medical knowledge and argued about whether his choice to support inoculation—a procedure that, at the time, had undergone little testing or analysis in the Western world—was truly forward-thinking or mere overconfidence, proven correct in retrospect. Meanwhile, while some studies have focused on the "superstition" that marked other areas of Mather's career, for example, his involvement in the trials of accused witches in Salem from 1692 to 1693, others look to Mather's engagement in medicine to consider his emerging "enlightenment" and its significance for secularization or, at least, for the decline of Puritan orthodoxy. The latter generally apply a false timeline to Mather's medical writings, suggesting that Mather's concrete advice on disease management usurped his earlier focus on the redemptive opportunity presented by disease. In fact, both themes dominate his medical writings throughout.[13]

Mather's involvement in the inoculation controversy must be considered in the larger context of his providential belief. This belief influenced Mather's understanding of the human body and soul, his approach to disease management, and his conviction that medical care was a crucial component of Christian benevolence and community. Mather described all of his work and ideas on the topic of inoculation in terms of providence. Although new visions of human benevolence were emerging in his time, Mather, along with many of his contemporaries, perceived medicine and benevolence as part of God's will for human work.

Mather understood physical sickness providentially. Like most Christians of his generation, he found the origins of sickness in the original sin of Adam and Eve. Physical health and spiritual health were intimately linked in Mather's mostly unpublished medical manual *The Angel of Bethesda*.[14] He saw more than a helpful analogy between, on the one hand, the medical terms of bodily sickness and treatment and, on the other, the spiritual understanding of sin and the work of repentance. Sickness was a symptom and reminder of human weakness and transience and an invaluable opportunity to encourage sufferers to reflect on their spiritual state and God's providential promise of salvation. By repenting and turning to God, sinners could heal their souls.[15]

Mather also believed that a healthy soul was the first step to physical health. In this conviction, Mather relied on medical opinions gleaned from his vast reading. He described, for example, an "Eminent Lady" with a "Chronical Malady," who was cured by turning *"herself wholly to God."* He also cited George Cheyne, a popular physician in early eighteenth-century England and an influential advocate of regimen in the promotion of bodily health. In a chapter on healing the soul, Mather quoted a passage from Cheyne's *Essay of Health and Long Life*, which described the importance of the soul and right belief to bodily health: "The *Love of God*, as it is the Sovereign Remedy of *all Miseries*, so, in particular, it *Prevents* all the *Bodily Disorders* the *Passions* introduce; by keeping the *Passions* themselves within due Bounds; and by the unspeakable *Joy*, and perfect *Calm* . . . it gives the Mind, it becomes the most powerful of all the Means of *Health* and *Long Life*." The soul that properly loved

God was the center of somatic well-being. It controlled the passions, prevented sickness, and promoted long-term health.[16]

Mather elaborated on the soul's role in bodily health in a chapter called "*Nishmath-Chajim,*" or the "Breath of Life," which was the only part of Mather's medical manual to appear in print during his lifetime.[17] According to Mather, God created the Nishmath-Chajim as an intermediary between the rational soul and the body; it was akin to the lower soul of the animal world, providing physical "Safety and Welfare" and manifesting itself as "*A Meer Instinct of Nature.*" Mather's prime examples were a nursing infant and mother, who do "Very Needful and Proper Things, without Consulting of *Reason* for the doing of them."[18] Mather was not alone in his understanding of a mediating, animal nature; it had long been a central part of the natural philosophy of Christian Aristotelians, and was maintained by Flemish physician Jan Baptista van Helmont—with whose work Mather was acquainted—and by German physician Georg Ernst Stahl at the University of Halle.[19]

The Nishmath-Chajim, importantly, allowed Mather to incorporate newer, mechanistic notions of the body alongside historic Christian conceptions of the soul's role in physical health. Mather accepted, in part, the contemporary iatrophysical figuration of the human body as machine, but he resisted a purely mechanical notion of the body's operation: "There are many Things in the Humane Body, that cannot be solved by the Rules of *Mechanism.*" Without rejecting mechanism, Mather nonetheless perceived something else was at work in the body. He argued that the "*Machin*" of the body was regulated by the Nishmath-Chajim, whose "*Faculties*" and "*Tendencies*" were "imprinted" by God. The Nishmath-Chajim assisted when the "*Engine*" of the body faltered: "other Parts of the Engine Strangely putt themselves out of their Way that they may send in Help unto it." The body, as machine, relied on the Nishmath-Chajim to correct disorder.[20]

With the Nishmath-Chajim, Mather participated in contemporary religious and medical debates regarding God, the soul, and the origin of bodily motion. Mather posited that the Nishmath-Chajim was "the *Strength* of Every Part in our Body" and gave "*Motion* to it," thus accounting for the "Origin of *Muscular Motion.*" Like others of his time, Mather questioned the explanatory power of Cartesian mechanism or Newtonian physics for the origin of bodily motion. For example, in discerning the origins of motion, the physician Archibald Pitcairne, George Cheyne's teacher at Edinburgh, focused on the heartbeat and circulation and posited some divine intervention. Mather's reluctance to accept a fully mechanistic view of the body and his interest in the soul was not necessarily, as has been argued, an effort to buttress ministers' place in the sick room; clergy and medical practitioners alike were interested in God's role in the human body.[21]

Mather's smallpox writings reflected these eighteenth-century medical debates about the physical body and soul, medical treatment, and the role of God. For his part, in discussing smallpox in the *Angel of Bethesda*, Mather stressed both repentance and disease management. He introduced these dual themes with language from Job, whose "*broken*" and "*lothesome*" skin and "*Wearisome Nights*" were widely associated with smallpox.[22] Mather made vivid reference to Job's suffering and lament: "*Lord, From the Sole of the Foot, even to the Head, there is no Soundness in me; nothing but putrifying Sores.*" With Job, Mather situated the suffering of smallpox within a providential narrative of sin and a call for humble repentance and resignation to God's will. Yet Mather's providential narration did not end with sin and repentance; he went on to identify smallpox as the "Adversary" of Job's account—a formidable force against which humans were powerless but which God controlled. Mather exhorted his readers to courage against the "Adversary," exclaiming, "There is a way to Manage him!"[23] Mather used the Book of Job to stage smallpox as both an opportunity for repentance and a battle that required active human effort, an effort in which success nonetheless depended upon God's direction.[24]

For Mather, the joint role of the human and God in disease management was found in the soul and tied to the stomach, or bowels, which housed the Nishmath-Chajim. This understanding and location proved critical for his defense of inoculation.[25] The stomach was the place of digestion and the home of the passions, which were, significantly, the main faculties Mather attributed to the Nishmath-Chajim—the "*Main Digester.*" As the lower soul, the Nishmath-Chajim was responsible for both nourishment and the basic function of life. Because of its centrality to human life, the stomach, when disordered, represented the "*Seat of our Diseases, or the Source* of them." Medical treatment had to target the stomach, focusing on proper digestion and humoral balance. In describing smallpox treatment—before he knew of inoculation—Mather stressed care of the stomach. He encouraged inducing vomit in order to remove "Morbid Matter," which helped clear corruption, balance the passions, and diminish the disease within.[26]

In his attention to the stomach and the balance of the passions, Mather was influenced, on the one hand, by the writings of John Woodward, a controversial medical writer in early eighteenth-century England, who saw the stomach as the site of disease and the main target of treatment. On the other hand, Mather combined this focus on the stomach with his own grasp of humoral medicine. He was convinced that humoral balance and physical health could be achieved not only through corporeal treatment but also through attention to the emotions—or passions.[27] For Mather, finding emotional balance depended on the soul and on God. Comprehensive disease management demanded not only the physical intervention required to restore balance to the stomach—the seat of the lower soul, or Nishmath-Chajim—but also the religious reflection of the higher "*Rational Soul.*" The rational soul controlled the passions, the balance of which was essential to the health of the Nishmath-Chajim and the body more generally. Through reflection and "Serious PIETY," the rational soul effected "Wonderful Influences" on the Nishmath-Chajim. The Nishmath-Chajim, in turn, successfully mediated between the higher soul and physical body.[28]

With the Nishmath-Chajim, Mather bound piety and physical intervention closely together. This was evident in his approach to smallpox inoculation, where he focused on the stomach, home of the Nishmath-Chajim, in order to differentiate the way corrupted matter spread in naturally acquired versus inoculated smallpox.[29] Mather believed that the former was acquired through the air, went directly to the blood in the lungs, pulsed quickly into the heart and, soon after, passed into the "*Bowels.*" The "*Bowels,*" which Mather seems to have understood broadly to include the stomach, represented the "*Centre* of the Citadel." They housed the Nishmath-Chajim, which maintained the body as "machine" by balancing the passions, fighting off corruption, and restoring order. According to Mather, naturally acquired smallpox reached the bowels too quickly, which limited the Nishmath-Chajim's opportunity for active response and, correspondingly, the chance of survival.[30]

Inoculated smallpox, however, was acquired through the skin. Based on firsthand observation and their understanding of the soul, Mather and some of his contemporaries believed that acquiring smallpox through the skin affected the body's ability to fight off the corruption. Mather thought that inoculated smallpox worked more slowly and only approached "the *Outworks*" of the "Citadel." By keeping corrupt matter away from the "*Vital Powers*," or the bowels, they were better able to combat smallpox. That is, the Nishmath-Chajim had time to order the body, to turn to piety and to God, and to balance the passions. It could then "oblige [the inoculated matter] to *march out the same way as* [it] *came in.*" Mather's metaphor here alluded to his firsthand observation: several days after inoculation, pus ran from the incisions made as part of the procedure. He interpreted this running as a sign of corruption exiting the body. Though inoculated smallpox was not harmless, according to Mather it left no scars through which it could return, and the patient could be "sure of never being troubled with [smallpox] any more."[31]

In early America, the state of one's soul was reflected in the body; complexion reflected both the physical health achieved through balanced humors and the spiritual health reflected in right behavior.[32] Mather and another prominent Boston minister, Benjamin Colman, pointed to the relative lack of scars on inoculation patients compared to the common and often disfiguring scars suffered by those who survived naturally acquired smallpox. They appealed to this widely experienced and highly visible evidence when promoting inoculation in print. These ministers interpreted scars as a visible sign of corruption beneath the skin. Colman argued that, when contracted naturally, smallpox left scabs that—together with the corruption they covered—prevented "free perspiration by the Pores" and left a "foul mass upon" the body. In this scenario, Colman reasoned, the smallpox could return and lead to the "second fever," which defined the confluent and more fatal smallpox. Inoculation incisions, on the other hand, released the disorder and prevented scars and lingering corruption.[33] A clear complexion implied that the vital power of the body, the Nishmath-Chajim, together with the higher, rational soul, had successfully fended off corruption.

Like Mather and Colman, anti-inoculators also attempted to explain their position to the public with tracts that appealed to visible evidence of corruption in the body. John Williams, drawing on his own experience and observation of smallpox and inoculation, argued that the running of pus at the incision was not a sign of corruption leaving the body. Rather, it signaled the living and more venomous corruption physicians had foolishly inserted into the body. The corruption of inoculated matter was evident, Williams believed, in its smell, which some witnesses reported as "worse than ever they smelled." Such a smell was "contrary unto nature."[34]

The observation of inoculation's effect in individual bodies was encouraged by the tradition of empirically based medicine and affected how writers interpreted inoculation as an activity of God's providence within the broader social body. Williams saw inoculated matter as corrupt. While he did not interpret preventive medicine (like bloodletting or a purge) as against God's providence, he could not see the application of corrupt, inoculated matter as preventive or providentially ordained. Williams argued that, instead of preventing disease, inoculation actually spread disease and corruption; the incautious inoculated patient could, in fact, give the natural and more dangerous virus to her neighbors. "To have it brought to them by a voluntary Motion of their Neighbour," Williams wrote, "is more hard to be born by their injured Neighbour, than if it came to them in or by the common way; (the Providence of God casting it where and when he will)."[35] In addition to introducing corruption to an otherwise healthy person, inoculation, in effect, intentionally introduced corruption into an entire neighborhood.

For his part, Mather interpreted the protests against inoculation as evidence of a community suffering from evil and corruption, determined to undermine a procedure that was providentially designed to save lives and prevent suffering. After his house was targeted by a homemade grenade (that failed to trigger) at the height of the controversy, Mather described anti-inoculation protests as the work of the devil, who was attempting to undermine Mather's efforts on behalf of his community's welfare. He prayed for God's compassion "to a Town already under dreadful Judgments, but ripening for more," and hoped that God would "yet appear to rescue and increase my Opportunities to do good, which the great Adversary is now making an hellish Assault upon." Inoculation was, as Mather's journal repeatedly echoed, a "good devised." Influenced by German Pietists, Mather had increasingly sought out God-given opportunities to engage in such good doing, or Christian benevolence. As his own son, Samuel, underwent inoculation, Mather outlined plans to recommend the procedure abroad in order to save more lives, believing that "a World of good may be done to the miserable Children of Men." The phrase "children of men" is a scripturally laden reference to humankind's sinful nature and God's loving and redeeming intervention in times of distress.[36] Inoculation, in Mather's view, was the most recent example of God's providential care and guidance for human activity on behalf of others.

Mather defended and promoted inoculation as a God-given public good, as an effective way to assist a soul-driven body in maintaining health, and as an empirically tested procedure that prevented and purged corruption in both the individual and social body. While Mather was certainly, as scholars have argued, motivated by his desire for authority and his confidence in his own expertise, his outspoken role in the inoculation debates also—and more importantly—reflected his engagement in the central questions animating his medical and Christian contemporaries. Mather responded to these questions not only by reiterating his commitment to the importance of repentance in sickness, but also by positing that active medical intervention in a proven form could actually assist the soul, or the Nishmath-Chajim, in fighting disease. Mather, his supporters, and his opponents appealed both to providence and to traditional medical emphases on observation and experience as they explained how physical symptoms signified internal corruption within the individual body. They extended these observations to their understanding of the spread and treatment of disease within the social body.

Both sides of the inoculation debate sought to comprehend God's providence in their response to smallpox. For Mather, inoculation was a gift of God to help his neighbors. For anti-inoculators, it dangerously introduced corruption and could inadvertently spread disease, which was not, they believed, God's plan. In the end, each side saw a central connection between the human soul and medicine, a connection defined by their efforts to discern providential direction and to devise good for suffering humanity.

Ebenezer, Georgia: Pietist Mission, Medicine, and Survival

In his insistence on medicine as a form of Christian benevolence and mission, Mather had been influenced by the Pietist movement centered around the Francke Foundations in Halle. Pietist missionaries would soon after make their way to North America, with one of their earliest settlements founded in Ebenezer, Georgia, in 1734. The Francke Foundations, together with the Society for the Promotion of Christian Knowledge (SPCK) and the Georgia Trustees, sponsored the mission and its pastors, and they were also committed to the support of a missionary physician, recognizing the central place of physical care to the success of Christian mission in the colony. This support was expansive: the second missionary physician sent by the Foundations, Christian Thilo, received preliminary provisions and a stipend as well as medicines free of charge. Thilo, who had trained at the medical university in Halle, came highly recommended, but over the course of his thirty years in Ebenezer, his approach to medicine came to be a source of constant stress for the ministers and wider community.[37] While he and Ebenezer's ministers agreed, fundamentally, on the importance of medicine in missionary endeavors, they differed over the role of the soul in bodily health and, correspondingly, appropriate treatment methods.

As in Cotton Mather's inoculation-frenzied Boston, Ebenezer's ministers and physician divided on how to pursue God's work in the medical care and treatment of individuals in their community. Like Mather, Ebenezer's first ministers Johann Boltzius and Israel Gronau intervened frequently. Their interventions touched on larger theoretical debates in formal medical education, while also engaging in less-formal networks, including women's medical knowledge and the popular press, as they endeavored to keep community members alive. Like Mather, Boltzius and Gronau interpreted their medical activity in terms of Christian mission. They embraced a Pietist impulse to do good, convinced that a healthy body allowed the human soul to pursue its work in the world, to promote the kingdom of God, and to exemplify Christian piety in colonial America. While many historians have told the story of Mather and 1720s Boston, however, few have examined the history of medicine in Ebenezer, despite its rich trail of sources.[38]

The trouble with Thilo began early, long before he arrived in Ebenezer. His behavior and preparation shocked the men he met in London, en route to North America, including important representatives from the Francke Foundations, the SPCK, and the Georgia Trustees. They reported that Thilo suffered miserably from a lack of provisions during his passage from Holland to England: he expected the voyage to be a mere twenty-four hours, not a full seven days. Further, they worried that Thilo—although well educated in the method of Georg Ernst Stahl under the instruction of Johann Juncker at the medical university in Halle—was unprepared in essential medical practices, including bloodletting and surgery. Alarmed by these reports from London, Gotthilf Francke, the Foundations' director in Halle, sent a letter to the Ebenezer ministers explaining that Thilo suffered from hypochondria, of both the body and the spirit, which was worsened by problems on his journey. The ministers were to welcome him, nonetheless, with love and gentleness. Francke opined that Thilo was a better physician for Ebenezer than one who sought honor, money, and good living.[39]

When Thilo finally arrived in Ebenezer in February 1738, he was met with great anticipation. As they had not yet received Francke's letters, the community was unaware of any problems and thrilled to have a physician after going two long years without. Shortly after Thilo arrived, however, he had an argument with Boltzius, the lead pastor. The argument ended, according to Boltzius, with Thilo running into his room, lying on his bed, and throwing a fit. Boltzius, meanwhile, fell to his knees in the courtyard and prayed to God for mercy and wisdom before he called Thilo to him. Running outside, Thilo pulled off his wig, put his head to the ground, and, according to Boltzius, mumbled perverse things. Thilo ceased going to church services, suggested the ministers were idolatrous, dallied with married women, and offered nonsensical reasons for refusing to provide a medical treatment one day but allowing it the next. Boltzius reflected with disappointment over the arrival of "such worthless material to sadness and moans."[40]

While Boltzius's frustration with Thilo's behavior was extensive, the most significant problems emerged in Thilo's medical approach to malaria, a disease that had constantly threatened Ebenezer since its founding in 1734 and the treatment of which was frequently debated. In narrating Thilo's response, Boltzius revealed both wide-ranging theoretical disagreements and immense diversity in how medicine was understood and practiced on the ground in desperate colonial contexts. Malaria's effect on early Ebenezer had been disastrous, prompting an almost immediate relocation after first settlement. Nonetheless, the malaria outbreak of 1736 proved even worse, spreading widely among adults and children.[41] Reports were so dreadful that sponsors in Europe, who annually published the ministers' journals for eager audiences, delayed publication of the 1736 journal until it could be prefaced with more encouraging news. Desperation was widespread, and some threatened to move away.[42] Ebenezer's stability and success were at risk.

The first record of the community's treatment strategies for malaria is from 1740. On May 29, Boltzius wrote Francke to thank him for medications and the advice of Halle physician Johann Juncker on the "*Fieber-Kuchen*," or the hard knots that formed in the left side of the abdomen in those affected by malaria. Boltzius hoped Thilo would implement Juncker's treatment and prayed for God's blessing on the cure.[43]

Boltzius continued by describing past advice the community had received for malaria treatment and his resulting debates with Thilo. Augsburg minister Samuel Urlsperger, an important Ebenezer benefactor, had at some point shared his own physician's advice. As Boltzius explained, however, the advice posed a problem: not only was the prescription difficult to fulfill with ingredients available in Georgia, but Thilo had also refused to follow it, because it did "not seem to follow the *method organica*." Boltzius explained that Thilo particularly objected to the use of "*cortex peruvianus*." Frustrated, Boltzius concluded that he "certainly does not take an active interest in the patients."[44]

Thilo's response to "*cortex peruvianus*" and alignment with the "organic method"—which was associated with the medical practitioner Georg Ernst Stahl in Halle—point to a significant theoretical debate over the place of the soul in medical practice and bodily health. In the eighteenth century the most effective treatment for malaria was the bark of the Cinchona tree (*cortex peruvianus*, or Jesuit's Bark), which contained quinine, but this treatment had its detractors, who feared that quinine's effect on fevers did not correspond with humoralism. As in Mather's Boston, humoralism was still an influential theory of medicine in Halle and its network. Because humoralism was centrally focused on balance, a medicine designed to reduce a fever (a main symptom of malaria) was expected to produce a corresponding form of evacuation. For example, bloodletting was understood to release the corruption causing a fever. Quinine was problematic because its use did not produce an evacuant, leading to the fear that the fever—or corruption—was simply suppressed and lingered within the body.[45] This fear echoed debates surrounding smallpox inoculation in 1720s Boston and the significance of the pus—the evacuant—observed to run from the site of implantation.

The debate over quinine in Ebenezer was shaped by professors at the medical university in Halle, whose approaches reflected different theories of the soul's role in bodily health. In the late seventeenth century Friedrich Hoffman, an iatromechanist, experimented with quinine and concluded that it neutralized the acidity in the blood, which he interpreted as the cause of fevers. Hoffman's colleague, Georg Ernst Stahl, however, was wary of mechanism. Stahl favored the "organic method." For Stahl—like Mather—the soul directed healing, and fever represented a normal release of corruption that should not be repressed. Because quinine prevented fever, Stahl and his students, including Johann Samuel Carl and Johann Juncker—Thilo's teacher—rejected its use in malaria treatment.[46]

Carl, Juncker, and, eventually, Thilo went beyond Stahl in emphasizing the soul's role in healing and, correspondingly, in promoting "gentler" and more selective treatments. In cases of malaria, for example, Carl recommended gentle dietary measures to aid the soul in removing corruption. Thilo, meanwhile, avoided treatments such as bloodletting and relied "on the course of nature." In a letter to Gotthilf Francke, Juncker described Thilo's long-standing fixation with patients' spiritual states, reporting that while Thilo was still in Halle, he occasionally extended appointments several hours, seeking to ascertain the condition of his patients' souls. In 1738, Boltzius reported that, in treating patients in Ebenezer, Thilo could change treatment midcourse, depending on "inspiration."[47]

Despite Thilo's formal medical training in Halle—and his support from the Francke Foundations—Boltzius and his assistant minister, Israel Gronau, found his treatments and methods unreliable and were spurred to action. Like Mather, they were influenced by wide reading, personal observations, and a providential sense of Christian mission centered on survival and the growth of God's kingdom. In the case of malaria, the Ebenezer ministers apparently used quinine despite Thilo's objections. Francke reprimanded them in 1743 and 1745, astonished at reports of quinine use. He warned the ministers with language grounded in his own humoral and empirical observation: he argued that quinine "plugs" or "jams" fever and, despite appearances, left dangerous corruption beneath the skin. He also worried that quinine had aggravated the symptoms and sickness that the minister Gronau described himself suffering.[48]

Even if the Ebenezer ministers did not appreciate the theoretical medical debates behind Thilo's treatment methods, they knew enough about medicine to understand Francke's humoral concerns. Nonetheless, when it came to the persistent diseases that threatened communal stability, they proved willing to intervene and try new treatments. Both ministers had received some medical training in Halle and used it, particularly when Ebenezer lacked a doctor in its early years. After Thilo's arrival, the ministers remained highly involved. In light of Thilo's dislike of bloodletting, Gronau practiced it, and Boltzius dispensed medicines, because Thilo rarely used the medicines freely provided to him from Halle.[49] They also recruited the help of Johann Ludwig Mayer, a 1741 immigrant from Swabia, who favored the use of quinine in treating malaria.[50]

The ministers were focused on their community's survival; the success of their God-directed mission in Georgia ultimately depended on their physical health. Ministering to a community originally made up of Protestant refugees from Salzburg, they found, like the Puritans and Separatists of New England, a symbolic pressure to survive and witness God's providential mercy. Disappointed in Thilo's lack of active intervention and trying to care for as many as he could, Boltzius repeatedly turned to other networks of medical knowledge, including women.

Although the only evidence we have for Ebenezer is from Boltzius's writings, it is important to remember that women as well as men participated in empirical medicine and that, although certain conditions highlighted discretion, this participation was often joint and interconnected. In July 1749, Boltzius wrote two letters regarding the poor health of his wife, Gertraud Boltzius, to Henriette Rosine Goetze, the mother-in-law of Gotthilf Francke. Boltzius wrote that he would have asked Thilo to submit a report, but Thilo was "rather inexperienced in women's conditions." In this instance, Boltzius diplomatically did not mention his dissatisfaction with Thilo, who had proven unreliable in treating Gertraud Boltzius. He had, early on, refused to treat or even see her; he sent medicine via a child messenger and also declined to bleed her, explaining vaguely that "the bloodletting must occur tomorrow and not today." Boltzius wrote to Goetze not only because he found Thilo's spiritual direction in medical treatment unpredictable, however, but also because he listened to his wife, who told him to contact Goetze. It is unclear what Goetze's medical knowledge and training were, but she had arranged for medical books to be sent to Ebenezer.[51]

Boltzius couched his request for help in his wife's case in the familial language of marriage, maternity, and providence, but his wife clearly assisted him in the composition of medical details related to her case. He opened by explaining that his active intervention in his wife's health was motivated by love—the love he and his children had for a "helpmeet" and mother given by God. He recognized that the outcome of Goetze's counsel would depend ultimately on God's mercy.[52] He then continued with detailed information regarding Gertraud Boltzius's condition in order to improve the likelihood that Goetze could recommend or refer the case for effective treatment.

Boltzius wrote that his wife had read a book on medicine by David Samuel von Madai, *Unterricht der bewehrten Hallischen Artzeneyen* (*Instruction Concerning the Tried and Tested Medicines of Halle*), which Goetze had included in a recent shipment to Ebenezer, and he requested specific medicines based on his wife's reading.[53] Urged by Gertraud, he also described her long-standing health problems. These began around age seventeen, during her first childbirth, when she was "very damaged . . . by an unscrupulous midwife." He described Gertraud's "distressful gynecological (*hysterischen*) incidents" with care, hoping that such detailed observations would assist in a cure: "Her stomach has become so weak through the many ebullitions of the blood that she feels almost every bit of bread and the lightest food, and must, after eating, if it can be said, vomit. . . . Please excuse me for mentioning out of necessity yet one particular condition. She indeed has always had her menstrual period, but irregularly; for example, every 3 weeks, sometimes too much, sometimes too little." Despite his discomfort with the level of detail, Boltzius hoped for Goetze's sympathy, and, "at the request of my helpmeet," he did not want to omit vital information.[54]

Boltzius's appeal underlines his dissatisfaction with Thilo and desire for active medical intervention, even if intervention required once again sidestepping professional networks of medical knowledge. Boltzius's account and its detailed observations further reflect ongoing participation in traditional empirical- and humoral-based medicine. He and his wife hoped their observations would allow for diagnosis and treatment. Unfortunately, Goetze died before she received the letters. Boltzius followed up with Francke, and in October 1750 Madai himself responded. Although unable to make a formal diagnosis based on Boltzius's account of the case, Madai suggested a treatment nonetheless.[55]

Gertraud Boltzius's sickness was not the only occasion in which Johann Boltzius alluded to a separate, or parallel, line of communication when it came to women's health and his perpetual disappointment with Thilo. During a 1750 epidemic, which has been variously identified as "Rothe Friesel," scarlet fever, or measles, Boltzius rarely mentioned Thilo and instead relied on his own observations and readings and Gertraud Boltzius's personal observations in trying to determine treatment.[56] Boltzius eventually determined bloodletting to be the best response. He reported that "adults who have this scarlet fever say that there is an extraordinary movement of the blood as if it is wished to break out of all veins." He wrote that the English said bloodletting was the best cure, and he noted that he had seen children regain health after suffering a nose bleed. Gertraud Boltzius, meanwhile, confirmed the overwhelming significance of blood in her observations of several women's experiences with the disease: "A grown girl had her first period during her paroxysm, but then it rose immediately to her breast as if it all wished to come out of her throat, and from this she suddenly died five weeks ago. . . . A pregnant woman in her first months was brought into mortal danger by the extraordinary motion of the blood in her body. However, because the blood broke out and she aborted, she soon recovered." Boltzius reported these, his wife's, observations as further evidence of the need for bloodletting.[57]

Boltzius turned to women's medical knowledge not only because it corresponded with his own humorally and empirically based understanding of the human body and the effects of illness, but also because it furthered the opportunity for intervention that he saw as critical to Christian mission. Despite his struggles and differences with Thilo, which stemmed in part from Thilo's fixation on the soul's role in sickness, Boltzius nonetheless was like Thilo in perceiving a spiritual significance in the practice of medicine and healing of the body. He maintained a Pietist-inflected perspective on good health: it represented a gift of God directed toward a spiritual end—to do God's work in the world. For Pietists like Boltzius, medical treatment made it possible, as historian Jürgen Helm has argued, for the sick person to "redeploy the body again in a condition that facilitated it to achieve the will of God and further it in the world. . . . [The body] served as 'guest giver' and suitable instrument of the soul. Because of this function, the body was necessarily worthy of preservation."[58]

Boltzius understood the healthy human body as a house for the soul, its spiritual work, and Christian mission, and he grounded his conviction in a providential understanding of Ebenezer. He longed for his community's survival, hoping to continue God's work in Georgia and to serve as an example of God's blessing on missionary work. Francke had shared this vision in a 1743 letter, invoking language from Matthew 5:14–16: "May the Lord therefore allow Ebenezer to be a city on the hill, and be a light on a glowing candlestick. May he then also grant to all inhabitants grace, to allow their light to be shone, through a spiritual and Gospel-worthy transformation, above all to the European inhabitants in America."[59]

After the Rothe Friesel epidemic of 1750, Boltzius envisioned a charitable institution designed for Ebenezer's physical and spiritual health: a hospital. The 1750 epidemic had been particularly bad: in a two-month period at least thirteen children, or about 5 percent of Ebenezer's population, had died.[60] Boltzius lost his oldest son, Samuel Leberecht, and his youngest daughter, Christiana Elisabeth. He was heartbroken. He accepted the loss as God's will and hoped for future retrospective clarity. In the top margin of a letter to Francke, he quoted John 13:7: "What I do thou knowest not now; but thou shalt know hereafter." Boltzius also dwelled on the sheer number of deaths among children in Ebenezer since its founding: "If all the children who were born and baptized sixteen years ago in Old and New Ebenezer were still alive, how large our congregation would be!" In hope, Boltzius envisaged "a beautiful troop of chosen and transfigured children from the Ebenezer congregation . . . resplendent before God's throne," but he also suffered acute grief.[61]

In responding to the loss of children, Boltzius envisioned the construction of a "spacious sickbay," which would provide protection for poor families in winter. When inhabitants became sick during this time, he wrote, "their quick recovery is hindered, and they also contract long-lasting sickness and consumption." Although physicians and medicines were freely provided, such a sickbay would transform the experience of illness in Ebenezer: "much good would accrue from it to the congregation and the whole country under the influence of God's blessing."[62]

Ebenezer could not survive without children, and if Ebenezer did not survive, what did that mean for its providential call to serve as an example of renewed piety and Protestant mission in America? Although Boltzius's sickbay never materialized, his vision of a congregation and country transformed by a benevolent institution—approved by God's providence—demonstrates the power he saw in the Christian commitment to medicine and care. Disappointed in Thilo and his fixation on soul-based medical care, Boltzius displayed his own deep desire to intervene actively among the sick. His concerns were both practical and providential. Far from centers of learning and medicine, he engaged—through correspondence, popular print, conversation, and experience—the medical knowledge and treatments available and sought to act upon this knowledge with the urgency impressed by his situation. His writings illuminate both the medical debates within Pietist academic medicine and the central Protestant concern with providing physical relief in the hope of survival, spiritual renewal, and Christian mission.

John Wesley: *Primitive Physic* and American Mission

In 1789, a new preface was added to the twenty-first edition of John Wesley's *Primitive Physic*, a medical manual first published in England in 1747. The 1789 edition was published in Philadelphia, and the new preface was written by Thomas Coke and Francis Asbury, bishops of the recently formed Methodist Episcopal Church. They began their preface, "The grand interests of your souls will ever lie near our hearts, but we cannot be unmindful of your bodies."[63] More than forty years after Wesley made bodily health a central part of his renewal movement within the Church of England, his writings on the subject remained central in the new American denomination he and his followers shaped.[64]

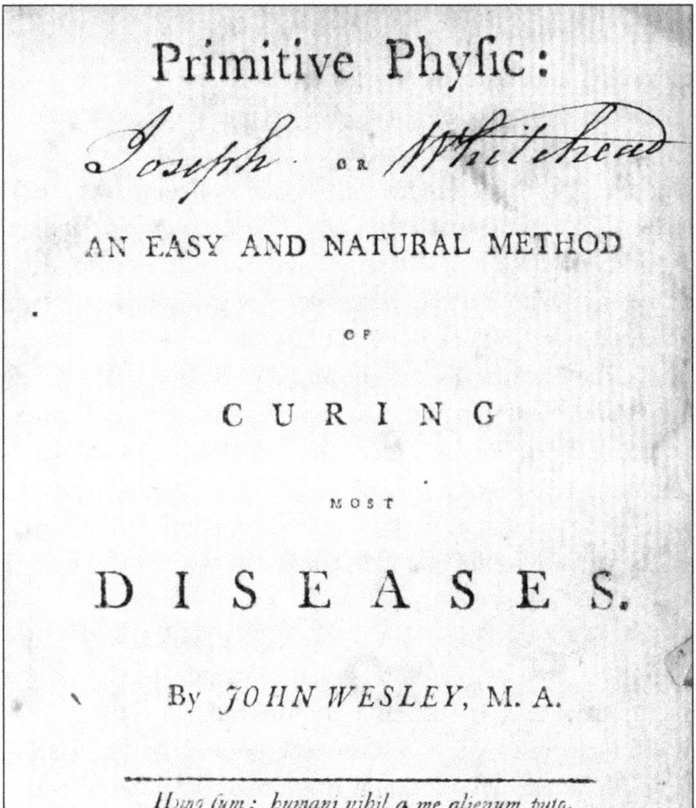

Primitive Phyſic:

Joseph or *Whitehead*

AN EASY AND NATURAL METHOD

OF

C U R I N G

MOST

D I S E A S E S.

By *JOHN WESLEY*, M. A.

Homo ſum; humani nihil a me alienum puto.

THE TWENTY-FIRST EDITION.

PHILADELPHIA:

PRINTED BY *PRICHARD & HALL*, IN MARKET STREET,
AND SOLD BY *JOHN DICKINS*, IN FOURTH STREET,
NEAR RACE STREET.

M DCC. LXXXIX.

Figure 3.2. Title page of the twenty-first edition of John Wesley's medical manual, printed in Philadelphia. An owner, Joseph Whitehead, inscribed his name within the title page text. John Wesley, *Primitive Physic* (Philadelphia: Prichard & Hall, 1789). National Library of Medicine (U.S.), https://wellcomecollection.org/works/fh33w55c, Public Domain Mark.

Like Mather and Boltzius, Wesley's interest in medicine was tightly bound to contemporary medical debates and Christian reactions to them. Wesley believed that theoretical medicine had developed at odds with God's design for human health. Following George Cheyne, Wesley emphasized the importance of piety in the maintenance and restoration of bodily health, and like Mather and Boltzius, he also saw a clear connection between Christian benevolence, medical care, and mission. In his commitment to the empirical tradition, Wesley, like Mather and Boltzius, learned from wide reading and observation. Wesley, however, took his commitment to mission and empiricism one step further. In an explicit critique of theoretical medicine, which had grown too complicated for the average sick person's participation, Wesley printed an inexpensive medical manual, seeking to make medical knowledge widely available to all. In this effort—and its success—Wesley surpassed Mather, Boltzius, and, indeed, all Christian authors on medicine of his time.

Wesley's *Primitive Physic* was immensely popular, with more than thirty-seven editions printed in the English language between 1747 and 1859, including at least twenty-four editions published in America. According to historian G. S. Rousseau, the book "was found in almost every English household, especially in those of the poor, usually beside the Bible." Notes and alterations to surviving American editions suggest that the book was well used, shared, and passed on.[65]

Primitive Physic and the general Methodist commitment to good health were important manifestations of Methodist theology in both eighteenth-century England and America.[66] Wesley's writings on medicine were premised on a providential understanding of the fallen human soul, the corresponding condition of sickness, the gift of medicine from God, and the place of medicine and treatment in the Christian mission to the larger community. Scholars, however, have overlooked the commitment to providence evident in Wesley's writings and in the broader Methodist movement; this oversight results from the efforts of scholars—and early Methodists themselves—to distinguish Methodism from Calvinism through reference to the Methodists' Arminian stress on human effort, action, and practice. Methodist theology and writings on medicine were deeply shaped by providential views, however, highlighting the important parallels in medical interest and practice between Methodists and other religious communities, including Puritans and Pietist Lutherans. One historian has termed Wesley's ideas as "Christian enlightened thinking," implicitly binding his attention to medicine to modern enlightenment, but this characterization fails to acknowledge his deep dependence on historic and contemporary Christian understandings of providence and healing.[67]

Wesley's interest in medicine was shaped by his participation in both formal and informal medical networks. From his own family history and the models set by other ministers, he knew medicine could serve as a useful parallel career for English clergy. His medical development was also influenced by his time as a missionary in the colony of Georgia in 1736 and by his relationship with George Cheyne, who treated Wesley on his return to England. Cheyne's straightforward writings on diet and exercise and his attention to piety affected Wesley just as they had Cotton Mather. In the 1740s, Wesley opened a medical dispensary in London, seeking to serve the poor free of charge, but it was costly and difficult to operate effectively. He redirected his efforts, and in 1747 he published *Primitive Physic*, an accessible book on medicine that was inexpensively distributed to interested readers in London and beyond. Recognizing the value of print in Christian evangelism, Wesley joined the already expansive medical marketplace that had emerged in eighteenth-century England.[68]

In the preface to *Primitive Physic*, which remained unchanged through over a century of new editions, Wesley articulated a story of sickness and healing that originated in the sin of Adam and Eve. Both sickness and healing were ordained by God as a result of humanity's sinfulness, and both were transmitted from generation to generation—the former by nature and the latter by education. Wesley told this story in providential cadences, explaining to readers the fall of humanity and the origins of sickness, God's gift of medical knowledge and its proper use, and the importance of making medicine available to everyone. Wesley's preface thus welcomed readers familiar with a traditional providential view of the origins of sickness in human sin, while also explaining medical education and action in providential terms. In so doing, the preface offered an important Christian commentary on the contemporary state of medicine in England.

Wesley argued that God had ordained medical knowledge, together with other expertise, to pass seamlessly from parent to child—similar, in a way, to original sin. Medicine was traditional: "every father delivering down to his sons, what he had himself in like manner received concerning the manner of healing." God had ordained not only sickness, but also the human ability to accumulate, share, and pass down knowledge for the promotion of cures and health. For Wesley, Native Americans offered an unadulterated example of this process; they passed knowledge to the next generation and participated in the foundational and God-ordained activities that prevented disease in the first place: exercise, diet, and temperance. These activities were key components of the physical regimen that, according to Cheyne, accompanied spiritual discipline and health. Only recently, Wesley wrote, had Native American temperance been corrupted, but their medicines, which had passed from father to child, remained "quick, as well as, generally, infallible."[69]

Wesley's preface detailed how medical knowledge was a part of God's providential plan to heal fallen creation. What might seem an "accident" was in fact how the "Author of nature" taught fallen humanity the means of medicine: "doubtless numberless remedies have been . . . casually discovered in every age and nation."[70] God's order shaped human experience and corresponding knowledge of medicine. As long as "physic was wholly founded on experiment," Wesley wrote, it reflected God's created order and was oriented to "common humanity."[71]

From this description of God-designed medical practice, Wesley turned sharply to criticize what he considered the contemporary corruption of the process. This corruption included theoretical approaches to medicine, which, he added, made profit rather than Christian humanity the orienting motive of the medical profession. When "men of a philosophical turn" ceased to be "satisfied" with the experimental approach to medicine, they turned increasingly to "hypotheses" and "theories" as they "inverted" the "whole order of physic." In so doing, these men forgot the simples—medicines consisting of a single herb—that had long dominated medical therapy in order to promote compound medicines, which contained multiple ingredients and came with complicated rules for use. Together with compound medicines appeared an ever-increasing supply of difficult books, which were inaccessible "for common people." Medicine "became an abstruse science." It involved anatomy, natural philosophy, and even astronomy and became, thereby, "quite out of reach of ordinary men." The new, theoretically obsessed medical profession was focused on "honor and gain" and apt to be territorial and corrupt. Compound medicines, Wesley wrote, were designed "to swell the Apothecary's bill," indeed, "possibly on purpose to prolong the distemper, that the doctor and he may divide the spoil." Meanwhile, the rest of humanity was left "utterly cut off from helping either themselves or their neighbours." The cost and inaccessibility of small-pox inoculation, for one instance, were important examples of the contemporary situation spurring Wesley's support of alternative remedies. Medicine, he was convinced, had been diverted from the God-ordained method of experience and goal of helping all in need.[72]

Wesley's intent in writing *Primitive Physic* was to return medicine to what he considered its providential design in experience-based knowledge oriented toward Christian mission to fallen humanity, including the most "common man." Wesley cited others who wanted to "explode" from medicine "all hypotheses, and fine spun theories," particularly Thomas Sydenham, George Cheyne, and physicians who avoided complicated compound medicines, such as Herman Boerhaave. But Wesley went further, attempting to make medical advice widely available to even the lowest classes. Common people could promote good health by following the straightforward and simple remedies Wesley provided as well as by eating temperately and exercising regularly. Wesley reminded readers, "above all," however, of the importance of prayer, "that old unfashionable medicine." It was prayer that turned humans away from their own ego and knowledge, away from the dangerous enticement of theory and medicine oriented to private gain, and reminded them to "have Faith in God, who *killeth and maketh alive, who bringeth down to the grave and bringeth up*." By echoing Hannah's praise of God's faithfulness and power over humanity in 1 Samuel 2, Wesley reiterated to readers the importance of remembering and trusting in the ultimate arbiter over human health and sickness.[73]

Within this trust in providence, Wesley was not against reading widely in medical literature and, with the goal of helping others, he participated actively in many of the scientific and medical developments of his time. Regardless of his rhetorical promotion of "ancient and contemporary 'popular' medicine," Wesley, as historian Deborah Madden has shown, "adopted, elaborated and simplified those authoritative medical sources that were validated by leading contemporary physicians."

As new editions of *Primitive Physic* were produced, Wesley occasionally added notes and described new treatments. He began adding an asterisk, for example, if he had personally tried or observed a remedy, or he appended a note if he found a person's testimony particularly compelling. For example, under the third treatment option listed for the condition "The Bite of a Mad Dog," Wesley wrote, "Mix a pound of salt, with a quart of water. Squeeze, bathe, and wash the wound with this for an hour. Then bind some salt upon it for twelve hours. N.B. *The author of this receipt was bit six times by mad dogs, and always cured himself by this means.*" Wesley was actively engaged in attaining medical knowledge, most famously in his use of a personally built "electrical machine," which he began using to treat patients in 1746. He used electricity to treat a variety of conditions, including deafness and obstructed menses. By 1760, he added a prefatory remark on the benefits of electricity as "*far superior to all the other medicine I have known.*" While Wesley's participation in the medical world was wide-ranging, however, he always wrote with clear and simple language that he couched in personal experience, and he stressed that the outcome of human medical activities relied, ultimately, on the "blessing of God."[74]

Wesley ended the preface with a citation of "a few plain, easy rules"—gleaned from Cheyne—which focused on the importance of balancing passions for the maintenance of bodily health. Like Mather, Wesley quoted Cheyne's admonition that "the love of God" assists in "keeping the passions themselves within due bounds." Such love represented "the most powerful of all the means of health and long life."[75] Following Cheyne, Wesley also argued that the passions were both animal and spiritual, and that both influenced the physical body. Indeed, Wesley saw the passions as motivating the body and its activity in a way similar to how gravity affects matter. Here he was shaped by Cheyne, who in a post-Cartesian world and influenced by Newtonianism, was centrally interested in the soul's driving force in the body and its health. Cheyne's thought was itself intriguingly similar to that of Georg Ernst Stahl, but, unlike Stahl, Cheyne—and later Wesley—perceived a mutual influence, a mutual force between body and soul. This connection between body and soul was a two-way street; following John Locke, Cheyne believed external stimuli could have internal effects. Thus, as his treatment methods developed, he came to stress—and Wesley agreed—that "discipline of the body was an essential counterpart to discipline of the soul."[76]

This mutually influential interrelationship between soul and body remained the driving impulse behind the publication and distribution of *Primitive Physic* in the United States: "the grand interests of your souls," Coke and Asbury had written, required attention to "your bodies." The 1789 *Primitive Physic* was not the first appearance of the book in the United States, but it was the first from the newly opened publishing house of the Methodist Episcopal Church: the Book Concern.[77] The Book Concern was founded in 1789 in Philadelphia as part of an effort to build Methodist community in the rapidly expanding denomination. In the United States, Methodist membership grew dramatically between the years of 1784 and 1791: from fifteen thousand to seventy-six thousand. Publication became a central focus of American Methodists; aware of both the opportunity and the dangers of this amazing growth in such a large geographic space, leaders saw books and periodicals as a means to contain and control the denomination's teachings and practices. The opening pages of the *Arminian Magazine*, a Methodist periodical first published in the United States in 1789, explained to readers the importance of publication efforts on the "extensive continent" of the United States. Popular print, including journals, hymns, poems, and letters, represented an opportunity to enunciate the doctrines of Methodists and to differentiate them from Calvinists on the one hand and Universalists on the other. It is significant that among the first books published by this new publishing enterprise were *Primitive Physic* and *Imitation of Christ* by Thomas à Kempis, which represented the two sides—physical and spiritual—of holistic care that Wesley himself had long identified as essential for every Christian household and pastor.[78]

Although early Methodist publications in the United States were not overtly theological, they contained nonetheless the central components of Methodist theology: human sinfulness, God's providential grace to all humans, and a mission to care—both physically and spiritually—for the sick and needy. In the early Methodists' involvement in hospitals in England, they understood their work as an opportunity not only to heal physically, but also "to reclaim the souls of the sick." Participating in charitable medical endeavors was, further, important for the healer, as it provided an opportunity for Christian usefulness. Medicine was a chance to engage once again in the human-to-human transmission of medical knowledge ordained by God as the healing counterpart to disease transmission. *Primitive Physic* became a way for Wesley to encourage widely the impulses of healing, evangelism, and spiritual growth, and the publication proved vital for Coke and Asbury in the development of the Methodist community in the United States.[79]

Wesley's *Primitive Physic* offered an important critique of the contemporary medical world and the growing prominence of theoretical medicine. Like other Protestants of his time, Wesley articulated a Christian understanding of the soul's role in sickness and bodily health and the importance of medicine for Christian benevolence and mission. *Primitive Physic* was a work of practical piety, but its preface also taught fundamental theological principles of human sinfulness, charity, and—above all—God's providence over creation. For Wesley, medicine was tightly bound to God's providence and was most successful when pursued with attention to the providentially ordained method of experience, the generational transmission of knowledge, and the goal of helping others both physically and spiritually. The enduring popularity of *Primitive Physic* in both England and the United States demonstrates the appeal and significance of Wesley's arguments and providential perspective in shaping early Methodist communities.

* * *

Eighteenth-century Puritans, Lutherans, and Methodists participated in an ever-changing and diverse world of medical knowledge. Contemporary debates on the nature of the human soul, spurred by emerging mechanistic conceptions of medicine and the body, demanded a response. Some Protestants, like Wesley, joined these debates directly and responded forcefully and publicly to theoretical and profit-driven medicine. Wesley saw medicine as God's gift for all humans to share intergenerationally with the intent of Christian healing.

Other eighteenth-century Protestants were less concerned with the increasing theorization of medicine and corresponding limitations on its accessibility and more focused on integrating traditional Christian conceptions of the soul within the new mechanistic understanding of the body. Mather promoted smallpox inoculation because, like Wesley, he felt a providential call to "do good" in the world. But, unlike Wesley, Mather was unaware of or inattentive to the practical aspects of inoculation that affected its accessibility to all of society. For Mather, God's providence would see to inoculation's implementation for the good. For Wesley, God's providence required intentional work on the part of Christians to make sure medicine truly promoted the common good.

In Ebenezer, Georgia, meanwhile, the minister Boltzius grew impatient with Thilo, the missionary physician in his community, and his soul-focused medicine. Like Wesley and Mather, Boltzius read widely and felt a Christian duty to help those who suffered, and he also valued firsthand observations and experiences of symptoms and treatments as he pursued cures for his entire community. Unlike Wesley, Boltzius did not contemplate his work and intervention as a response to the theoretical debates within larger eighteenth-century medicine—debates that were, in ways, personified by the frustrating Thilo and his pursuit of a "gentler" medicine. Like Mather, Boltzius sought to implement treatments and cures that would ensure his community's survival. Like Wesley, he actively worked to make sure these treatments were available to all, and—due to the small size of his community and the discrete nature of his mission—this direct intervention was achievable in a way it was not in Mather's colonial Boston or in Wesley's wide readership.

These differences are important, but eighteenth-century Protestants were nonetheless unified in significant ways. Regardless of their soteriology or stance on predestination, these Protestants actively pursued medical care, disease prevention, and health maintenance. They combined knowledge from their own humoral or empirical understandings of the body, from informal medical networks that included enslaved Africans and women, and from the burgeoning medical print culture as they sought to help the sick in the most effective and efficient way possible. They understood their interventions in terms of a Christian mission of benevolence, recognizing that physical care was closely linked to the spiritual renewal and rebirth of both the individual and the community.

Mather, Boltzius, and Wesley—along with their correspondents and contemporaries—are a crucial part of the story of eighteenth-century medicine. They have been overlooked because scholarship has assumed, based on caricatures of their theologies, that they could not have participated in the eighteenth-century transformations in medicine. Yet their focus on the soul's influence on bodily health was not a theological, antiempirical Christian maneuver, but a serious participation in contemporary medical conversations based on observation and theory as well as religion.

Mather, Boltzius, Wesley, and their circles actively shaped the physical and medical worlds of their communities in concrete ways. Through treatments and writings they promoted medical care as an essential component of Christian benevolence and mission. Their ideas reflected not a simple story of dawning Enlightenment or declining theological commitment but rather their contemporary medical world and deeprooted Christian beliefs in God's providential direction over the human body, soul, medicine, and mission.

4

Providence and Benevolence in Philadelphia's Yellow Fever Epidemic

On the evening of September 13, 1793, the Lutheran pastor Heinrich Helmuth "wrestled before God." "My Jesus," he wrote in his journal, "has fled from me." Living and working through the yellow fever epidemic that had enveloped Philadelphia, he felt spiritually barren and "cheated" in his hopes for a decline in deaths. He buried seven people from his congregation that day; an eighth was buried at midnight.[1]

One of the hardest questions to ask—and to attempt to answer— about the yellow fever epidemic is why people stayed and worked with the sick and suffering. Not everyone had the means or opportunity to leave the city, but many Philadelphians went to great lengths to flee the misery, chaos, noxious smells, and death.[2] Yet some chose to stay and serve their sick neighbors willingly. Helmuth was one: throughout the epidemic, he continued to serve his congregants of St. Michael's and Zion, the largest Lutheran parish in North America. He preached, he visited, he buried, and he baptized. His work was unrelenting: in the evenings he struggled with his faith, dreading sleep punctuated by disturbing dreams.[3]

And yet, Helmuth forged on. He lived in an era interested in human sympathy, in medicine, and in the great potential for human institutions, organization, and bureaucracy. He and his fellow Philadelphians were shaped by this emerging faith in humanity. But Helmuth—like many— also remained deeply influenced by his Christian faith in God's providential management over human affairs and by a deep consideration of what God's providence required when it came to human action and response.

Occurring at the cusp of the modern political era, in a world transformed by the free exercise of religion, the yellow fever epidemic offers a brief but vivid window into how religious commitment continued to shape American individuals and communities in their response to the sick and suffering. The epidemic was a momentous event in the history of the new United States and its capital city, Philadelphia, and while numerous studies have explored the epidemic's implications for early national politics, medicine, literature, and race relations, none has provided a close analysis of the epidemic's significance for early American religion.[4] Responses to the epidemic magnify broader trends in America's religious history, including the privatization of charity and the emergence of humanitarianism in the nineteenth century. Although scholars have seen such privatization and humanitarianism as critical to the development of a secular age, Christian narratives of God's providential direction—both in sending sickness and in encouraging acts of charity and service—defined benevolent endeavors in early national Philadelphia.[5]

Religious and Secular Stories of Benevolence

Accounts from Philadelphia's yellow fever epidemic represent a wide and diverse engagement with Christian and Enlightenment questions about benevolence, sympathy, and the role of God in humans' actions to alleviate suffering. Along with Helmuth, others wrote vivid accounts of their responses to the yellow fever, including the Committee to Attend to and Alleviate the Sufferings of the Afflicted with the Malignant Fever, African American ministers Absalom Jones and Richard Allen, and John Redman, a physician and the first president of the College of Physicians of Philadelphia. These accounts reflect a variety of interpretations of human duty and compassion from both religious and (what some might call) "secular" professions.[6]

When scholars study the religious history of early American benevolence, they often look to New England Puritans or their successors, men like John Winthrop, Cotton Mather, or Samuel Hopkins. They generally overlook the important contribution of other traditions, such as German Pietists,[7] African American Methodists,[8] and Presbyterians.[9] Studies of the Enlightenment story of benevolence and the rise of humanitarianism, meanwhile, generally focus on a handful of elite male intellectuals, such as David Hume, Francis Hutcheson, and Adam Smith.[10] The influence of these men is undoubted, but other men and women—including ministers, physicians, and concerned citizens—also reflected on the origins and significance of human benevolence and developed passionate concern for doing good.[11]

The 1790s yellow fever accounts do point to important changes in Christian responses to sickness over the course of the eighteenth century, and, correspondingly, in how Christians interpreted their responses to sickness in writing. Early eighteenth-century pastoral manuals on sickness had urged repentance and trust in providence. While trust in providence remained a central theme in the 1790s yellow fever accounts, repentance was often overshadowed by the accounts' emphasis on immediate physical and social action in response to suffering. Further, while early and mid-eighteenth-century Christian medical manuals and missionary medical endeavors had focused on the possible conversion and future Christian life of the patient or recipient, accounts of the yellow fever often stressed the spiritual development—or, indeed, happiness—of the benefactor.

The idea that humans might find happiness or pleasure in doing good works—in helping others—was contested in the eighteenth century, as philosophers, novelists, and ministers alike sought to articulate the virtues of "sensibility" and "benevolence." One contemporary defined sensibility as "a temper which interests us in the concerns of our brethren; which disposes us to feel along with them." This language of sensibility worried Christians who were anxious about motivations for compassion rooted in human feelings rather than in God's command. "Benevolence," meanwhile, had long been a term associated with God's goodwill toward creation, but had more recently been used to describe human efforts to do good. Christian clergy on both sides of the Atlantic, including Samuel Hopkins and John Brown, argued for a notion of "disinterested benevolence," which attempted to alleviate concerns over potential motivations of self-interest by grounding charitable endeavors in self-sacrifice. The term "benevolence," however, has never escaped skeptics who saw—and see—it rooted in selfishness and a desire for power, both over recipients and through social reputation.[12] For most eighteenth-century Protestants, the debate spoke centrally to the concern of finding pleasure in good works. They worried such pleasure betrayed sinful self-interest and insisted that charitable enterprises should spring from a commitment to God's providence.[13]

Accounts from the yellow fever demonstrate that, between the extremes of Christian self-sacrifice and sinful self-interest, eighteenth-century Americans had many perspectives on benevolence, its motivations, and its rewards. Those who wrote about yellow fever described their motivations for benevolence as grounded in a sense of duty, informed by both Christian conviction and human sympathy. Their benevolence was rewarded by the sense of fulfillment or happiness they found in performing this duty. Some interpreted this happiness in Christian terms of God's providence, perceiving their good works as manifestations of their faith or of their own free will to work toward salvation. Others found their happiness beyond human reason to explain and, while not always explicitly religious, turned to Christian themes of self-sacrifice even in an otherwise secular account. All of the authors narrated their actions with reference to familiar forms of Protestant sickness writing. They adopted a retrospective—and sometimes providential—perspective on both the trauma of yellow fever and the significance of their response in the story of their lives.

"Die süße Pflicht"—"The Sweetest Duty"

For the Philadelphia Lutheran pastor Heinrich Helmuth, writing provided an essential comfort and resource during and after the yellow fever epidemic. He filled his daily journal with details of suffering and also, when the epidemic was over, published an account looking back on the experience. Despite his moments of despair and doubt—or, perhaps, because of them—Helmuth persistently conveyed his conviction that God led him to know his duty during the epidemic and guided him in fulfilling it. He wrote in terms of God's covenant, citing Genesis 17:1 (*"wandle vor mir und sey fromm,"* or, "walk before me and be pious"). Helmuth perceived his actions and faith as significant for his Christian journey toward salvation and accepted that God directed him in ways that, while not immediately clear to his human perspective, would be evident in retrospect. Helmuth's account of duty was also shaped, however, by the commonsense philosophy that pervaded contemporary conversations of benevolence. He acknowledged that humans had an innate sense of sympathy: the desire to do good—to act benevolently—was a natural instinct. But despite his openness to this new optimism about human nature, Helmuth retained a deep sense of human sin. He realized that any innate benevolence could be thwarted by other human instincts, including fear, without God's providential intervention.[14]

Echoing generations of Christians before him, Helmuth perceived the epidemic as God's chastising hand upon a city of sinners and, based on this interpretation, attempted to discern the human response sought by God. In his well-known published account of the epidemic, *Nachricht von dem sogenannten Gelben Fieber* (1793; translated into English in 1794 as *A Short Account of the Yellow Fever*), he began with an extensive discussion of God's righteous chastisement of the city, evoking at one point Jesus's lament over Jerusalem from the Gospels. Helmuth bemoaned Philadelphia's godlessness, apparent in its sinful luxuries, theater, and circus, but his deepest concern was the city's corresponding lack of care for its widows and orphans. God wanted sinful men and women not only to convert but also to help others. By turning his account on the pivot of charity, Helmuth claimed that the *"reflecting Christian"* would recognize that the fever was the result of social breakdown. In a society that privileged folly and amusements over compassion for its neediest members, the reason for God's stinging judgment was clear.

Helmuth's diagnosis came with a straightforward treatment: take care of your neighbor.[15]

Helmuth's interest in charity predated the yellow fever epidemic. As a child, he had been a charity student at the orphan house of the Francke Foundations and the University in Halle. He eventually taught at the orphan house before accepting a call to Pennsylvania in 1768. These experiences informed his concern about how the city of Philadelphia cared for its poor. Following the lead of both the Francke Foundations and Philadelphia's English speakers and their blossoming mutual aid and voluntary societies, Helmuth and members of his congregation founded Die Gesellschaft zur Unterstützung der redlichen Hülfsbedürftigen Haus=Armen (the Society for the Support of the Honest Needy Poor). Officially formed in 1790, the society met monthly, gathering money and organizing for the relief of the poor. There was a fee to join the society and a collection at each meeting. Even in informal, pre-1790 meetings, the society pulled in twenty dollars a week, and by 1796 it was incorporated. It received money from donations, bequests, and publications, including Helmuth's *Short Account of the Yellow Fever*, and directed its funds for the food, fuel, and clothing of those in need—the "honest poor" of its title—including widows and orphans.[16]

Helmuth's society affirmed a duty to relieve the suffering of the poor. They located this duty both in God's direction as well as in human compassion, the latter of which reflected a contemporary philosophical interest in sympathy. Although predating the word "humanitarianism," the idea that humans' inborn affections directed their responses to suffering was already widespread in the eighteenth-century Atlantic world and engaged thinkers such as Anthony Ashley Cooper, the third earl of Shaftesbury, William Wollaston, Francis Hutcheson, and Adam Smith. An increased faith in human nature had important implications for understanding social evils and for perceptions of God: increasingly, the ills of the world were seen as eradicable through human effort, and God was understood as a benevolent overseer. Yet even for those thinkers with the most general understanding of God's involvement in human life, a concept of providence nonetheless remained central to their view of compassion: it was God who endowed humans with the instinct of benevolence.[17]

Helmuth and his society assumed the new philosophical language of human compassion as a natural instinct, and they grounded it firmly in providence. Their tract spoke, however, not of a general providence in which a distant God creates at the beginning or rewards at the end of time, but of a particular or special providence in which God took an active role in human affairs. Compassion was an instinct and a duty that Christians must undertake on their journey toward salvation, but this journey was directed not by their own activity or desire for happiness but always by God. As the society sang in a hymn,

> How beautiful indeed is the band of love,
> there one fulfills the sweetest duty;
> there one, from gentle, compassionate instincts,
> assuages the pain of the poor brother.
> This is the path, upon which one
> can become an image of the highest.
>
> God creates a happiness of eternalness
> He cultivates the faculties of the soul

He himself will lead us to truth
He makes us happy on this path:
He gives enlightenment to the mind,
The heart enhances its hand.[18]

This hymn described a providential direction of human compassion. With its language of "instincts" and a God who "cultivates the faculties of the soul," the hymn merged Enlightenment and providential language. It promised happiness and enlightenment to those who traveled the path with God and helped the "poor brother." Each line of the second stanza, however, reiterates that the primary actor here was God, creating, cultivating, and leading the human, heart, soul, and mind.

It is not clear if Helmuth saw where his society and his writing echoed and diverged from new ideas and language about innate human sympathy. He was generally aware of and skeptical of Enlightenment thought, particularly when it stripped God of too much power in the lives of sinful humans. He and his colleague in Philadelphia, Johann Schmidt, were anxious about attempts to rationalize Christian faith. They worried about the attitudes of "atheism and the contempt and derision for the means of grace," which seemed to be taking the "upper hand" in "western lands." They were especially dismayed by reports of the arrival in Philadelphia of Joseph Priestly, a scientist and dissenting English minister who sought to bridge Enlightenment thought and Christianity and did so, according to Helmuth, by rejecting the divinity of Christ.[19]

When it came to the yellow fever, Helmuth's writings struggled between his implicit acknowledgment of an innate human compassion and his belief in providence. The yellow fever demonstrated, for him, the breakdown of human sympathy without God's direction and intervention. In his published account he remarked not only on the "instances of humanity and hospitality" he witnessed, but also on the "unfriendly conduct, sometimes even inhuman brutality," which "will remain a stain upon humanity." As evidenced in his private journal, Helmuth's encounter with inhumanity led to increasingly fervent calls to his congregation and community to fulfill the commands of Scripture even in a time of desperation. On Tuesday, September 17, for example, Helmuth urged his congregation not only to endure the evil around them for the sake of their salvation, but also to "shake yourselves up and place yourselves in the fissure."[20]

By "fissure," Helmuth meant the chaos, the social disintegration, and the lack of basic human care that he daily witnessed in the city under the epidemic. He told his community not to flee or hide but rather to dig into this misery, despite the terror and inhumanity, which he made no attempt to elide. He wrote in his journal of a terrible smell he encountered while accompanying a corpse through town to its grave. A companion explained that the smell, near a house on the main thoroughfare, was from a man dying unaccompanied. Disturbed by the thought of people dying alone, Helmuth confided in his journal, "My God! What is becoming of us miserable worms!" His published account of the epidemic expressed the conviction that many people died from solitude. Without the attention of human compassion, "the fear of death overpowered many and actually killed them."[21]

To step into the fissure, then, meant to cross that boundary of fear and to respond with compassion to suffering. Helmuth recognized the difficulty of this task when fear had overcome the most basic of human instincts: the innate love and affection found particularly among families. He told of anxious relatives standing at a distance, reluctant to approach an ailing beloved. Distress was, fortunately, alleviated by courageous individuals who "at other times did not properly make it their business to attend the sick." While physicians like Caspar Wistar and Benjamin Rush assisted as they were able, Wistar contracted the fever and Rush's house was overflowing with patients. Thus those who had the least of occupations—those who tended the dead—proved most significant. The congregation's "inviter" (who managed funerals) and the driver of the hearse were willing to touch the dead, place them in coffins, and offer a final human dignity. These men and Helmuth were often the only people to attend the dead to their final rest. The funeral procession of three men, he wrote, was a marked difference from the norm.[22]

Helmuth cared about service to the suffering, but he recognized that, with the exception of a few brave souls, his community had been paralyzed with terror, unable to perform the basic functions of human compassion. He was not alone in his concern for the limits of innate human sympathy. The Scottish Common Sense philosopher Thomas

Reid had delineated a difference between benevolence as an affection and benevolence as a virtue. The former was "a propensity to do good, from natural constitution or habit, without regard to rectitude or duty." The latter was "a fixed purpose or resolution to do good when we have opportunity, from a conviction that it is right, and is our duty." For Reid, the answer to a breakdown in benevolence was to root it not in the passions but in a "fixed principle," grounded in human reason and judgment.[23] For Helmuth, the answer to such a breakdown was to turn to God. He meditated on Christ's passion: "I pushed myself as a poor poor sinner in the wounds of Jesus. A right poor worm." Through such meditation, Helmuth confirmed his dependence on God's direction and mercy and his need for repentance; he also emerged refreshed for further work.[24]

Helmuth found hope and a calling in God's providence over the epidemic and in his corresponding sense that the experience of God's providence was not bound by human emotions and time. "The world," he wrote, "disappeared before my eyes like a shadow." The epidemic swept away the immediate and familiar; those left behind had to make meaning of a life transformed. Helmuth urged his congregants not to fixate on earthly mortality and instead to follow Jesus, who was "the primary path to have peace, courage, and yieldedness [*Gelaßenheit*] in these dangerous days."[25] Helmuth's published account of the epidemic likewise highlighted stories of how faith in God's providence lifted himself and his community—not so that they might avoid earthly sorrow but so that they could act with compassion unhindered by fear.

St. Michael's and Zion continued to meet and worship throughout the epidemic, despite criticism from some that this could further contagion. Helmuth defended such meetings in a place of worship, arguing that they did much to temper fear: the congregation took precautions with spaced seating and opened windows and supplemented a shortened worship and prayers with the latest news and means of prevention. Through their mixture of spiritual and practical ends, the meetings distracted from fear, and, Helmuth wrote, "experience has shewn how hurtful fear has been to the inhabitants of this city." Turning to God and the church community in the midst of the yellow fever was not a way to avoid the epidemic's reality—it was a way to encounter the disease with courage.[26]

Helmuth recognized that his community's actions during the epidemic had far-reaching, transcendent significance for their spiritual lives and for their posterity. This significance depended, however, on an adequate record and interpretation of the events. He began this interpretive work the moment he announced his decision to stay. Adopting a retrospective framework, he expressed his decision to remain in the city by voicing, at the same time, his conviction of the outcome: "See me," Helmuth had declared from the pulpit, "as a dead man."[27] He had every reason to suspect his service during the epidemic would kill him; yet his pronouncement did not, in fact, fix his death date. His reference was to a universal, inevitable mortality—a reminder that the end of Christian life was not physical survival but spiritual growth. This perspective shaped all of his writing on the fever; it was an opportunity to discern and do God's will and to grow spiritually, regardless of physical danger. This was true for not only Philadelphia's Christians but also those "distant brethren" Helmuth addressed in his published account. He called on all who witnessed the epidemic and its suffering—firsthand or through narrative—to recognize it as a providentially ordained call to humans to reflect and to serve, and, ultimately, to turn to God in faith with the promise of salvation.[28]

Helmuth's conviction of God's intention and grace in sending the epidemic also allowed him to comprehend his personal experience and emotional turmoil. His journal described long quiet nights among the graves—the "newly raised hills"—and his sense of Jesus's presence "among the tombs." Helmuth wrote of Jesus as looking for the "possessed," a reference to Luke 8:27. The Gospel account describes a man bound by evil spirits and forced to wander in a cemetery. Freed by Jesus, the man returned to the city, proclaiming Jesus's words. Helmuth's published account echoed his journal's story. The thought of Jesus's presence in his own cemetery, Helmuth wrote, was "reviving . . . to my soul!" and made his time among the graves "sweetly solemn." Looking back, he interpreted his sense of peace in the midst of death as God's means of rescuing him—like the possessed man in Luke—from evil and restoring and refreshing him for ministry in the city.[29]

Helmuth attributed both his faith and service to God, and he recognized with joy that his experiences during the epidemic would define his Christian life and career. He wrote,

And I—the most unworthy of the servants of the Lord, who had been so unprofitable, so little useful, during the whole time of my office, I may cherish the unmerited hope, that the Lord graciously made use of me, to lead many a soul to salvation, who else would have strayed and been lost—and oh! my God what happiness! To be instrumental in saving a soul! not for a world, would I barter the personal advantage which I have derived from the mortality in Philadelphia. Forget not oh my soul! what the Lord has conferred upon thee, unworthy as thou art![30]

While Helmuth saw and felt the misery of the epidemic, he also recognized and valued that it changed his life. The epidemic would forever be part of his reputation as a Christian minister, and Helmuth's published account ensured that. There is an air of Enlightenment self-interest in his description of the happiness and "personal advantage" he received from his good works, yet Helmuth took care to offer such an account with an explicitly Christian interpretation.[31] He called himself an "unworthy servant," in reference to Luke 17:10, explaining he had merely done his duty; his faith and his service in furthering the Christian faith of others were the true focus. Helmuth's "happiness" was not the happiness of more skeptical Enlightenment thought—a happiness found in personal fulfillment and this-worldly ends. He grounded his happiness, rather, in the fact that his retrospective account confirmed God's providential guidance over his life, his faith, and his service to others.

Helmuth believed that his actions during the yellow fever were inspired by God. Despite his acceptance of a natural instinct of human sympathy, he recognized that this instinct could be thwarted by fear. He believed the only way to transcend this fear was to turn to God in dependence and humility, praying for God's direction in earthly work and in salvation. He narrated the epidemic by stressing God's active intervention in the community, their dependence on this intervention, and the rewards offered for those who, like him, found grace in surrendering their lives and duty to God's service.

"Their Sympathy Is Balm to Our Wounds"

As Helmuth worked among the German-speaking Lutherans, a group of English-speaking men gathered in City Hall to address the organizational and political vacuum created by the epidemic. Many political leaders had fled the city, and by early September the mayor, Matthew Clarkson, along with those overseers of the poor who had remained, placed an advertisement in the city's papers seeking the assistance of "benevolent citizens." The city needed volunteers who were "humanely disposed" to "aid in the present distress." The advertisement appeared on September 10, 1793, and on September 12, the new Committee to Attend to and Alleviate the Sufferings of the Afflicted with the Malignant Fever gathered. It met daily in City Hall until the epidemic abated in late October and continued meeting periodically until March 1794.[32]

Like Helmuth, the Committee members recognized that sympathy and compassion were not enough to encourage people to fulfill basic human duties during the epidemic. Unlike Helmuth, the Committee focused its attention not on God but rather on its responsibility for reestablishing order. The Minutes stressed repeatedly that with good order people might again behave with consideration toward their neighbors. The Committee did turn, eventually, to a general sense of providence in its efforts to comprehend fully the extent and meaning of the epidemic and its actions. While this sense of providence profoundly shaped the narrative of the epidemic, it was secondary in the early sections of the Committee's Minutes.

Upon its formation, the Committee acted immediately, citing a joint commitment to sympathy for suffering citizens and a great concern for order. They first focused attention on the hospital at Bush-Hill, where they achieved success with dedicated volunteers and attention to detail. By September 14, only two days after its initial meeting, the Committee received a report on the miserable state of affairs at the hospital. Two members, Stephen Girard and Peter Helm, volunteered to lead efforts to reform the hospital, "commiserating the calamitous state to which the sick may probably be reduced for want of suitable persons to superintend the Hospital." Moved by sympathy, Girard and Helm made efficient improvements to the hospital's cleanliness, staff, and patient care. These had immediate effects; for example, reports on September 18 showed many patients were not visited daily. By noon of the next day, the Committee recorded that all patients had been visited that morning, with the help of a newly hired doctor, Deveze. By September 24, the Minutes reported that "all the sick are in bedsteads, and furnished with suitable bedding, that the rooms are all numbered and that the whole house is in regular order."[33]

Establishing the "good order" of the hospital was essential to easing the epidemic and its effect on the city. Once the hospital was in order, the Committee encouraged those who were sick to "admit themselves" as soon as they experienced any symptoms, ensuring that "the lives of many might be preserved." Likewise, the Committee took charge of the burial of the dead: after hearing citizens' complaints, the Committee changed the carters' route from the hospital through town, urged coffin makers to take more care, and reported on burial grounds.[34] Although the Committee did not understand the cause or transmission of yellow fever, it was convinced that proper care of both the living and the dead would benefit the city's overall health.

The Committee also cited a "duty incumbent" to look after the orphans created by the epidemic. It organized a committee to care for them, found a suitable house for them—eventually in the old Loganian Library—and coordinated donations from "fellow citizens." By October 24, 159 children had been admitted to the orphan house. They had a matron, Mary Parvin, ten assistants, and a doctor, Samuel Duffield; thirty-one had already been released to relatives, and only eight had died. The Committee was cautious about releasing children, anxious that "improper persons may" claim "they are connected" with certain children. The Committee instituted a ten-day waiting period on such claims and insisted on retaining oversight.

In some cases, the Committee's interest in the orphans may have stemmed from class anxieties—related, of course, to its focus on reestablishing order. The first orphans mentioned in the Minutes were the fifteen-month-old twins of Joseph Mercier and his wife, reported dead on September 16. The infants were left with no one to care for them but a servant girl of "unknown" character. The Merciers also left behind property. The Committee took the property into possession, "until legally called for," and found a "very suitable place" for the infants. Perhaps the Committee feared that the Merciers' servant would be tempted to steal or take advantage of the infants' property. Yet the Committee's care for orphans seems to have been expansive. Among the diverse children admitted, for example, was "Billy Dee a mulatto."[35]

It could be argued that the Committee's efforts to reestablish order were motivated by an interest in social control and economic concerns, an argument made about charity and benevolence in other historical eras.[36] The endless lists of names—of those admitted to the hospital, to the orphanage, to the potter's field—certainly evidence how the epidemic created an opportunity for modern bureaucracy. A similarly reductionist account would suggest that charitable responses represented an effort to enforce a Protestant ethic of discipline, criticizing the idle and extolling the productive and industrious citizens who went about their duty.[37] Alongside such interpretations, however, it is important to remember that in the immediate context of the epidemic, the order and leadership exhibited by the Committee were also essential to relieving distress: they ensured that the sick would be visited, corpses would be carted away and buried, and orphans would be cared for.

It is impossible to know the motivations of those who worked on behalf of this order, but their writings offer insight to manifold, overlapping concerns. These included not only human sympathy and economic and political interests, but also conceptions of divine judgment and Christian duty. Scholars have highlighted that the men on the Committee were lay professional men, mostly of "middling" backgrounds. Not normally included in civic leadership or government, they had an opportunity to shape the city when most government officials had fled. They were anxious to prove themselves and their civic-minded beneficence, but their records also indicate an intense apprehension about the future—of the city, the nation, and the individual—which often manifested itself in explicitly providential terms.[38]

Behind the detailed accounting of time and resources, the Committee's Minutes often pulsed with a larger narrative of divine punishment and the redemption of the nation. This narrative is especially evident in the records of donations the Committee received (the Minutes recorded both the letters that accompanied donations and the Committee's responses). When other towns and cities—in Pennsylvania, New York, and New Jersey—donated money and goods to Philadelphia, they described God's judgment on the city as a judgment on "fellow citizens" of the "American Nation." This providential and national framework was crucial to the responses of cities and individuals throughout the Northeast. Through their sense of shared divine judgment, they were drawn together in charity, dismayed by the incontrovertible fact that the capital city of their new nation suffered such a setback.[39]

What could it mean that the political center of the young United States was hit with such misery? On October 12, 1793, Richard Varick wrote to the Committee on behalf of the Common Council of New York City. He sent five thousand dollars and offered more, if necessary. The New York Council bemoaned the disorganization the epidemic wrought. They were "deeply impressed with the awful judgment of the Almighty on the American Nation, in permitting a pestilential disease to lay waste and disorganize that once populous, well regulated and flourishing sister city, the seat of Empire, by destroying the lives of many valuable patriots and citizens and by driving many others of its numerous and very opulent and useful inhabitants into exile." Varick concluded with a reference to a biblical plague, praying that God "speedily stay the progress of the desolating disease and say it is enough" (2 Samuel 24:16; 1 Chronicles 21:15). He also praised the Committee members, who had "remained faithful to your trust," and prayed that they "be the peculiar care of Heaven."[40] The New York Council saw in Philadelphia's suffering a judgment not only on Philadelphia but on the entire nation. God's judgment, visible in the sickness of one community or family member, demanded the pious reflection of all.

The Committee's response to the New York Council turned likewise to providence as it tried to comprehend both the suffering in Philadelphia as well as their neighbors' sympathy, which transcended civic boundaries. In some of the most explicitly religious language of the Minutes, Clarkson, the mayor of Philadelphia, acknowledged gratefully the donation "on behalf of our suffering fellow citizens," explaining that the New York Council's benevolence and sympathy "is balm to our wounds," a scripturally laden reference to healing. Clarkson described the "divine interposition" that touched their lives—not only in sending the epidemic, but also in seeing that "the hearts of so many around us have been touched with our distress and have united in our relief." He prayed that "the Almighty disposer of all events" protect others from the disease.[41]

Some scholars have interpreted the Committee's use of phrases like "Almighty disposer of all events" and "great Ruler of the universe" as an example of the adoption of "fashionable Deistic terminology" and a sign of growing secularization. But the God who disposes all events is different from the God who is a clock maker or final judge. As the Committee and its benefactors discussed the meaning of the epidemic and the charity and compassion of fellow humans and citizens, they in fact maintained a Christian providential framework. One historian has tried to divide epidemic accounts that relied on "a traditional religious framework" of divine judgment from accounts that offered a "more hopeful interpretation" of human effort and the possibility of communal recovery.[42] With its detailed Minutes, full of compassion, order, accomplishments, and gratitude, the Committee and its work could almost fit into this latter, secular narrative: its work typified an Enlightenment-infused optimism about human nature. Yet the Committee itself did not describe its work in this way. It relied on both narratives—on human effort *and* divine judgment. It relied on providence.

In the Christian tradition of providential thought, there is no narrative distinction between judgment and hope—they are bound closely together. For those suffering and serving during the epidemic, within the experience of God's judgment there was also to be found hope and a call for human effort. In his thanks to the New York Council, Clarkson accepted the divine judgment on his city, writing, "We humbly kiss the rod and improve by the dispensation." Deistic as his language might sometimes seem, Clarkson relied on a providential interpretation of transcendent judgment, human repentance, and the hope of redemption, which was, indeed, already evident in the bonds of human sympathy.[43]

As with Helmuth, members of the Committee relied on retrospection in order to narrate their experiences during the epidemic. When the yellow fever waned in late October, the Committee's Minutes signaled gratitude for survival as well as sadness over the loss of so many. The Committee thanked "Divine Providence" for the "agreeable prospect of returning health to our long afflicted city" and adjourned for a day in order to allow members to attend "their respective places of worship." The Committee's final report from March 1794, which was copied into the Minutes, acknowledged the deaths of four Committee members and reflected, in the report's last lines, on the epidemic's meaning: "Yet while we look back with mournful regret to the loss of our companions, gratitude to the supreme disposer of events requires our acknowledgment of his interposition in the preservation of our own lives, and those of so many of our fellow citizens."[44] After pages of detailed Minutes accounting for human efforts and failures as well as survival and loss, the Committee concluded by looking back with a final appeal to providence.

The writing of a Committee member, the publisher and author Mathew Carey, offers insight into one individual's experience of participating in the Committee and interpreting the epidemic. Although Carey fled the epidemic for a period of three weeks, his time in the city affected him.[45] In a popular publication, *A Short Account of the Malignant Fever*, he sought to make sense of how the epidemic revealed human nature. Influenced by contemporary philosophical understandings of benevolence, Carey remarked that those who served the sick performed the "kindest offices of disinterested humanity." He surmised that responders who had gained acclaim, such as Helmuth, "would have done the same," even if they had been "remote from the public eye" and had no promise of fame. Carey knew their reward was a "self-approving conscience," but he sought to give them, further, the "approbation of our friends and fellow men" by placing their names in print. He hoped his account would provide examples for subsequent generations "to emulate." He found in this work of narration the "highest consolation I have ever experienced."[46]

In addition to finding meaning in writing and in reputation, Carey also reflected on a divine overseer as he contemplated human actions. Carey depended on a very rational, creator God, whom he invoked in his criticism of those who, like Helmuth's Lutheran congregation, continued to worship in the midst of the epidemic. He argued that the "mistaken zeal" of those who worshiped in church rather than at home actually furthered the contagion, pointing out that churches with the most crowded worship services suffered the highest number of dead. Such action exemplified an incorrect understanding of God's providence, he argued. Instead of focusing on God's law, that is, God's commandment to worship, humans should focus on another kind of law, "implanted" in their very nature: the "law of self-preservation." This law was written "in indelible characters by his divine hand, on the breast of every one of his creatures." Breaking the fundamental law of self-preservation was no proper way to adore "the maker and preserver of mankind." Carey suggested that the law of nature, implanted by God, supplanted the law of the Old Testament.[47]

Carey's rational, general overseer differed from Helmuth's active, intervening God. Vestiges of a Christian providential framework nonetheless remained in Carey's account when he described the feelings of joy he experienced in comprehending a meaning in suffering and in human efforts to ease suffering. He concluded with "thanksgiving to that Supreme Being, who has, in his own time, stayed the avenging storm, ready to devour us, after it had laughed to scorn all human efforts." Human efforts were, in the end, nothing without a supporting transcendent force. Carey likewise turned to God in narrating the self-sacrificial efforts of those whose dedication surpassed all reason. He could not adequately describe his emotion, he wrote, without comparison to the divine. He wanted his reader to share in the "pleasure" he found in witnessing such human charity: "When we view man in this light, we lose sight of his feebleness, his imperfection, his vice—he resembles, in a small degree, that divine being, who is an inexhaustible mine of mercy and goodness." Carey "rejoiced" to be "a witness and recorder" of such human behavior in approximation of the divine, even in the midst of misery.[48]

Like Helmuth, Carey found a sort of "personal advantage" in his work among the sick. Unlike Helmuth, he was unwilling to attribute his "pleasure" to God's intervention, but he nonetheless perceived in the divine being a model of "mercy and goodness" for humans to emulate. Carey's difference from Helmuth on providence, while significant, was subtle compared to later changes. In a letter written four decades after the epidemic, in 1834, Carey returned to this mysterious pleasure, explaining that his work on the Committee remained "some of the most tranquil and happy hours of my existence," and he remarked that his colleagues on the Committee felt "pretty much the same."[49] He still wondered how such an emotion could exist in the midst of the terrible social breakdown that accompanied the epidemic. But in 1834 Carey did not turn to divine example or a general providential framework. Instead he turned to science. He wrote that his feelings of enjoyment were "curious" to him, and he invited a "physiologist" to investigate how he could find such happiness in a time of misery.[50]

In the immediate context and aftermath of the yellow fever, however, Carey and the Committee still relied on providence to make sense of the suffering around them and their responses to it. Although more general than the providence that pervaded Helmuth's writings, the divine, the "Almighty," or the "Supreme Being" that appeared in the Committee's Minutes and Carey's account played an important role. It allowed them to express their conviction that both the suffering and their benevolent actions had significance beyond the immediate event. They were part of a plan to help the city, its inhabitants, its neighbors, and themselves. Their accounts suggested that while humans might fail, there was a timeless model for compassion in divine mercy and goodness, a model that could inspire renewed efforts and hope.

"Instruments, in the Hand of God"

As a printer, Mathew Carey seized the opportunity to publish the first account of the yellow fever epidemic and released multiple editions in the early aftermath. His prompt publication gained authoritative status, privileging the story of the Committee's response and the leadership potential of its tradesmen and artisans. While extolling the Committee, however, Carey not only disregarded but also degraded the contributions of other communities, including black nurses.[51] In response, African American ministers Absalom Jones and Richard Allen published their own account of the yellow fever, defending black nurses from charges of misconduct, extortion, and theft. Shaped by their years in the Methodist Episcopal Church and participation in Philadelphia's zeal for voluntary societies, Jones and Allen explained the black community's response as a result of their own free will and God's providence, and as an example of their civic belonging and participation in the era's central concerns of human sympathy and benevolence.[52]

Black nurses and workers were a central part of the response to the yellow fever. These men and women cared for the dying, nursed hundreds back to health, and buried the dead. And, despite erroneous medical claims that blacks were immune to yellow fever, many became sick during their efforts and died alongside white Philadelphians. While Carey briefly praised the efforts of Jones and Allen, who organized the nurses, and William Gray, who took charge of the burials, he mostly disparaged the efforts of black responders. He claimed that they took advantage of their suffering and desperate patients and a city in disarray to steal and charge high fees for their services.[53]

Jones and Allen responded to Carey's narrative with an account of their own: *A Narrative of the Proceedings of the Black People, during the Late Awful Calamity in Philadelphia, in the Year 1793*. Scholars have highlighted the significance of the *Narrative* as a "first"—the first published account in which African Americans responded directly to white accusations—and as a "polemic" that expressed blacks' frustrations and anger with Carey's characterization of their behavior and with their situation in Philadelphia and the new nation.[54] Although scholars have emphasized the uniqueness of Jones and Allen's *Narrative*, in important ways it is not unique at all: it confirmed that the black community was also guided by principles of Christian charity and human sympathy, overseen by God's grace and mercy. Though the *Narrative* should be read as a unique expression of a community's frustration and anger, it also inhabits a familiar form. Like Helmuth and the Committee, Philadelphia's black community was a community of Christian and civic-minded human beings, dedicated to serving their neighbors and doing God's will.[55]

In the late eighteenth century, Philadelphia's free black community was the largest in the United States. The community had grown steadily after Pennsylvania had passed a law for the gradual emancipation of slaves in 1780. Despite its size and the sympathy of antislavery white Pennsylvanians, the community's position remained precarious. Because emancipation was gradual, many blacks remained enslaved for their whole life or for twenty-eight years, depending on when they were born, while some had worked or continued to work in order to purchase their own freedom. Blacks "bore the costs and burdens of emancipation" and knew it. Among white reformers, there was also growing interest in colonization programs, which would resettle blacks in Africa or elsewhere. Although not unpopular in some black communities, colonization was unappealing to Philadelphia's blacks in this era and represented an unwelcome alternative to true citizenship. Further cementing the need for leadership and organization in Philadelphia's black community, finally, was the passage of the 1793 Fugitive Slave Act, which required the return of escaped enslaved persons and also, some feared, promoted the kidnapping of free blacks.[56]

From this context, several black leaders emerged, including Jones and Allen. Both formerly enslaved, they were instrumental in the development of the Free African Society, a mutual aid and burial society, and a new African Church, institutions that mirrored white efforts and communities in Philadelphia. Problems nonetheless continued for Philadelphia blacks: some white clergy did not approve of the new African Church and retaliated by segregating black parishioners. With construction of the African Church under way, meanwhile, some benefactors who had initially pledged money to the construction withdrew their funds in order to support plantation owners escaping to Philadelphia from the uprising of enslaved peoples that began in Saint-Domingue in 1791.[57] The irony and capriciousness were not lost on Philadelphia's black community.

The yellow fever epidemic of 1793 occurred in this period when Philadelphia's free blacks were striving to emerge as an autonomous and organized community. They recognized that their response to the epidemic was an opportunity to demonstrate their role in and relationship to the city. Thus, in their narrative, Jones and Allen relied on language that would be familiar to all Philadelphians. On the first page, they wrote, "We found a freedom to go forth, confiding in him who can preserve in the midst of a burning fiery furnace, sensible that it was our duty to do all the good we could to our suffering fellow mortals." From "confiding" in the God of the scriptural "fiery furnace" to citing a "duty" to "fellow mortals," the *Narrative* showed that Philadelphia's free black community voluntarily participated in the same tradition of human affection and providential guidance that characterized white efforts and writings.[58]

From early in the *Narrative*, Jones and Allen explained black workers' duty in response to the yellow fever as a matter of free choice—much like the men who served on the Committee. The newspapers had published a "solicitation" in early September, asking "people of colour to come forward and assist the distressed, perishing, and neglected sick." This solicitation was the result of the common—though mistaken— belief that black people were immune to yellow fever. After meeting and discussing the matter with others, Jones and Allen decided to act with a public appeal. In their narrative, they emphasized that their response was entirely their own: it was a "charge we took upon us." Not as slaves, but as "fellow mortals," Philadelphia's black community freely sought to help the suffering. After consulting with Mayor Clarkson, Jones, Allen, and William Gray directed their service first to recruiting nurses and second to the removal and burial of the dead.[59]

Jones and Allen emphasized the voluntary nature of their work for two reasons. First, influenced by Methodist teachings, they believed that humans had free will in matters of salvation, including in the good works they chose to do as they sought a life of sanctification. Their efforts during the fever exemplified a conscientious Christian choice to do good and to live a holy life. Second, they emphasized that they also participated in the era's culture of voluntary and mutual aid societies. They performed their duties, they wrote, out of a "real sensibility;–we sought not fee nor reward." This statement was, in one sense, a direct response to Carey's damaging accusation that black nurses charged extortionate fees for their services, but the language of sensibility also stressed their connection to wider benevolent networks. Indeed, their commitment to mutual assistance and compassion was not limited to an immediate community of black Philadelphians but shared with the wider community. As nurses they engaged in the "finer feelings" and "acts" of "humanity" in their care of patients both black *and* white. The same could not be said of most white Philadelphians. As it turned out, blacks were susceptible to yellow fever and "suffered equally with the whites." Yet even though "our distress hath been very great," Jones and Allen wrote, it was "much unknown to the white people. Few have been the whites that paid attention to us while the blacks were engaged in the other's service." In serving both black and white communities, black workers exemplified Christian good works and benevolence to a greater extent, they argued, than most whites.[60]

Jones and Allen did describe the attention of one white man: the physician Benjamin Rush, who encouraged their work and connected them to understandings of Christian service within Philadelphia's contemporary medical society. Rush taught them how to bleed patients (for better or worse), to prepare medicine, and to call on him or another physician when situations required. Jones and Allen learned from Rush's model of diligent service to the sick: "We feel a great satisfaction in believing, that we have been useful to the sick, and thus publicly thank Doctor Rush, for enabling us to be so. We have bled upwards of eight hundred people, and do declare, we have not received to the value of a dollar and a half, therefor: we were willing to imitate the Doctor's benevolence, who sick or well, kept his house open day and night, to give what assistance he could in this time of trouble."[61] In Rush, Jones and Allen chose a well-known and respected model of Christian benevolence for their work as nurses. Rush had studied medicine first under the Philadelphia physician John Redman, a Presbyterian from whom he learned a respect for medicine as a work directed by God for the good of humanity. Rush's memoir of Redman highlighted the pious underpinnings of his medical work, evident even in the concluding lines of his medical dissertation: "God grant that my studies and labours may be directed to the glory of his name, and to the welfare of my neighbors."[62] Jones and Allen likewise explained their nursing work as directed by God. "When a physician was not attainable," they wrote, "we have been the instruments, in the hand of God, for saving the lives of some hundreds of our suffering fellow mortals."[63]

By placing themselves in the company of Christian physicians like Rush, who accepted pay, Jones and Allen also pointed to the value of their work and the conviction that economic self-interest and Christian benevolence could go together. Though they reiterated that they "sought not fee nor reward," they also seem to have respected individual black workers' decisions to choose their compensation.[64] These decisions were shaped by perceptions of human duty and God's providence. Anecdotes suggest that a few nurses avoided payment. One female nurse refused pay, saying, "If I go for money God will see it, and may be make me take the disorder and die, but if I go, and take no money, he may spare my life." Such stories suggest an anxiety about the nature of good works and how underlying human motivations might affect God's acceptance. Because Methodists believed they were free to contribute to their salvation, they also believed they could lose their salvation. The examples of nurses refusing pay highlight the seriousness with which black nurses considered their actions, their freedom, and their salvation. These examples do not mean, however, that black nurses understood their work as a "recusal from Philadelphia's commercial society," as has been argued. Alongside accounts of those nurses who refused pay were those who "charged with exemplary moderation."[65]

In the case of those who did accept extra pay, Jones and Allen did not condemn but offered understanding and sympathy. When recruiting black nurses, they had arranged pay of six dollars a week, but the desperate sick often offered more. Jones and Allen could not restrain the nurses from accepting more pay: "It was natural for people in low circumstances to accept a voluntary, bounteous reward; especially under the loathsomeness of many of the sick, when nature shuddered at the thoughts of the infection."[66] Jones and Allen condemned acts of pilfering or mistreatment, of which—they pointed out—both white and black people were guilty, but they recognized that no intervention on their part could change the inflated wages some nurses collected. They saw, and the mayor agreed, that wage inflation was created by the epidemic and the difficult working conditions, not by innate evil impulses on the part of black nurses.[67]

The social breakdown caused by the yellow fever pushed Jones and Allen, as it had others, to action and faithful trust in God's providence. Like Helmuth, they recorded human cruelty and the failures of compassion: men and women abandoned to die "unseen, and unassisted" and orphans and widows left helpless. The *Narrative* described this "barbarity" and reported that it was "with reluctance we call to mind the many opportunities there were in the power of individuals to be useful to their fellow-men, yet through the terror of the times was omitted."[68] Many of the people who fled—including Carey, who had so unfairly criticized the black community—were white. And, in responding to Carey, Jones and Allen were at pains to point out that whites along with blacks were guilty of petty crimes and inhumanity. Yet, like Helmuth, Jones and Allen also allowed for the powerful effects of fear on human actions: "We ascribe such unfriendly conduct to the frailty of human nature, and not to willful unkindness, or hardness of heart." The only way to overcome this frailty and fear, they argued, was with God's assistance. "Truly our task was hard," they wrote, "yet through mercy we were enabled to go on." God "was pleased to strengthen us, and remove all fear from us, and disposed our hearts to be as useful as possible."[69]

The *Narrative* depends on this trust in God's providential direction. Although Jones and Allen stressed human freedom in pursuing good works, they nonetheless, like Helmuth, perceived and narrated God's presence guiding their activity through the epidemic's misery. This is evident in the first page of the tract, where they wrote, "We found a freedom to go forth, confiding in him who can preserve in the midst of a burning fiery furnace." They refer here to Daniel 3, a story of three

Babylonian Jews who, refusing to worship their king's gods and golden image, were sentenced to death in a "fiery furnace." Once the sentence was enacted, the king saw not three but four men walking in the furnace. He was astonished and realized that "the form of the fourth is like the Son of God." The king ceased the punishment, and the three men emerged unscathed. Jones and Allen imagined the presence of God in their own sojourn into the "fiery furnace" of yellow fever, trusting in this presence to "preserve" their lives and, perhaps, their reputations as they served their "suffering fellow mortals" from their own free will and journey toward salvation.[70]

The epidemic reminded Philadelphia's black community of God's providence and the salvific significance of all their work and action, whether rewarded in this life or not. These themes are reiterated in Jones and Allen's publication by a series of paratexts that ended the work. One was a significant antislavery appeal, "An Address to Those Who Keep Slaves and Approve the Practice." In this address, as historian Richard Newman has shown, Allen expertly appealed not only to white sensibilities of reform, liberty, and justice but also to Old Testament stories of God's sympathy with—and ultimate salvation of—the oppressed. The next paratext, "People of Colour," urged enslaved peoples to "put your trust in God, who sees your condition, and as a merciful father pitieth his children, so doth God pity them that love him." Christian love, the text argued, would endear the enslaved to masters and "promote your liberty." And, if masters proved cruel, God was not: God would favor those who loved and worked with affection for others, even in the context of misery. The "chief end" of life was "to be prepared for a better." This end was true even for those who had been freed and carried resentment toward "the white people." Allen urged forgiveness, admonishing readers to recognize that "very many of them are instruments in the hand of God for our good[;] even such as have held us in captivity, are now pleading our cause with earnestness and zeal." The appended texts ended, finally, with a hymn urging ministers to preach repentance and to emphasize the shortness of time and the dangers of waiting in a world with unexpected crises.[71]

These paratexts offered important messages of freedom, forgiveness, consolation, and justice—as well as otherworldly rewards for those enslaved in hopeless situations. But why mention enslaved persons at all in a pamphlet describing the work of Philadelphia's free black community during the yellow fever? Jones and Allen had an audience and an opportunity to make a case against slavery. Perhaps, also, Jones and Allen wanted to suggest that, although free in body and will, the black men and women who served in the epidemic might nonetheless—like those still enslaved—have to wait for a deferred reward: that their work, though spurned by men like Carey, contributed to their salvation and had providential significance that would be fully realized only in retrospect.[72]

Jones and Allen concluded their main *Narrative* along these lines, reflecting on the vagaries of human memory and its implications for human compassion and faith. Citing an "old proverb," which they found "applicable to those of our colour who exposed their lives in the late afflicting dispensation," they wrote: "God and a soldier, all men do adore, / In time of war, and not before; / When the war is over, and all things righted, / God is forgotten, and the soldier slighted."[73] In the crisis of an epidemic, Jones and Allen recognized, men and women gained a unique appreciation for those who responded with commitment and attention to duty.

The yellow fever forced people to encounter human suffering and to ponder God's will, the freedom of humans to respond, and the meaning of their response. African American workers responded to the fever, and their work deserved credit from both their "fellow mortals" and their fellow Christians. They rightly feared their actions would be forgotten, especially when accounts like Carey's slighted them. Jones and Allen wrote their *Narrative* to defend and record their community's humanity, compassion, and service, born of their own free will and faith in God's providence.

"Your Duty to Venture"

The African American nurses who served in the epidemic represented one prong of the city's medical response. Yellow fever was also the focus of Philadelphia's professional medical community, which was thriving by 1793. The first medical school in the thirteen colonies was founded at the College of Philadelphia (later University of Pennsylvania) in 1765. In 1787, twenty-four physicians gathered to found the College of Physicians of Philadelphia, a professional medical organization designed to further knowledge and research in science and medicine. Within this community, heated debates developed over the cause of yellow fever, and scholars have given sustained focus to the medical, scientific, and even political nature of these debates.[74] Little attention has been given, however, to the ways in which medicine in early national Philadelphia was regarded as a benevolent and Christian enterprise.

During the 1793 epidemic, John Redman, president of the College of Physicians of Philadelphia, was the only physician who could offer an account of the yellow fever epidemic that had previously hit Philadelphia, in 1762. He gave a lecture to the college based on his experiences, which was subsequently published. Redman was an esteemed leader in the city's medical community, served as teacher, mentor, and correspondent of the influential physician Benjamin Rush, and was reelected president of the College of Physicians multiple times, serving from its foundation in 1787 to 1804. His lecture on the previous epidemic along with his manuscript correspondence offer a critical view of how an influential early American physician understood suffering, human duty, and God's providence in the midst of an epidemic.

Redman's medical career was deeply shaped by his Presbyterianism. He was early educated at the famous "Log College" of William Tennent alongside men famous for their role in the Great Awakening—the revivals of religion that swept the eighteenth-century American colonies. With this background, it is no surprise that Redman's medical writings were infused with piety. His presidential addresses to the college resounded with references to God's providential guidance over its work. In his inaugural address, he merged the language of rationality with the language of providence, citing Proverbs 3: "I am convinced that it highly becomes rational men in all their lawful enterprises and undertakings of importance . . . to acknowledge God to be their sovereign Ruler and the Over Ruler of all events."[75]

Redman described God's involvement in the college's undertakings as a covenant. The college held "obligations" to God "for giving us capacities for such an undertaking, and influencing our wills to engage in so good a design at this time." God, in turn, would bless their work and lead them to salvation. In the end, if they had "served our generation faithfully according to the will of God," Redman wrote, "we may be fitted for and admitted into his Kingdom and glory, through Jesus

Christ, our Lord and Saviour."[76] Like Jones and Allen, Redman stressed God's providence in the work of medical care. Unlike Jones and Allen, however, Redman, as a Presbyterian, did not stress human freedom to do good works and earn salvation through sanctification. The physician's ability to do good—in both the skills he employed and the service he pursued—was directly overseen by God. God "influenced" the human will in works of salvific significance, including medicine.

An Enlightenment language of sympathy and compassion also frequently punctuated Redman's writings and statements on medicine, although it was never far removed from his deep faith in providence. He reveled in the college's devotion to "*good work*" and the "cause of humanity." On one occasion Rush recorded a toast made by Redman: "to the Individual Practitioner, who makes the health, Comfort & happiness of his fellow Mortalls one of the chief Ends & delights of his life—And acts therein from Motives that ought Render him Superior to all the difficulties he may have to Encounter in the pursuit thereof."[77] Sympathy for patients and the easing of their physical pain, grounded in both Enlightenment and Christian compassion and charity, were essential components of medical work for Redman.

To rise above the inevitable "difficulties" of the medical profession—including witnessing the widespread suffering and death of an epidemic—the physician depended above all, according to Redman, on faith in God's providence. Writing to Rush in 1782, Redman again reiterated that their professional service was "according to the will of God" and that "though some storms should meet us, so common to all, in the voyage of life; yet having him who rules the winds, commends the raging waves silences the roaring billows & stills the tumult of the people, with us in our little weak & shatterd bark; and though he may seem to sleep, yet if we call on him in truth, He will soon awake arise, and silence our own tumultuous passions within, command a calm all around us, or overrule all for our best good, and so astonish & charm us with a view of his power & sense of his love." Redman found both motivation and solace in his piety, and it defined his medical care. One of his dying patients said to a friend that "death had nothing terrible in it when Dr. Redman spoke to her about it."[78] In his medical practice, Redman and his patients depended on both his reason and his faith.

Redman's account of the 1762 yellow fever exemplified how he merged his medical training, his concern for the public good, and his conviction of God's providential guidance. He offered extensive observations of the disease and practical advice regarding the use of vinegar and tobacco for their preventative benefits. He also included what he found to be the best advice of all: to be fearless and trust in God. Such trust, he wrote, had done him great good and made him of use to others. Redman reflected that God guided him through anxieties and fears, lifting him up to continue his work. "This much I know," he wrote, "that when that Light which shineth in darkness led me to the exercise of piety and virtue, it made me happy even in the midst of danger or troubles, and when slighted or neglected it rendered me miserable, tho' surrounded with every other circumstance capable of giving pleasure to the senses."[79] Like Helmuth, Carey, Jones, and Allen, Redman experienced a sense of happiness from his service. He was careful to differentiate this happiness from ephemeral pleasures, however, stressing that his work, success, and joy depended ultimately on his faith in God's grace.

In 1797, when yet another yellow fever epidemic hit Philadelphia, Redman offered a revealing glimpse of how closely he identified the practice of medicine with Christian ministry. His minister, Ashbel Green of the Second Presbyterian Church of Philadelphia, had asked Redman whether he should return to the city after fleeing to the outskirts. In reply, Redman said that he considered it Green's "duty to venture," writing, "We think that it be deemed improper or unjustifiable for Medical Doctors & Natural parents to Quit us at such times; It is equally if not more so, for our Spiritual Fathers to desert us altogether, or at least not occasionally to Aid the remainder of their flock who Cannot, or dare not Emigrate, in their Worship . . . on the present Calomitous [sic] occasion." For Redman, both physicians and ministers had the responsibility to stay and serve in times of epidemic; such crises demanded "more peculiar Exertions in duty," in "doing & promoting Good."[80]

While Redman—the physician—claimed that he sought not to "intrude on matters above my small Sphere," he continued his letter by quoting scripture to his minister. He chose Psalm 91:2–6, in a less-than-subtle way to remind Green of God's promise of providential guidance in times of disease: "I will say of the Lord, He is my refuge and my fortress: my God; in him will I trust. Surely he shall deliver thee from the snare of the fowler, and from the noisome pestilence. He shall cover thee with his feathers, and under his wings shalt thou trust: his truth shall be thy shield and buckler. Thou shalt not be afraid for the terror by night; nor for the arrow that flieth by day; Nor for the pestilence that walketh in darkness; nor for the destruction that wasteth at noonday."[81] Green's duty was clear, in Redman's view, and God's direction was obvious.

To walk piously, in covenant with God, was the profession of the Christian, whether physician or pastor, or, indeed, tradesman. In 1798, Philadelphia was struck once more by a yellow fever epidemic, and Redman again found himself writing to his minister Ashbel Green, who had this time fled to Princeton. The purpose of Redman's letter was not to advise Green on whether he should return to the city (presumably Green had learned better than to ask). Redman's letter was, rather, a report on the city and congregation Green had left behind. The Second Presbyterian Church had continued to meet every Sunday "but one," Redman reported, with "Messrs Eastburn and Faulconer" as officiants. Eastburn, a tradesman, had worked on both "the board of health and in discharge of Christian duties," proving essential "both to the souls, & bodies" of those who were sick or suffered loss. For Redman, Eastburn's presence in the city, with its joint benefit to human souls and bodies, could be seen as nothing other than "very providential."[82]

During the yellow fever epidemic, Redman confirmed and extended his well-honed conviction that medicine was a work done to relieve human suffering and was directed by God. Like others who stayed and served, he found happiness not only in his faithful pursuit of this work and his hope for salvation, but above all in his sense of the continuous presence of God's mercy in his life, even in times of immense trial. In his leadership, faithful service, and deep commitment to medicine, Redman exemplified the merging of Enlightenment-era conceptions of sympathy and advances in medicine with devout Christian faith in God's providence.

* * *

In 1929, the *Journal of the Presbyterian Historical Society* published a biography of Redman, a nearly forgotten alumnus of the Presbyterian Log College. Before his long and illustrious career as a physician, he was a schoolmate of Gilbert Tennent, the famed revivalist of American religious history. Further cementing his Presbyterian credentials, the article continued, Redman served as a trustee of Princeton from 1761 to 1778, along with other former Log College schoolmates. In an 1851 account of Log College and its famous alumni, however, Redman did not make the cut.[83]

Why not?

According to the 1929 article, "Dr. Redman's calling was a secular one."[84] By choosing medicine instead of ministry, the article suggests, Redman dissociated himself from a religious calling and from the religious world of his peers. Perhaps it is time to reconsider this assumed separation.

Redman did not perceive his care for the sick and response to yellow fever as separate from his sense of Christian calling and God's providential direction. Neither did Helmuth, the Committee, or Jones and Allen. Although they understood and represented their actions and motivations in different ways, depending on their individual work and religious beliefs, they all saw in the epidemic a call to human action and a need to reflect on God's providence. They described their actions with language from the Enlightenment, they reflected on an innate human sympathy, they grew troubled over the persistent failures of humanity, and they turned to God for direction, for models of service and sacrifice, and for narrative forms.

Although scholars have separated the religious and secular "genealogies" of nineteenth-century benevolence, these genealogies converge in the oft-cited shared sense of duty and conception of providence.[85] Recognizing this does not require an uncritical stance to the problems, prejudices, and blind spots of benevolence in the eighteenth century or as it developed in the so-called "benevolent empire" of the nineteenth century. Rather, understanding the ways in which benevolence developed from a commitment to providence can highlight both its motivating potential for good and its inherent dangers. Helmuth's zeal and determination, which were continuously reinvigorated by his providential faith, benefited his community and patients and his own spiritual journey and professional reputation. Carey's zeal and spin on the yellow fever, however, highlighted the salvific nature of the Committee's response and their innate compassion, while belittling the contributions of free blacks and suggesting a racialized, innate sinfulness and avarice in their work.

In claiming the greater benevolence for the white Committeemen, Carey relied on a powerful and appealing providential narrative.

Understanding how these religious and secular genealogies are, in fact, joined by providential thought also clarifies a common conundrum of scholarship on benevolence, which is the question, how could Christians expect or accept an earthly reward or benefit for doing good? Some scholars have suggested that such benefits—be they an enhanced reputation, the money earned from service, or the survival of a loved one—reveal a deep-seated and hypocritical self-interest and undermine claims to be motivated by God's providence.[86] At the same time, for scholars of secularization, such as philosopher Charles Taylor, the correspondence with self-interest was a critical turning point for the movement into a secular age, when the motivation for human actions began to come from the "human realm" and not God.[87]

As Helmuth, the Committee, Jones and Allen, and Redman all realized, doing good could be of "personal advantage." Their work certainly affected their reputations, careers, and income, and they were all aware enough of these benefits to record their actions in both private and public writings. But they also interpreted the advantages of their work in a way consistent with Protestant tradition: in terms of the spiritual fruits it wrought in their own lives and the lives of others.

In Christian tradition, doing good in the world is a part of the covenant with God. Such care was an obligation of the believing Christian with salvific significance. Although Reformation traditions transformed aspects of charity, in particular by insisting that good works are not in themselves salvific, Protestants nonetheless continued to understand charity as a central part of their Christian lives. For the Lutheran Helmuth, doing good was a reflection—or outpouring—of a Christian's faith in God and hope in salvation. Jones and Allen, as Methodists, understood that the good works they did of their own free will as faithful Christians contributed to their sanctification. For the Committee and Carey, their good works were motivated not only by sympathy but also by a sense that divine providence intended for them to benefit from the experience and the service. Redman, a Presbyterian, perceived God's direction of human service for others, including in medical and spiritual care.

Providence remained a powerful component in all of these accounts. It had not shape-shifted into a vague Enlightenment ruler or creator that implanted an innate sense of compassion in humans. Nor did it limit the authors to passive contemplation of God's judgment. Providence was, rather, the force that provided them with the meaning and motivation for activity in the midst of intense misery. In their service and writings, Philadelphians turned to providence with hope and happiness that their actions would not be lost to the moment of crisis or the passage of time. The epidemic reminded them of the limits of sympathy; yellow fever exposed human fear and the failings of human compassion. Yet these limitations and failures also opened an opportunity to tell of the possibilities of human struggle to overcome these obstacles with God's grace, to transcend the chaos through human action and faith.

5

Medicine, Providence, and Nature in Eighteenth-Century Maternity

When Elizabeth Fisher, a Philadelphia Quaker, died at age twenty-six on February 22, 1796, her husband Samuel Fisher wrote a brief account of her life. He described her conversion, her temperament, her commitment to her religious community, her struggles with illness, and her final words— all typical components of sickness narratives from this era. Within the account, however, Samuel also provided details about her maternity: in particular, Elizabeth's inability to nurse her four children and her corresponding grief. He wrote of her first childbirth, "During her Confinement a suppuration took place on her Breast, which occasioned it to be long & painful & prevented her giving Nutriment to her Infant. This latter Circumstance was a source of trouble to her delicate Mind, & seemed a greater trial of her fortitude than her own bodily pains." The account goes on to describe her continued disappointment at her "inability" and "incapacity" to breastfeed her subsequent children and her continued "grief."[1]

Elizabeth Fisher's struggles to breastfeed were part of her lifelong struggles with sickness, but her grief stands out. Her husband's use of terms like "ability" and "capacity" highlight his—and, likely, her own— view of breastfeeding as a physical act, a matter of mechanics, which was in line with contemporary medical writings on the human body and on how women should act in accordance with nature or design. Yet her grief over her inability, her sense that it was a trial, also points to the religious significance of both the experience of maternity and the capacity to fulfill a matter of human design and nature. From her experience of maternal and human limitation, Fisher could learn resignation and strength; she could repent and be redeemed.

We have seen how providential thought affected eighteenth-century Protestants' narratives of sickness, their views of the human body and soul, and their understandings of medicine and mission. The Philadelphia yellow fever epidemic was an episode that illuminates how providential ideas shaped accounts of extreme and widespread illness, of medical work, and of emerging ideas about benevolence in the Enlightenment era. Writings on eighteenth-century maternity—from theological to medical, from personal to political—further bring our themes together, highlighting the critical ways in which providential thought both persisted and was transformed in the eighteenth century.

Throughout the eighteenth century, providential thought remained an important way to figure the divine relationship to the human as well as the meaning of both spiritual and embodied suffering. This continuity is evidenced in writings on maternity; providence had long been imagined through maternal relationship. On the one hand, through biblical women like the Virgin Mary, maternity was a sign of human faithfulness and obedience, and, on the other hand, maternal love and sacrifice offered a glimpse—albeit imperfect—of divine love and selflessness. At the same time, maternity was a profound reminder of human limitation and dependence on God; no matter how great a mother's love and sacrifice, human relationships and love would always be characterized by mortality, suffering, and loss.

For Protestant theology, motherhood threw into relief the concerns of both the beginning and the end, corruption and renewal, dependence and strength. And it affected both women and men, as it provided concrete examples and metaphors for central religious ideas. The particularly fraught moments of pregnancy and childbirth made strikingly clear the narrow boundary between mortality and new life: as Puritan minister Cotton Mather once wrote to pregnant women, "your death has entered into you." Like many ministers, Mather deeply understood the medical realities of maternity; widowed three times, Mather had fifteen children, only two of whom survived him. Such lived experience provided vivid bodily language—from "miscarriage" to "travail"—for theological writings.[2] Maternity also, importantly, expanded beyond the immediate experiences of pregnancy and birth; it spanned the life course in a revered and idealized relationship of care for children as well as for extended family and community. In its intensity, intimacy, and physical embrace, maternal love represented both the full potential of human love and its ultimate limitation in comparison to the eternal, encompassing love of the divine.

Beyond the realm of theological reflection and metaphor—in lived experience—sources on eighteenth-century maternity highlight how providential ideas were adapted, transformed, and maintained in the medical and political developments of the era. As male professionals began to engage and, eventually, dominate midwifery practice, they brought mechanistic notions of the human body to their study and writings, and pregnancy, childbirth, and infant care developed into a science demanding specialized training, manuals, case studies, and anatomies. Yet these men grounded their observation and claims in an understanding of "nature" and the created world that was imbued with providential meaning; they adapted Protestant understandings of maternal humility and sacrifice into their scientific vision of correct motherhood.[3] These new scientific approaches to the maternal body and behavior—to nature and nurture—were, likewise, shaped by observations of motherhood in missionary, reform, and colonial settings. As providential thought infused the maternal body and activity with meaning in the medical realm, it contributed to emerging political ideals of womanhood and domesticity and, correspondingly, colonial and racialized ideologies of civilization. In their proper fulfillment of their design and caretaking responsibilities, inscribed by providence and medicine, women were critical to the success of the nation.[4]

Motherhood in Christian Thought and Society

Maternity is not a typical focus of intellectual inquiry into topics like providence, the enlightenment, and secularization; yet maternity is a widespread and significant human phenomenon, deeply considered in Christian thought and lived experience. Through biblical exemplars like Sarah, Hannah, and Mary, the mother of Jesus, Christian communities have both perceived and used maternity as an opportunity to teach about the relationship of God to humanity and the nature of human faith and relationship. While the Virgin Mary is often associated with Roman Catholic thought and popular Catholic piety, Protestants maintained aspects of Catholic tradition that saw Mary as the exemplar of motherhood oriented toward faith in God and God's will. Protestants recognized the importance of Mary's role in giving birth to, nursing, and caring for the redeemer, and they also saw in the humble and sacrificial nature of Mary's maternity—and of motherhood, more generally—a metaphor for the redemption made possible through Christ's sacrifice for humanity.[5]

With their relatable and evocative imagery and symbolism, it is no surprise that stories of the pregnancy and childbirth of Mary and other scriptural women continued to resonate in the writings of seventeenth- and eighteenth-century British, German, and (eventually) American Protestants. The Puritan Cotton Mather, for example, turned to Mary to describe the "dignity" God offered women through childbirth. The pains of childbirth were attributed to women's inheritance of Eve's original sin; Mary, however, gave birth to the savior of humankind, an act that—according to Mather—endowed childbirth and its suffering with sacred and redemptive significance for all believing women. The German Pietist Johann Arndt likewise highlighted Mary along with Hannah as role models of a joyful faith formed through complete dependence on God; their faith and dependence were rewarded in their experiences of motherhood.[6]

Mary's early care and nursing of the infant Jesus were, in particular, the subject of much artwork and theological commentary. Through her breastmilk, Mary's maternal love and sacrifice represented and prefigured Jesus's love of humankind. For centuries, breastmilk had been understood to be redirected blood; thus, through nursing, a mother in effect gave her infant her blood. It was a human experience that paralleled, however humbly, Jesus's lifegiving blood on the cross: through his death, sacrifice, and blood, Jesus fed and redeemed humanity. As Caroline Walker Bynum has shown, late medieval artwork of Mary breastfeeding the infant Jesus not only highlighted these spiritual themes of Christ's sacrifice but also shaped views of maternal love and sacrifice more broadly in late medieval society.[7]

Mary and the image of nativity remained important in Protestant art after the Reformation, including in England and North America, and even in non–explicitly religious contexts as it shaped views of domesticity and civilization. In British and American art, the nativity scene was often transformed to represent individual family members, reunion, and tranquility, rather than the exemplary relationship of the future redeemer of humankind and his mother, chosen by God. The Protestant John Singleton Copley, a well-known American artist, depicted Mary and Jesus in *The Nativity*, painted around 1776. Copley used his own

Figure 5.1. Hans Memling's *Virgin and Child*, ca. 1475–1480. Metropolitan Museum of Art, New York.

wife and child as the models for Mary and Jesus. This painting may have been influenced by the American Quaker Benjamin West's family portrait, which has been described as a kind of "secular" nativity. It depicts West's family reunited in London before the American Revolution. His wife and new baby represent the Madonna and child, his father and brother are filling the spot of the shepherds or magi, and the artist himself is painted into the background, as a sort of Joseph.[8] While Mary lost her place as an intercessor in Protestant thought, Protestants remained willing to imagine maternal experiences through her and the themes of faith, selflessness, and family evoked by her story.

Figure 5.2. John Singleton Copley's *The Nativity*, ca. 1776. Museum of Fine Arts, Boston.

Figure 5.3. Benjamin West's *The Artist and His Family*, ca. 1772. Yale Center for British Art, New Haven, CT.

As it was for Catholics, Mary's role as the mother of Jesus was important for Protestants, their theology, and their views of women, and they turned to the New Testament narrative to interpret and apply the significance of Mary's experience. Mary was a central early figure, for example, in the popular theological and devotional treatise *The Great Exemplar of Sanctity and Holy Life according to the Christian Institution*, first published in 1649 by Anglican Jeremy Taylor. Taylor was supported by William Laud, Archbishop of Canterbury, and began his career under King Charles I. While viewed with suspicion by Puritans and other dissenters, Taylor's writings on the life of Christ had lasting popularity. They were published in multiple editions and formats into the nineteenth century, including in North America. In 1829, Charles Francis Adams, the son of John Quincy Adams, recorded reading Taylor's discourse on Mary and nursing—albeit with some displeasure regarding the "sensual" nature of Taylor's imagination. Writing almost two hundred years earlier, however, Taylor found Mary's experience as a mother a helpful model of the "wholly practical" theology he sought to offer, perhaps particularly for the many laypeople in England still shaped by Catholic thought and practice.[9]

Writing in the midst of the English Civil War and an era of profound Christian fracture and disagreement, Taylor is an early example of a Protestant author seeking to uphold and maintain aspects of Marian piety as he advised Christians in their "daily office" and devotions. The book was meant to be a Protestant version of the *Imitation of Christ*, a devotional to which readers could turn as they attempted to imbue their day-to-day practices with Christian piety. In each section of his history of the life of Jesus, Taylor offered not only narrative but also short reflections, a prayer, and, finally, a discourse, in which he explained the practical lessons to be gained for the everyday life of believers. In his telling of the nativity, for example, Taylor explained Mary's saintly and exceptional status. He described how Mary's childbirth was atypical because she—alone among all women—avoided the pain that had accompanied birth since the punishment of Eve. As a sign of the painlessness of her birth and of her humble chosenness, Mary's only attendants in birth were angels. Following prophecy, further, Mary's body remained pure in both conception and parturition. Although Mary was unique among women, however, Taylor nonetheless drew useful "considerations" from the story of the nativity as he reflected particularly on her care for her newborn. He described how she swaddled her baby, rocked him, and "from this deportment she read a lecture of Piety and maternal care, which Mothers should perform toward their children when they are born, not to neglect any of that duty which nature and maternal piety requires."[10]

For Taylor, Mary was critical to understanding the nativity as a story of patience and humanity—and a story of God's plan and direction. Jesus was not "hasty" in his arrival; he did not try to "prevent the period of Nature" or to "break the laws of the Womb," established by "his own sanctions." His birth story was one of humility. He was surrounded by beasts and provided with the bare "necessities" of the human body: a "course Robe" and "a little breast-milk." Jesus's birth was a reminder to put off worldly pleasures and affluence and to consider that the savior "suck'd the paps of a Woman."[11] Mary's role in Taylor's recounting was carefully balanced. She was a paramount example, she was chosen; but she was also a sign—in her "paps" and alongside the beasts—of the material and earthy start of the incarnation story and a model of humble maternal care.

Mary figured as a significant model for Protestants beyond the English-speaking world as well, including in the German Pietist Johann Arndt's early seventeenth-century prayer book *Paradisgärtlein* (*Little Garden of Paradise*). This prayer book was widely distributed; it was frequently published with Arndt's popular *Wahres Christentum* (*True Christianity*) as well as translated, excerpted, and copied in subsequent pastoral writings and sent to missionary communities around the globe. Like many prayer books of this time, *Little Garden of Paradise* offered prayers to guide readers in specific circumstances of suffering and thanksgiving. In the prayers suggested for pregnant and childbearing women, Arndt pointed to scriptural women like Mary and Hannah; in their conceiving, childbirth, and infant care, they exemplified the highest levels of Christian faith and prayer. Mary, in her Magnificat, "prayed with the great joy and happiness of the heart," while Hannah's prayers were characterized by "loud, powerful sighs." Although one step below the highest form of prayer—union with God—Mary's and Hannah's maternal prayers nonetheless exemplified human faith through their acknowledgment of dependence on God as well as in the joy that accompanied such trust.[12]

Into the eighteenth century, Protestant pastoral writings emphasized Mary's role as the human mother of Christ and an example of God's grace and human faith. In a pastoral tract written for women nearing childbirth, for example, the Puritan Cotton Mather offered the figure of Mary as reassurance to anxious, laboring women. Referring to an oft-cited passage from 1 Timothy 2:14–15, he urged women to proclaim, "We are Sav'd thro' that Illustrious Child-bearing! O the Dignity put upon our poor Sex, in the Birth of such a Redeemer! O the Assurance which the Distressed Handmaids of the Lord have to find Help with such a Redeemer in their Time of Need!" For Mather, God offered women "dignity" through Mary's experience of childbearing and infant care: Jesus was "born of a Woman . . . and nursed by a Woman."[13] The role of a woman in the early life of the Christian redeemer offered all women security in future childbirth.

Because Protestant ministers found motherhood so evocative of redemptive trust and faith, they sometimes used maternal metaphors in catechism titles and other theological writings. One example is the Puritan John Cotton's popular 1640 catechism *Spiritual Milk for Babes*, which was available in both England and America. The use of "milk" in catechism titles is a clear reference to 1 Corinthians 3:2: "I have fed you with milk, and not with meat: for hitherto ye were not able to bear it, neither yet now are ye able" (cf. 1 Peter 2:2). Many English catechisms used "milk" in their titles, and it has been suggested that "milk" (as opposed to "meat") signaled that these were beginning catechisms, which even the youngest reader could draw on.[14] Yet these catechisms' audiences were not limited to children, a fact made clear by a significant German text, also titled after this tradition: *Geistliche Kinder-Milch* (*Spiritual Children's Milk*), by Philipp Adolph von Münchhausen. Münchhausen's subtitle describes his text as a "Christian house-pharmacy" with "wholesome medication for the soul," which Jesus, "the worthiest physician of the soul," loves. Münchhausen's text was reprinted several times, including in a popular evangelical magazine, and contained sermons, catechisms, and prayers for both children and adults.[15]

Both Cotton's and Münchhausen's texts suggest that their titles were not mere references to scripture, but rather that the language of maternity continued to have metaphorical power for key seventeenth- and eighteenth-century Protestant theological principles. The subtitle of

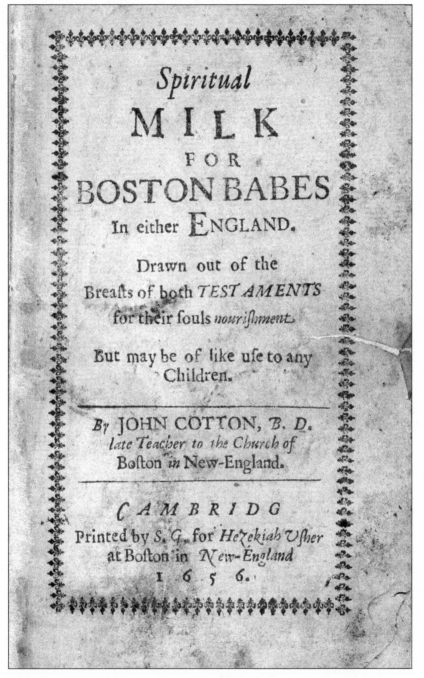

Figure 5.4. Title page of John Cotton's *Spiritual Milk for Boston Babes in Either England. Drawn Out of the Breasts of Both Testaments for Their Souls Nourishment* (Cambridge, MA, 1656). New York Public Library, Rare Book Division, http://digitalcollections.nypl.org/

Cotton's catechism points not only to simplicity but also to the Protestant emphasis on *sola scriptura*—the importance of unmediated, direct access to the Bible. The full title reads, "Milk for Babes: Drawn Out of the Breasts of Both Testaments."[16] Catechisms contain the main teachings of the church, often in question-and-answer format. Cotton's catechism also contained biblical references in the margins, next to each answer. With these references, readers could look up directly for themselves the roots of each teaching. These citations confirmed that the catechism sprung directly from God's word, as milk from a mother's breast to a suckling babe. Münchhausen's text likewise used the maternal metaphor to emphasize the immediacy and efficacy of Christian teachings. By comparing Christian teachings to not only milk but also medicine, Münchhausen explained the salutary effects of Christian learning and redemption in comprehensible, physical ways that could offer readers significant assurance.[17]

While maternal metaphors could point with hope to religious assurance, they were also utilized to stress timeliness and fearful consequences. Pregnancy provided a clear time frame for women who wished to participate in God's work of redemption through their own repentance and through the preparation of their future child. Mather stressed this by describing the quickly growing fetus: "It is a Child of God, that you have now within you . . . whose Bones are now Growing in the Womb. . . . It is, indeed a Member of [God's] Mystical Body, which is now Shaping in Secret, and Curiously to be wrought."[18] In his prayer for expectant mothers, the Pietist Arndt also used maternal language— taken from scripture—to describe the early stages of the Christian's journey from pregnancy through early infancy: "*Thou has taken me out of the Womb; thou didst make me hope, when I was upon my Mother's Breasts. I was cast upon thee from the Womb: Thou art my God from my Mother's Belly*" (cf. Psalm 22:9–10).[19]

Ministers used maternal metaphors of growth, parturition, and misconceptions to emphasize the need for timely repentance. Mather urged pregnant women to ask God to "wean" them from the world. They should reflect on every sin or "miscarriage." They should "be as much afraid of Leaving any Sin unconfessed, as you would be of having the *After-birth left in you*, after your travail." Should they succeed in repentance, however, they would be granted a *"New birth."*[20] The joint terror and hope of maternal metaphors was not new; they had been used to convey Christian suffering, urgency, and patient faithfulness since the writing of the Gospels. At the last supper, Jesus described his followers' sorrow over his departure in terms of a mother's travail—it would soon be forgotten in the great joy that follows birth (John 16:21)—a reference repeated by Arndt in his prayers for pregnant mothers.[21]

Experiences of pregnancy and childbirth offered women the opportunity to encounter and live the central Gospel teachings of sin and new life; as for the disciples, these teachings demanded great sacrifice and careful discipline. Women were not, after all, actually Mary; they still suffered from the original sin of Eve in their labor pains, and this sin shaped their future children as well. "I and the Fruit of my Womb are both by Nature Children of *Wrath,*" Arndt's pregnant woman was to pray, "but thou, O gracious Father, have Mercy upon us!" The pregnant woman should plead with God to cleanse her unborn child: to "purge" it "with Hyssop" and cleanse it such that "it shall be whiter than Snow." All children were "conceived in Original Sin" and faced humanity's shared corruption, but mothers—with their unmediated contact with the unborn—were especially dangerous. They should pray, "Keep me from Fear and Terror, and from the evil Spirits, whose Pleasure it is to destroy and ruin the Works of thy Hand." Pregnant women and mothers must be sober, be temperate, and avoid lust, which could "make a strange Impression on the Infant." A mother's fears, sins, and other experiences could harm an infant and cause it to be malformed, a common view of the early modern world.[22]

The maternal experience invited eighteenth-century Christian women to remember the story of Jesus's birth and its promise, but it was an experience that nonetheless remained overshadowed by human sinfulness. Maternity highlighted human weakness, the need to repent, and the goal of salvation. It served as a reminder of Mary's maternity and God's providence, as evidenced in her chosenness, faithful dependence, and obedience. It suggested that human love reflected divine love, but that reflection was always imperfect. Mary's maternity was relatable, but it also exemplified a more sacred and pure conception—that of Jesus— and, ultimately, the limits of human relationship.[23]

The Promises and Dangers of Maternal Love

Human relationships were the closest a living Christian could come to the experience of divine love, sacrifice, and redemption. They were also always needfully limited by the bounds of time and mortality, the constant reminders of God's providence and human dependence. Too much worldly love could be dangerous, but motherly love, when kept in proper perspective, could be a reminder of Christ's love. A mother, following Mary, should perform her appointed functions, including the mundane work of birth, care, and attendance at death. This work ensured the loyalty and commitment of her children—not, ultimately, to the mother herself, but rather to God and the Christian community. In cases of sickness and loss, a mother's dedication and love should be a humble human sign of a transcendent, sacrificing, and eternal love. It should invite all witnesses to focus on redemption.

Sarah and Mary Rhoads, a Quaker mother and daughter living in Philadelphia in the 1780s, highlight the challenges of balancing motherhood and human love, on the one hand, with the greater redemptive possibilities they were to represent and encourage. Sarah Rhoads wrote an account of her daughter Mary in a series of commonplace books she compiled for her granddaughter (Mary's niece). Commonplace books were manuscript copies of poetry, prose, memoirs, and other notes that were maintained and often circulated among families and wider communities. Sarah Rhoads's books were filled with excerpts from verse, theological treatises, letters, moral teachings, historical anecdotes, and reminiscences and condolences marking the deaths of her daughters and a grandchild. These manuscript books likely would have been shared with her community but were, in any case, intended as a record for her granddaughter. The included memoirs were a testament to a lost generation of women in the family.[24]

In her description of her daughter Mary's death, Sarah detailed the last months of Mary's life, including her sudden illness and decline. Mary was an adult in 1788, when the events described in the account occurred, yet as Mary neared death, she interacted with her mother in a way that emphasized—in physical terms—their mother-child relationship. The night before Mary died, she asked her mother to undress, climb into bed with her, and put her arm around her waist. Mary, in turn, wrapped her arms around her mother's neck. Mary knew she was dying and wanted to sleep her last night in her mother's embrace. She woke up periodically and spoke encouraging words to her mother and her aunt, who also served as a caretaker. At one point, she told them of a vision she had of herself "ascended as into the clouds," looking "down on the Earth" at her body, watching her aunt prepare it for burial.[25]

This is a scene of remarkable maternal intimacy, of an embrace between a mother and adult daughter, nearing death. But it is also a scene in which the daughter relates a vision of physical separation from her mother and aunt, as if to prepare them for a fundamental shift in their relationship. Of course, this is all from the perspective of Sarah—the mother. Her account of these last moments with her daughter pivots between, on the one hand, her bond with her child and the joy and love she found in this maternal intimacy, and, correspondingly, the agony—and necessity—of preparing for her expected loss.

Sarah portrays Mary, the daughter, as anticipating her death by some months and as seeking constantly throughout that time to help her mother to prepare, in part, by focusing on this physical maternal bond. Sarah recorded one of Mary's dreams, in which Mary stood at a broad river, trying to reunite with her deceased father. She was prevented from crossing the river, however, because her mother "held her fast." As Sarah retold Mary's dream, she emphasized its application in her own life: she knew she needed to release her daughter from this maternal grasp, to resign herself to God's will, and to set about continuing her earthly life and duties with cheerfulness.

In the end, Sarah wrote that she met her daughter's end with prayers and hope for her salvation and strength. Moreover, Sarah described her experience of loss in terms of her own personal redemption. She wrote that her "very soul seemed to ascend with [Mary's]." Through her experience of maternity, including, ultimately, her physical loss and sacrifice, Sarah felt that God had redeemed her.[26]

The loss of a child was difficult for early American women, and it could be challenging to understand it in terms of God's providence and hope in redemption. Yet many exerted great effort to do so. The Philadelphia Quaker Sally Logan Fisher was devastated by the loss of her eleven-month-old son in September 1780; she had also previously suffered a miscarriage. She was "greatly supported, thro' this severe trial," but found her "endeavor to keep my mind quiet . . . almost in vain." She spent time "alone, thinking of my dear Baby, who is gone to a Happier world, how can I be so selfish as to wish him back, in this scene of trouble." Fisher believed her son was redeemed and sought to overcome her grief by emphasizing this and, in turn, recognizing her selfishness. Later, in both November and December, she believed she was pregnant again, only to be disappointed. With the new year, she redoubled her effort to come to a new outlook on her experiences: "Oh how thankfull I shall be to be resigned, & to esteem my domestic Blessings as they really are precious Gifts of Providence." Fisher's resignation did not imply any passivity. She worked constantly to interpret her experiences. She wrote that she could not "help sometimes regretting my precious little Lambs," though she knew it was wrong, "for they are happy, safely landed from all storms." Her maternal losses made her cognizant of God's grace as well as the difficulty of overcoming the maternal bond: "the strong ties of Nature how hard they are to break." She had another baby within the year.[27]

In 1777 Abigail Adams, who was married to John Adams, delivered a stillborn daughter. Stillbirths and pregnancy losses affected women of all classes in colonial America; Adams, like Fisher, had the means and the ability to record her loss. Her letters to her husband conveyed that she was at once prepared for the death and terribly shaken by her fears surrounding the birth. She had been sick a few days before and "very apprehensive that a life was lost." The next evening, she wrote John that she was not at ease, but also not "ill enough to summons any attendance." Her anxiety by that point was heightened by concerns over her own health. She wrote, "I pray Heaven that it may be soon or it seems to me I shall be worn out." She knew how dangerous her condition was—so much so that she had to pause from writing: "I must lay my pen down this moment, to bear what I cannot fly from—and now I have endured it I reassume my pen and will lay by all my feelings and thank you for your obligeing Letters." Later the next day she would deliver. When she wrote her husband again, five days later, she began with her own survival— "spaired and carried thro Distress and danger although the dear Infant is numberd with its ancestors." Her life—as a wife and a mother to four living children—continued. Though her "Heart was much set upon a Daughter," she was reminded of "the uncertainty of all sublinary enjoyments." A Unitarian of Congregationalist upbringing, Adams reflected on the religious significance of her experience. She sought to be thankful "amidst my sorrow" and reflected on her maternal limitation—"so short sighted and so little a way can we look into futurity"—in light of "the dispensation of Heaven," to which "we ought patiently to submit." Her maternal attentions focused anew on God's grace and her older children, praying that "Heaven continue to us those we already have and make them blessings."[28]

The death of a child or mother and the profound fears surrounding childbirth itself were difficult to overcome. The challenge created by maternal intimacy and loss, however, was used to highlight God's greater love and providence, as seen in the accounts by both Sarah Rhoads and Abigail Adams. This perspective could also be found in the loss of a mother or grandmother. In the mid-eighteenth century the New England Congregationalist Sarah Pierpont described her grandmother's death in such terms. She imagined, first, the reunion between her grandmother and her mother and, second, her grandmother's meeting with Jesus. In her journal, Pierpont recorded, "What a joyful meeting she would have with her Child (my Mother) as also with Her Friends & Acquaintances, But above all with Her Jesus." When Abigail Adams lost her mother in 1775, she also mourned the loss of "earthly comforts," but found hope in "a more permanent consolator who has bid us all call upon Him in the day of trouble." The joy of the mother-child relationship was great, but not as great as the love of the redeemer.[29]

Maternity offered believing Christians a human glimpse of the love, dependence, and sacrifice that, on a greater scale, were to typify their commitment to their community and, ultimately, their trust in God's providential consolation. The vagaries of human loss and grief were important reminders that this human relationship and understanding were always limited and could even be dangerous, as when they prevented humans from resigning an earthly love and fully trusting in God's providence.

As historian Phyllis Mack has shown, the theological emphasis on assurance, self-denial, and discipline within the Methodist movement of Protestantism could be especially challenging for women approaching childbirth. Women who feared birth could be crippled by the added anxiety "that they would be damned if they died in a sinful state of doubt or despair." The potential death of a child or separation from children could also create conditions ripe for "religious crisis." The Methodist leader John Wesley himself offered "little spiritual assistance" to those who grieved children; in 1791, he chided Adam Clarke, a minister, for his expressed sadness over the loss of an infant: "But you startle me when you talk of grieving so much for the death of an infant. This was certainly a proof of inordinate affection; and if you love them thus all your children will die." Yet others in the movement, including John's brother Charles Wesley, displayed intimate concern with children and family, and Methodist hymns often described, on the one hand, a maternal Christ whose side wound nourished followers, and, on the other hand, an infant or suffering Christ in need of motherly care.[30]

Methodist women lay leaders and preachers often embraced maternal experiences alongside a visionary piety. In 1811, the lay preacher Mary Taft wrote of undergoing labor while her eight-year-old daughter, Mary Ann, seemed to be on her death bed. Taft waited beside her sick daughter and hoped for a vision of her own mother, who had recently died. Eventually, Taft had to leave her daughter Mary Ann's side in order to give birth. Later, however, Mary Ann, who had survived her illness, reported receiving the vision her mother had longed for. Mary Ann had seen her recently deceased grandmother—who had also been a Methodist leader—accompanied by two women friends, "all with crowns on their heads." Mack argues that the embodied experience of childbirth was not, in fact, central to Taft's account; rather Taft's narrative focused on the "supernatural experience" of her sick daughter, who "validated the women's spiritual authority."[31] Nonetheless, childbirth and maternity set the stage for an intense story of women's visions, prophesies, and authority, a story grounded in generations of maternal relations, life, death, and hope.

Eighteenth-century women who lost children and family may have been comforted by these visions of reunion, of God's greater love and plan, and of a sense of their purpose fulfilled. And yet the theological pressures surrounding death could also raise fearful specters of damnation and separation. When the New England Congregationalist Sarah Osborn lost her son Samuel, for example, she was filled with anxiety over her too-intense love for her child as well as concern over his conversion and state of grace at death, as historian Catherine Brekus has shown. Osborn had long identified with the Sarah of scripture, referring to Samuel as her "only Son," but at his death this reference contained a new significance in its echoing of the mourning calls of Jeremiah and Amos or perhaps of the "many 'only sons' whom God had chosen to rescue from death, including his 'only begotten son,' Jesus Christ, who had been resurrected." Osborn's vision of her son's election was never certain, but she did emerge from the experience of his death and her grief with an insistence on her own relationship with God, her "Father."[32]

In their experiences of maternity, eighteenth-century Protestant women identified with the stories of scriptural women and with Christ. They experienced love and loss in their human relationships that allowed them to imagine the love and sacrifice of God. They were also continually reminded of their mortality, inadequate perspective, and deep-rooted temporal and physical affection. Theological visions of God's providence and future reunion could be comforting, but they could also cause intense anxiety over the sinfulness of inordinate human love, as well as the danger of despair, grief, and doubts about election or salvation. Maternal love and relationship were reminders of both divine grace and human limitation, and of the providential hope to be found in sacrifice, faith, and redemption.

Maternal Bodies: Nature, Duty, and Knowledge

In Protestant theology and lived experience, maternity served as a key metaphor and symbol for repentance and salvation, and this spiritual significance remained crucial even as maternity came to be investigated as a natural, medical, and scientific phenomenon. By the eighteenth century, medical tracts depicted the maternal body as a machine, one that could be touched, maneuvered, and dissected by practitioners who were increasingly male. Lactation and early infant care were, likewise, beginning to be treated as matters of science and mechanical skill. And yet male midwives and early obstetrical practitioners built from a language of "nature" that in the seventeenth century was grounded in a joint enterprise of science and theology. The scientific and medical communities of this era developed from a reconciliation of mechanism with a providential worldview—as evidenced in the originating work of the Royal Society of London for Improving Natural Knowledge, founded in 1660.[33]

The earlier redemptive discourse of motherhood reverberated in the emerging scientific and medical discussions of maternity, lending a providential valence to debates over instinct, duty, and design. Practitioners claimed their scientific knowledge was a natural stepping stone in human progress, as they wrested maternal care from women's supposed superstition and weakness in the face of the luxury and corruptions of modernity. At the same time, the "naturalness" of women as mothers and caregivers as developed in the Christian tradition provided fuel to the other side. Critics of male midwives charged them with both seduction and effeminacy as they pursued a practice long dominated by women. What was "God's design" or "natural" for human knowledge and practice in maternity was up for debate, but all agreed on the need to protect women—and Christian civilization itself—through the providential ideal of humble, virtuous, and self-sacrificing motherhood.

Writings on lactation and wet nursing reveal an early and easy merging of religious understandings of God's design, on the one hand, with the mechanical language of instinct and women's "natural" role as caregivers, on the other. Jeremy Taylor's discussion of nursing in his treatise on the life of Christ offers one seventeenth-century example. Taylor dedicated his practical "discourse" on Christ's nativity to a lengthy treatise on lactation, titled, "Of Nursing Children in Imitation of the Blessed Virgin Mother." In promoting maternal nursing over wet nursing, Taylor relied on Christian understandings of duty, reason, and law, studies of the natural world, and medical ideas of the relationship between body and soul. Starting with Mary's maternal care for Jesus, Taylor expanded to discuss nursing, more generally, as a basic human action, albeit with moral significance. He argued that nursing was both a natural instinct and a higher obligation or law, "exalted by grace." Humans, like all beasts, were designed by God to nurse their offspring through instinct, yet human inclination raised above mere "nature" and this "impulsive force." While all animals nursed by instinct, humans had reason and knowledge concerning the act of breastfeeding, making it a duty as well. With reason, humans could see that women were gifted by nature with "two exuberant Fontinels." According to Taylor, a mother's breasts served both for nursing and for "cradl[ing] in the entertainments of love and maternal embraces." History had shown that wet nurses could not love a child as a mother did, nor could they "endure the inconveniences, the tediousnesses and unhandsomnesses of a nursery" like a birth mother, endowed with "natural affection."[34]

In his devotional text, Taylor linked maternal nursing to the dutiful pursuit of human reason, which recognized not only the instincts but also the natural gifts and affections of the human body. Nursing was further a matter of law because, according to Taylor, it was a matter of justice and charity. "With all their powers which God to that purpose gave them," mothers owed it to their children to "promote their capacities and improve their faculties." Offspring could not thrive with the nourishment of another mother. Taylor turned to "naturalists," to remind the reader that animals that nursed from other animals changed in their physical properties, as fleece became hair when a lamb nursed from a goat. Through such observation, humans could plainly see how the "Instrument"—the body—was liable to change depending on nutrition and care. Such transformation posed a major problem, further, for the soul, which suffered without "its proper Instruments"—that is, when its body was altered by foreign, external factors. In order to promote a child's virtue, Taylor argued, mothers must therefore "secure [the child's] first seasonings; because, whatever it sucks in first, it swallows and believes infinitely, and practices easily, and continues longest." While hired wet nurses might be able—at the most mechanical level—to deliver milk, they tended to limit their sense of duty to basic nourishment and cleanliness. A mother, however, "cannot think herself so easily discharged." She must provide the "spiritual milk" necessary for her child's development in piety and virtue.[35]

Taylor's notion of nature's role in the design and function of maternal bodies reflected both an ancient Galenic idea of "a provident nature" as well as the general approach of many in the scientific community of Taylor's own era.[36] The Royal Society of London for Improving Natural Knowledge, writing a decade after Taylor's writings on the nativity first appeared, had as its explicit goal "to illustrate the providential glory of God manifested in the works of His Creation." Many of its early fellows "grappled" with how to relate "the providential deity of Christianity" with a natural world increasingly understood in mechanical ways—including a human body imagined as a predictable and observable "machine."[37]

While Taylor's writings were theological, moving from Christian exegesis to practical piety, they were not far removed from contemporary medical and scientific discussions and debates over women's bodies, childbirth, and lactation. Human actions in body and health had long been viewed as a central part of Christian practice, charity, and mission, and maternity was a key part of this conversation. This "evangelical" trajectory was, as historian Ruth Bloch has argued, one wing of the ideal of "moral motherhood" that developed by the late eighteenth century. The "enlightenment" formed the other trajectory. Taylor's treatise on nursing is an early example of this merging. The long tradition of Christian interest in a humble, natural, and dutiful maternity, here voiced by Taylor, was critical to how seventeenth- and eighteenth-century midwifery manuals imagined women's bodies, childbirth, and lactation and the place for practitioners' roles and interventions. As midwifery manuals were increasingly authored by men and for men—the emerging class of male midwives and early obstetricians—they claimed medical knowledge gained from lectures, autopsies and dissections, medical models and diagrams, and detailed case studies of preternatural births, nutrition, and infant care. They argued that such knowledge was based in nature and trumped the humble traditional knowledge of women midwives and family members, whose new duty was to follow the advances developed through human reason, endowed by the creator. Despite their dedication to scientific empiricism and improvement, however, this new fleet of male practitioners often couched their medical explanations in terms of "nature," "design," and duty that were in fact deeply rooted in providential and moral views of human knowledge, health, and right motherhood. This providential foundation, combined with Enlightenment reason, had far-reaching implications for notions of civilization—as evidenced in the philosophical writings on nature and childrearing by men like John Locke and, later, Jean-Jacques Rousseau.[38]

Eighteenth-century midwifery manuals reflected an ongoing effort to understand the design of the maternal body—by providence, "Nature," or a "Creator"—and what that meant for human knowledge and intervention in childbirth and infant care. In a preface to Hendrik van Deventer's *Art of Midwifery Improv'd*, published in London in 1728, for example, an "eminent physician" explained that childbirth was a matter of mechanism, designed by providence, and required little intervention. The "great Providence" of the "Creator" had "contrive[d] the most necessary Machines" of the human body to be "least liable to Accidents and Error." Medical practitioners nonetheless still played a critical role; the "various Machines" within the human required constant attention in order to stave off "decay" and mortality. The machines of "Generation," for their part, required the attention of a midwife. Through "her *Knowledge* and *Practice*" a midwife ensured "a Child's Passage into the World." A midwife was not always strictly necessary, because "Almighty God has ordered this Passage the most Safe," such that a mother "or any Woman who had once brought a Child herself" could deliver safely. Yet there were instances when a midwife's knowledge was crucial, due to the "preter-natural *Bulk*, or *Shape* of a *Child*; the wrong *Posture* of the *Womb*, or of the Child in it; and an ill Make of the *Os Sacrum*, or some other of these Bones." Deventer nonetheless questioned the recent rise in male midwifery and the use of "dilating instruments," which he viewed as more likely to harm or kill an infant than to help. He called for "Humanity" and restraint in midwifery and a "Vindication of divine Providence."[39] Deventer emphasized providential design, then, while allowing a limited role for human intervention.

In his popular *Synopsis Medicinæ* of the early eighteenth century, John Allen likewise emphasized the mechanical design of the "Creator" in order to argue against aggressive intervention in childbirth. Allen offered an analysis of the female human skeleton in comparison to the male. He observed that "in a Female . . . the lower Parts of the Sedentary Bones are generally further distant from each other, and don't bend down so much towards the *Os Coccygis* as in a Male one." This basic mechanical difference, Allen wrote, was by design: "The most wise and beneficent Creator thus contrived to obviate the many Difficulties of Childbirth." There were, nonetheless, cases where assistance was necessary, and Allen outlined how a midwife could touch or use a hand—not instruments, which were relatively new and disputed—to assist "humanely" with childbirth.[40]

By the mid-eighteenth century, an aggressive new emphasis on mechanism and human intervention in childbirth emerged with William Smellie, a British male midwife who sought to reform midwifery. Smellie argued that his interventions could save the lives of women and children who, under earlier approaches, would have been lost to the superstitions and "ridiculous prejudices" of the "fair sex." In his provocative work, *A Treatise on the Theory and Practice of Midwifery*, published in three volumes between 1752 and 1764, Smellie was outspoken in his promotion of male knowledge, hands-on investigation, methodological progress, and medical instruments. He based his work on extensive experience in practice, particularly among "poor women," and in teaching. For purposes of instruction, Smellie had even devised and constructed a "machine" to mimic a woman's body, with a doll for a fetus that could be positioned in various ways. For publications, he included detailed anatomical plates, based on pregnant cadavers, whose dissection and artistic presentation he carefully curated. Smellie told a history of midwifery in which women were almost entirely absent because, he argued, "none of their writings are extant." He also, however, had little use for female knowledge. He decried what he described as the secret knowledge that had long defined the work of childbirth, particularly when the practice was limited to women. He wanted, instead, a story of progress and of the expansion of knowledge through experiment and publication.[41]

Midwifery, by Smellie's account, was about the public good and the preservation of life, which required a redeemed human knowledge. It should not be limited to women's superstition but rather expanded through investigation and mechanical intervention. After losing "several children, and sometimes, the mother" in his early practice, Smellie had set off to create a "better method of practice," always with "a view of saving" women and children, "honour[ing] . . . the profession," and promoting "the good of society." His calls for intervention, however, shocked the sensibilities of his contemporaries. An entire section of his treatise is titled "Of Touching." It begins, "Touching is performed by introducing the fore-finger lubricated with pomatum into the *Vagina*." Smellie detailed the use of instruments such as fillets, forceps, and scissors, and offered cases discussing how to intervene in what midwifery manuals labeled "preternatural births." He offered explanations and illustrations of how to cut apart conjoined twins in the womb, how to drain the head of a fetus suffering from dropsy in order to deliver it and save the mother, and how to perform a Caesarian operation after the mother's death (always with a witness who could confirm the death). Smellie's work was not theological but incredibly mechanical in its description of the pregnant and laboring woman and of the midwife's work. Women—like the impoverished Parisian women at the Hotel Dieu—were featured not as fellow practitioners but rather as "opportunities" for surgeons to improve their knowledge.[42]

Smellie's work provoked both extreme criticism and support. On both sides, authors turned to long-standing ideas of providence and nature as they outlined appropriate forms of human intervention. The debates over male midwives and instruments raised questions about practitioners' character, motivations, sexuality, and knowledge, patients' purity, and, at base, morality and civilization. One of Smellie's detractors questioned the naturalness of male midwives, finding them effeminate and foreign in origin. Beginning in France and spreading elsewhere, male midwives stifled the work of "Goody Nature." They sought "haste," celebrity, and money and, more sinisterly, hoped to steal the virtue of unsuspecting wives, whom they unnecessarily touched in examination. They pursued unwarranted procedures with "iron instruments," perhaps leaving "the woman's person less *agreeable*, and often loathsome to her husband," and thus undermining sexual relationships, domestic life, and familial stability. Nature had been sufficient for "many generations" and "scarce ever errs." Providence was careful in the preservation of even "brute creation" in the process of gestation and parturition; how could one doubt the care of providence for "the noblest part of her production?"[43]

Smellie's anonymous critic here blamed not only the male midwives but also the larger community that had been seduced by the "fashion" of male midwifery, blind to its unnaturalness and threat to family and civilization. The fashion of male midwifery gave lie to its honor and revealed its corruptive influence on the natural order. Male midwives were not natural; they were "mongrels" and "amphibious." They were like the male staymakers and hairdressers of Italy, another place of questionable civilization. Mysterious and dangerous, male midwives seduced women, touched women, and destroyed women both in body and in marital fidelity—all with the consent of unsuspecting husbands.[44]

While this anonymous critique was rather hyperbolic, later defenses of Smellie's work suggest there were widespread concerns regarding nature, human knowledge, and the morality of male midwifery. Jean-Louis Baudelocque, a French obstetrician, was influenced by Smellie's work and helped popularize his writings and techniques for both European and American audiences. In an advertisement introducing the English edition of Baudelocque's *A System of Midwifery*, the surgeon John Heath responded to recent publications and criticisms of male midwifery. He critiqued those who emphasized "the powers of Nature" to the point "that a young student might be led to believe the whole art may be reduced to this single precept, *do nothing*: and that in this particular instance man is dispensed from the exercise of that reason with which the Creator has endued him."[45]

At issue here was the meaning of "Nature" and design. Most Christians had long accepted that God's providence—or design—did not limit human intervention in the realm of medicine. Rather, God gave humans reason to explore the natural world, to learn, and to heal. In the debate over obstetrical instruments and male midwives, Heath relied on a similar logic: a commitment to "Nature" and design required a commitment to the workings of the reason bestowed upon humans by "the Creator." A practitioner needs "a real and accurate knowledge of the parts concerned in delivery, and of the mechanism by which it is performed." Such knowledge "enable[s] the operator to assist Nature when [Nature] is at fault."[46] Heath refers to births that were classified as "preternatural" in midwifery manuals, meaning they were "outside the ordinary course of nature."[47] In such instances, male midwives could help through their use of naturally endowed reason and study of nature. Baudelocque, whose work Heath was here promoting, claimed a place for Nature and design in both the maternal body and the male practitioner's knowledge, reason, and intervention.

Endowed with reason, humans were called to improve their knowledge of the natural world, including through formal instruction on the machine and workings of the human body. This learning was—by the late eighteenth century—limited to men. Women midwives were told they had no claim to a natural knowledge of childbirth; their former alleged understanding and practice had advanced merely by "accident" through personal experiences. There were exceptions, however. By 1800, faced with the continuing practice of female midwifery and resistance to male midwives, New York surgeon Valentine Seaman decided to offer a course on midwifery for female practitioners. Seaman, who was physician extraordinary to the Lying-In Ward in the Alms House, nonetheless made clear his low opinion of women's knowledge and skill as midwives. He emphasized midwives' lack of formal medical education and their corresponding ignorance of the inner workings of the human body: "I much doubt whether one out of twenty of them have ever seen the bones that support and pro-

Figure 5.5. Plate highlighting the dimensions of the pelvis, from Jean-Louis Baude-locque's *A System of Midwifery*, trans. John Heath (London: Parkinson, 1790). Library of Congress, Rare Books and Special Collections Division. Photograph by author.

tect the womb: indeed I cannot but suspect whether some even know, that, in being born, a child has to pass through a bony passage." Although he was willing to work with those who availed themselves of his teaching, Seaman consigned the rest "to grope on in their original darkness."[48]

Seaman promoted scientific learning as a Christian response to the corrupting forces of the modern world, made visible in fashion and luxury and their deleterious effects on not only society but also the female anatomy. While he advocated for the scientific practice of midwifery, he also acknowledged that it became necessary only when civilization decayed from an earlier state of humility, nature, and order. "Probably in the early ages," he wrote, "before the pampering stews of luxury had taken the place of the salutary calls of nature in diet, and before the warping trammels of fashion had taken the lead of comfort and convenience in dress, seldom, very seldom, was there any disease in childbearing, or difficulty in travail." Luxury and fashion had distorted society and the female body as designed.[49] Gone was the humble childbirth of Mary; women had been distracted from their ordained maternal roles. Christian charity and scientific progress called for a learned response, based on knowledge carefully gained from observation of the natural world.

Many obstetrical and child care reformers, like Seaman, developed their skills, expertise, and authority from their practice in poor houses, hospitals, and orphanages. They used this experience to claim knowledge of the innate design of a mother's body; impoverished women, unencumbered by contemporary fashions, were imagined closer to "nature." They also pointed to their work among the poor in order to insist that their practice and scientific expertise were based on a firm foundation of Christian benevolence and the social order it promoted. Seaman ended his tract with reference to Proverbs 28:27, "*He that giveth unto the poor shall not lack.*" He urged his readers to pursue the profession of midwifery not from the "sordid motive" of riches but rather from the "desire of doing good": to pursue industry, enlightenment, and order, through "the judicious establishment of regularly instructed midwives." Male or female mattered little in the end; important was education, mechanical practice, and a calling "to relieve the major part of the community."[50]

Eighteenth-century midwifery manuals reveal a world in motion. Mechanical views of the human body and medical intervention permeated depictions of the maternal body as well as debates over male practitioners and the use of instruments. And yet these debates took place within a larger framework of design—be it providential, natural, or both. The resistance to male midwives and instruments could almost be grounded in Jeremy Taylor's idealized depiction of the nativity: Jesus's patient gestation and humble birth were a far cry from the "haste," ego, profit, "fashion," and seduction of male midwifery. On the other hand, those who defended male practitioners emphasized human reason—provided by the Creator—and, like Taylor, suggested a duty for humans to utilize their reason toward the ends of charity. Through knowledge and practice, appropriate intervention in childbirth was an opportunity to "do good" and redeem humankind from the excesses of luxury that had warped maternal bodies and God's creation.

Maternal Nursing: Design, Morality, and Civilization

As with childbirth, eighteenth-century medical discourse surrounding lactation was shaped by mechanical questions of design and related social and moral concerns. Yet the religious overtones in medical discussions of nursing were, if anything, stronger. Eighteenth-century

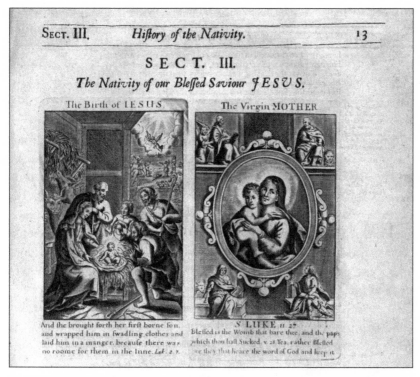

Figure 5.6. Plate introducing "Sect. III. The Nativity of Our Blessed Saviour Jesus," in Jeremy Taylor's *Antiquitates Christianæ: or, The History of the Life and Death of the Holy Jesus*, 7th ed. (London: Macock and Flesher, 1684), 13.

midwifery manuals, medical correspondence, and clerical writings all strongly advocated maternal nursing. To nurse one's own infant was a chance to avoid potential vices, to fulfill a maternal instinct and religious duty, and to serve society. These views on nursing and infant care also shaped how missionaries, reformers, and colonists imagined race and civilization.

Central to Jeremy Taylor's discourse on Jesus's nativity had been a religious vision of the nursing mother and her contribution to social stability and progress. Nursing was an obvious practical application of Mary's maternity. While Mary had not suffered the pains of childbirth, no one doubted her full human experience in the work of infant care. Mary thus served as the epitome of moral, charitable, and economical motherhood. Taylor expanded quickly from this ideal with other examples from scripture and antiquity to make an argument about the role of mothers in ensuring stable domestic families and civilizations. To nurse your own child was to ensure loyalty; history offered countless cases where vain and careless mothers had been grim portents of coming decline. In ancient Rome, Taylor argued, a woman's refusal to nurse her own child—to instead dry up her milk "with artificial applications" like a puppy—was a sure omen of social and political disintegration. At one point in his text, Taylor further graphically describes "that many tyrants have killed their mothers, but never did violence to [their] nurse; as if they were desirous to suck the blood of their mother raw, which she refused to give to them digested into milk." Taylor decried the "softness" of his own age, "above the effeminacy of *Asian* Princes," by which people rejected their children in favor of "custom and fashion" and against the "Laws and prescriptions of Nature." Such selfishness and vanity in mothers undermined nature, order, and society.[51]

Within the field of medicine, meanwhile, scientific investigation concerning the suckling of an infant had been under increasing, if inconclusive, investigation; many medical writers continued to rely on a concept of providence or design. That is, unsure how exactly nourishment was delivered to the fetus in the womb and then, after birth, to the infant via the breasts, physicians and medical practitioners often turned to divine knowledge or nature. *The Compleat Midwife's Practice*, a popular late seventeenth-century midwifery manual, offered detailed scientific discussion of conception and the development of blood vessels and major internal organs, complete with reference to the medical work of well-known physicians such as William Harvey and Isbrand de Diemerbrock. Faced with the conundrum, however, of how the "nutritious juice" would know "after the Child is born, and instead of going down to the womb, rise up to the breasts?" the authors concluded that, like "many other things in nature," the reason was "only known to Almighty God, the maker of all things."[52]

When medical practitioners and authors appealed to providence and design in order to explain the natural function of the maternal body, they both reflected and undergirded a growing cultural consensus of innate maternal affection. By the end of the eighteenth century, as historian Nora Doyle has shown, nursing your own infant was viewed as critical to the cultivation of true motherhood in the Atlantic world. And this was a category increasingly limited in terms of class and race to those women who had the time and resources to provide and reserve milk for their offspring—and their offspring alone.[53] This cultural consensus both shaped and was shaped by medical and religious writers who, throughout the seventeenth and eighteenth centuries, debated how the act of nursing was learned. *The Compleat Midwife's Practice* had posited that infants must have learned to suck in the womb. A century later Baudelocque rejected such an "ancient" idea and recognized that the source of in utero nutrition was the umbilical cord. He nonetheless still remarked on the "inclination of a newborn to suck" and could offer no explanation for this "great aptitude." In the early eighteenth century, the New England Puritan Cotton Mather, who wrote extensively on the topic of medicine, had likewise turned to the language of "instinct" to understand the infant's ability to suck at birth. Mather, writing from his own observation and embodied knowledge of infant care, found such instinct to be an operation of the human's lower soul, implanted by God with the express purpose of protecting creation. Mather viewed nursing with "astonishment." It was a manifestation of a soul imprinted by God and integrated into the human body for the purposes of its material survival. He merged this providential view of nutrition with the contemporary medical-moral concern over luxury, urging women to follow *"Nature"* and *"Suckle your infant your Self if you can."* For those who refused, Mather remarked that, it was *"Unnatural"* to "complain of a State, whereinto the *Laws of Nature* established by God, have brought you."[54]

While Mather, as a minister, was forthright in his view of the spiritual significance of breastfeeding, his views of the naturalness, rightness, and obligation of maternal nursing were shared among many medical writers. Breastmilk was purgative, healing, and transformative. "No aliment is fitter for a child than its mother's milk," Baudelocque wrote. "There is nothing equal to their mother's milk," Seaman argued. When mothers "suckle their own children," Smellie explained, they avoided further medical problems and interventions. "Superfluous fluids" like the lochia were "drained off" by nursing, without further need of evacuation. Mothers who nursed also were more likely to avoid "milk fever." Breastmilk itself was purgative for the newborn, "carry[ing] off the black matter contained in its bowles," and preempting the need for the "gentle" medicinal purges recommended for clearing meconium. Breastmilk could also help in the treatment of thrush and proved effective for the mother's health, more broadly, relieving her from conditions such as hysteria, nerves, and general weakness. According to some, the stimulation of lactation could even be a "cure for barrenness."[55] Nursing was not only an instinct and by design but also salutary in its effects of restoring and preserving the balance and function of both maternal and infant bodies.

Medical interest in nursing was part of a larger discussion of the "intentions of nature" in newborn care, including questions over head shape, child care, and clothing. In the mid-eighteenth century, for example, Smellie had argued that male midwives could, with their hands, "reduce" newborn's heads into their "pristine shape"; Baudelocque later cautioned against this technique, "for the head soon recovers its natural form of itself." Medical writers, further, began to emphasize nature and simplicity in newborn care when warning against luxury in clothing and food. Physician William Cadogan, an eighteenth-century reformer and director of the foundling hospital in London, pioneered such efforts. His 1748 *Essay upon Nursing* revolutionized knowledge of lactation; he urged women to follow "nature" and breastfeed from birth (thus contradicting prevailing ideas that colostrum, a mother's first milk, should be avoided). These efforts contributed to changing ideals of motherhood throughout the Atlantic world, as historians Nora Doyle and Marylynn Salmon have shown.[56]

In his discussion of lactation and newborn care, Cadogan took nature as his authority in his critique of women's knowledge and control of maternity and children's health. He envisioned both the corruptive and redemptive possibilities of knowledge—particularly women's dangerous, "traditional Prejudices"—and thereby defended his intervention into an area long dominated by women's practice and authority. Although women might "fancy that Nature has left a great deal to their Skill and Contrivance," they "often do much harm." His own system of knowledge was more firmly based in nature, he explained: "The Art of Physick has been much improv'd within this last Century; by observing and following Nature more closely, many useful Discoveries have been made, which help us to account for Things in a natural Way, that before seem'd mysterious and magical; and which have consequently made the Practice of it more conformable to Reason and good Sense." Through observation of natural processes and the field of medicine, Cadogan argued, it was possible to redeem the problematic oral and communal knowledge that had characterized women's practices surrounding maternity and child care into the eighteenth century. Cadogan insisted on modern science; nature was "exact," and humans were "her chief Work." Nurses who did not follow "Reason" corrupted this order, causing irreparable harm and even death.[57]

Cadogan defended the interventions of medical learning into an area of women's health by arguing explicitly from design and the laws of nature—or providence—which demanded human activity and progress through investigation of the created order. In so doing, he portrayed counterarguments, like appeals to long-standing tradition, as corrupted interpretations of the natural order that had descended into superstition. Unlike his contemporary John Wesley, the Methodist leader and author of *Primitive Physic*, Cadogan did not hold such generational and popular knowledge with much respect. He did not consider that women's knowledge also grew from a measure of experience and observation. In fact, if pressed, Cadogan gave a profoundly moralizing critique of women's knowledge—or superstition—in health care: their claims were grounded in their vanity, their susceptibility to corruption, and the seductions of fashion.

Cadogan applied to maternity and child care the concerns of the larger religious and medical world obsessed with diseases of flesh and fashion and the corresponding moral failing thought to attend them. Combined with Christian—and, increasingly, medical—ideas of innate maternal instincts, his views on nursing and infant care placed enormous attention on the mother, her morality, and her potential to corrupt the child in diet, clothing, and care. He cautioned that his advice on breastfeeding was for active, temperate women, "whose Fountains are not greatly disturbed or tainted." While women were designed by nature to be mothers, this design could easily be degraded by foolishness and pride. This was too often the case for Cadogan, who was dismayed women did not follow his "plain natural Plan" due to their shortsighted selfishness: "Most Mothers . . . either cannot, or will not undertake the troublesome Task of suckling their own Children . . . were it rightly managed, there would be much Pleasure in it, to every Woman that can prevail upon herself to give up a little of the Beauty of her Breast to feed her Offspring."[58] Cadogan was not alone in his understanding of nursing as a natural good or of women as the vain creatures who defied nature. Cotton Mather had also worried that, even knowing its benefits, women evaded nursing and its inconveniences. He urged them not to avoid reason, nature, and God's will: "Be not such an *Ostrich* as to Decline it, meerly because you would be One of the *Careless Women, Living at Ease*."[59]

To follow nature was to live truly into a healthful, humble motherhood. Even in seemingly hardened circumstances, nature's power was visible. Like many of the male midwifery writers, whose observations were shaped by their experiences among the poor, Cadogan worked in a foundling hospital. He also pointed to the "lower Class of Mankind," who, despite hardships, had healthy infants: "The Mother who has only a few Rags to cover her Child loosely, and little more than her own Breast to feed it, sees it healthy and strong, and very soon able to shift for itself." The wealthy child, on the other hand, was "puny." Further removed from nature, it "languish[es] under a Load of Finery," stuffed with "Dainties," "till he dies a Victim to the mistaken Care and Tenderness of his fond Mother."[60] Closer to nature and with a mother free from the corruptions of fashion and vanity, the poor baby thrived.

Cadogan's romanticized image of "nature," captured in the image of the impoverished but robust mother and newborn, points to an emerging economic and racialized discourse of motherhood and civilization in the colonial Atlantic world—as well as the providential and moral language that undergirded this discourse. Poor women's supposed proximity to nature meant they were best able to demonstrate the salutary effects of nursing; they were a test case, an extreme. They were not, actually, perceived as the ideal but rather served as examples of the strength afforded by measures of simplicity and humility. Prowess in motherhood could, in fact, be dehumanizing. As historian Jennifer Morgan has shown, African women's bodies were considered—or made—savage in part through depictions of their natural ability as mothers who conceived easily and labored "painlessly" and whose breasts were so grotesquely large they could nurse their infants over their shoulders. If they did not suffer the labor pains associated with Eve, as Morgan argues, it was easier to consider African women as animals or a different species—and easier to enslave them.[61]

The image of the infant reaching over the shoulder to nurse also worked to separate African women from the ideal vision of the nursing mother within Christianity. The African child was not depicted like Jesus, nestled at Mary's bosom—or, as Jeremy Taylor wrote, "to the breast where naturally . . . the child is cradled in the entertainments of love and maternal embraces."[62] When useful to the purposes of European colonists, nonetheless, colonized women could be portrayed in such a maternal pose. In his painting *Penn's Treaty with the Indians,* for example, Benjamin West depicted a nursing Native American woman in the lower righthand corner, an idealized scene of domesticity balancing the political and economic negotiation occurring at the painting's center. In contrast to his nativity-like portrait of his own family, reunited in England and centered around his wife and newborn, here West reduces the nursing native woman to a small prop in the greater story of America and its place as a setting for peaceful encounter.[63]

Colonial discourses of race, class, and civilization are made further visible by debates over wet nurses and their characteristics, which joined medical and moral concerns. While maternal nursing was recommended, midwifery manuals offered advice on selecting a wet nurse, advice that reflected concerns of nature or design, maternal affection, and the potential for corruption. A midwife should be chosen based on a variety of factors, these manuals advised, including complexion, hair color, age, and other indicators of the nurse's humoral constitution, which ideally should be in sympathy with the birth mother and the child. Manuals also urged attention to "the qualities of the mind" and external characteristics such as bad breath, decayed or false teeth, and crooked noses. Many manuals also warned of negative consequences should the nurse engage in sexual activity. The general assumption was that the child would suck in the "disorderly" qualities of the nurse—be it the mother or someone else—with lasting consequences for the child's health and temper. In some cases, a "good wholesome nurse" could correct for the "ill complexion of the Mother," although the mother was almost universally preferable. The stakes were high; children often died or became diseased, and writers claimed that "the chief cause is the Nurses milk." Such tragedies (and logic) were explained by recourse to scripture, as Jane Sharpe's 1671 *Midwives Book* explained: "If a nurse be well complexioned her milk cannot be ill; for a Fig-Tree bears not Thistles: a good Tree will bring forth good Fruit."[64]

By the eighteenth century, as historian Nora Doyle argues, the almost-obsessive concern with wet nurses' physical characteristics meant they were "defined by their utilitarian physicality, while middle-class and elite mothers"—the presumed audience of such advice—"were described in terms of their morality, sensibility, and sentimentality." The detailed instructions on a nurse's appearance, fraught with racial and economic overtones, demonstrated a continuing concern with the long-standing relationship perceived between matter and spirit. In the case of maternity, this concern had for centuries contributed to worries over bad or dangerous wombs, through which deviant mothers could harm a developing fetus.[65] In an era increasingly fixated on the naturalness of maternal care, such concerns over how the corporeal affected morality contributed to corresponding unease with wet nursing. Parents, relatives, friends, and missionaries fixated on a nurse's appearance, including her age, heartiness, potential "disorders," level of "common sense," offspring, "contentedness," morality, and sexual activity.[66]

Missionary accounts offer glimpses of how these European and Christian ideals of motherhood were translated into colonial contexts. In one particularly telling example from colonial India in the 1730s, lengthy letters between German Pietist missionaries and physicians described anxieties over Tamil wet nurses. These concerns had come to light due to instances of syphilis, adultery, and abortion. When the local missionary, Christian Pressier, investigated, he learned that Tamil women, who often worked as wet nurses among wealthier neighbors, avoided sex with their husbands and pregnancy because they feared harming the nursing child and, correspondingly, their employment. It is unclear whether these fears stemmed from local warnings, threats from their masters, or Pietist teachings; other Europeans had previously worked and lived among this community. The women and their families depended on the income from wet nursing; indeed, one woman was reportedly "rented" from her "heathen" husband as a wet nurse. Another woman was described as a "bonded servant."[67]

In a letter revealing the religiously charged nature with which nursing was imbued, Pressier wrote to August Hermann Francke in Halle about these cases, seeking medical advice. He first explained that the vast majority of the mothers could, "without doubt, themselves give breast to their Children." He then went on to detail a few examples of the problems emerging from wet nursing as practiced in their missionary settlement. One man, whose wet nursing wife refused to have sex, had turned to "whores." Meanwhile, a wet nurse, fearing the loss of her job, followed the "evil" advice to abort her three-month pregnancy by swallowing a mixture of talcum and cobwebs. Pressier described conflicting views from Tamil women regarding the danger of continuing sexual relationships or becoming pregnant while nursing a child. Some believed it affected their milk supply and caused the suckling infant to become sick and perhaps die. Others thought a sexual relationship was fine, so long as it did not occur too often.[68]

The end of Pressier's letter included extensive "theological and natural" questions about nursing, pregnancy, and sex, questions that highlighted the complex ways in which Christian and providential views of motherhood mapped onto political and economic questions of colonization and civilization. Pressier's chief concerns were about motherhood and sex: he asked whether women should hire wet nurses at all if they were not medically necessary and whether a husband's desire to continue a sexual relationship was compelling enough reason for securing a wet nurse. He was also curious about the medical, economic, and domestic aspects of wet nursing. Could a continuing sexual relationship—or resulting pregnancy—truly harm a nursing child? Did the Indian women of the community have the economic right to sell their services as a wet nurse? Even if a husband approved of such a sale, should the missionaries intervene? Pressier wanted direction as a missionary responsible for the spiritual welfare of his community, but his questions reveal a complex web of theological, medical, and economic concerns, as well as a paternalistic attitude toward the women in question.[69]

Johann Juncker, a physician and professor associated with both the medical university in Halle and the missionaries' home institution of the Francke Foundations, responded. He commented extensively on the spiritual virtues and vices at stake in pregnancy and nursing. He argued that physicians and theologians agreed that it was "faithlessly dealt if a mother without urgent need denies her child milk." Through a wet nurse's milk, a child was exposed to "vices," just as a "mother can implant evil in her child through nutrition in utero." Juncker insisted that the state of the nurse's soul was paramount—and had clear physical ramifications. Arguing from what he called "purely scientific grounds," he claimed that a woman outside of the state of grace would have "harmful, bitter, and fleeting milk."[70]

While some contemporary scientists denied Juncker's insistence on the unity of spirit and matter, he was far from alone in his conviction. He insisted on both a medical sense of maternal design and a missionary concern that this design could be corrupted in places of questionable Christianity and civilization. Sounding remarkably like Cadogan, Juncker insisted that nursing was natural and turned for evidence to the "experience" of impoverished people, who could not afford to hire a nurse "and yet have the healthiest children." He did not see a relationship between a woman's menses or pregnancy and any disruption to the nursing child. The evidence was overwhelming, especially, again, in the extreme case of poor women, who could nurse and support a pregnancy at the same time. Juncker nonetheless urged the missionary Pressier to exercise caution when it came to wet nurses and the potential for corruption that they posed.[71] The physician's advice here was, in ways, general; he was not singling out Tamil women. Missionary reports from India had, however, expressed alarm over an apparent lack of maternal feeling among the local women. That perception, along with Pressier's reports over sexual misconduct and disease, may have contributed to colonialist apprehensions about Indian mothers and whether Indian wet nurses could provide the innate maternal care necessary for both the physical and spiritual health of their infant charges.[72]

Nursing was, in the end, not only a duty for which nature had designed mothers but also a religious act; each was essential to a mother's key service to the larger political community and its success. Both medical and religious writings highlighted these political consequences of maternal nursing. Popular midwifery manuals, such as Jane Sharpe's *Midwives Book* and Nicholas Culpeper's *Directory for Midwives*, had turned, like Jeremy Taylor, to scriptural and classical examples of exemplary maternal care producing dutiful children, who were, in turn, essential to the defense and development of civilizations. The strength of the Germans and the Spartans came through nursing mothers; maternal nursing—not birth order—likewise determined succession among the Lacedemonians.[73] In his *Essay upon Nursing*, Cadogan stressed the importance of nursing as not only natural but also a necessary means to promote infant health and survival. The mortality rates in England for those under the age of five were abysmal: "Half the People that come into the World, go out of it again before they become of the least Use to it." Cadogan insisted that the wholesome milk of a loving mother could prevent corruption and death, and, after all, a "Multitude of Inhabitants is the greatest Strength and best Support of a Commonwealth."[74] Cadogan's language was not rife with religion, but his concern with nature and maternal duty and their implications for survival, usefulness, and society echoed Taylor's language of the previous century. Taylor had ended his discussion on nursing by applying it to the example of the two mothers arguing over a babe before King Solomon: The "true mother" was she who would not see her child divided; according to Taylor, she kept her child whole and completed her duty by *both* bearing *and* nursing her child. A nursing mother fulfilled not only her natural design but also her pious and political duty.[75]

Society rested on maternal sacrifice in the nourishment and education of its virtuous citizens. It depended on the dedicated and moral mother, acting according to nature and with little thought for luxury or herself but rather for the humble and domestic comfort of her children, family, and community. These ideas, heavy with providential symbolism and significance, contributed in crucial ways to the figuration of womanhood in the eighteenth-century colonial world.

* * *

Maternity is, in the ways it is explored here, not always a health condition, an encounter with sickness or suffering. And yet, as experienced by women and men in the eighteenth century, maternity speaks importantly to the interconnecting themes of providence, health, and medicine pursued in this book. Maternity—in terms of pregnancy, childbirth, lactation, and the care women extended to family and neighbors—was something that was deeply considered and narrated in terms of God's providence and human dependence. It was, theologically and metaphorically, both a reminder of human limitation and sinfulness and a foretaste and glimpse of God's greater love and commitment to creation. Maternity was a constant, universal, and corporeal reminder of human loss and disappointment as well as of divine sacrifice and the hope of salvation.

In the eighteenth century, maternity was also increasingly definable in terms of medical conditions. In midwifery manuals, male practitioners sought scientifically to categorize and explain conception, miscarriage, natural and preternatural births, lactation, and infant care. They debated their work and the nature, progress, and purposes of human knowledge, and they sought to understand the natural world, its design, and the appropriate use of human instruments and interventions. This medical discourse, however, was not devoid of religious ideas and implications. In medical practitioners' understanding of nature's design, as well as in the practical application of this knowledge, the woman's body became not simply a machine to be studied but also a place where innate maternal characteristics, almost always with continuing religious significance, could be fulfilled—particularly in nursing and infant care.

A providential commitment remained embedded in both the theological and medical views of maternity that dominated the eighteenth-century European-American world. This commitment was crucial to cementing and supporting the developing concepts of nature, virtue, and civilization central to colonial endeavors. The conviction of a God-ordained mission and nation depended on a dutiful, sacrificing, and virtuous populace. And it rested on the providential narrative of the transcendent significance of human suffering and redemption, made visible in motherhood.

Epilogue

I wanted to come, and if I hadn't, they would have been all
alone, and nobody would have ever known how frightened
and brave and irreplaceable they were.
—Connie Willis, *Doomsday Book*

In Connie Willis's 1992 novel *Doomsday Book*, historians of the future do
their work through time travel. The main character, Kivrin, is a young
scholar of medieval European history who, after extensive preparation,
finally has her chance to visit the Middle Ages. Unbeknownst to her,
however, she and her coordinators are exposed to a deadly flu epidemic
shortly before she time travels. She arrives in the past terribly ill and
disoriented, and her team—likewise affected by the virus—has mistakenly dropped her in the wrong year: 1348. With the help of the medieval
villagers who find her, she recovers from the epidemic illness of her
own time just in time to witness them succumb to a historic one: the
Black Death, the plague that killed approximately one-third of Europe's
population.

Doomsday Book is a work of science fiction, based on the premise
that historical knowledge is best achieved through time travel. The
past comes alive in the book, however, not merely through the feat of
time travel and the firsthand encounter with historical events but also
through the universal reality of human suffering and human responsiveness to suffering.

Moving between epidemics past and future, the reader, on the one
hand, learns how the human experience of suffering is inextricably defined by historical circumstances like medical knowledge, environment,
political and social institutions, class, and religious teachings. And yet,
on the other hand, the reader also perceives that the experience of suffering can transcend historical context. In both the past and the future,
humans' perspectives and actions in times of sickness are shaped by

emotions like vulnerability, grief, and hope, as well as by long-standing Christian teachings about God's providence, ethics, and community.

When we place sickness and bodies at the center of our historical inquiry, in other words, we see change and continuity. We see different medical treatments, for example, but we also see familiar conceptions of benevolence and self-sacrificing care. This continuity in the midst of change disrupts our traditional, linear narrative of progress from a cruel and irrational religious past to a modern and rational medical future. Kivrin's experience of the plague completely countered what she had been taught: that medieval villagers were "panic-stricken and cowardly during the Black Death, that they ran away and wouldn't tend the sick, and that the priests were the worst of all." Living in the midst of their suffering and caring for them—as they had cared for her—she concluded that "it isn't like that at all."[1]

Like Kivrin, we are surprised by our encounter with stories of sickness and health. While our empathy might be heightened by our experiences living through the global pandemic of COVID-19, such empathy can be a hindrance if we do not recognize eighteenth-century women and men in their own richly contoured lives and contexts. It is easy to assume much about their theologies rather than seeing how they actually lived these theologies. When we read widely of eighteenth-century Protestants—their pastoral manuals, letters and journals, medical advice, missionary reports, meeting minutes, epidemic narratives, and midwifery manuals—we see them engage medicine while at the same time relying on providence. We realize the flaws in our received narratives of early American passivity in the face of suffering, of the decline of providential thought in light of medical advances, and of the corresponding secularization that began in the eighteenth century.

While most scholars of religion have acknowledged and described a much more complex narrative of secularization, historians of eighteenth-century medicine, benevolence, politics, and women's history too often continue to assume a story of religious decline and secular progress that both belies the continuing significance of religion in the lives of individuals and overlooks the important ways Protestant Christianity shaped medicine, politics, and gender into the modern era. The story of religion and medicine in the eighteenth century is complex and deserves to be treated as such. Protestants of America and the Atlantic world held together various strands of their spiritual, corporeal, and social lives even as they changed. They continued to depend on long-standing Christian convictions of God's sovereignty, human sin and guilt, and Christian mission as they engaged religious practices of writing, medical transformations, missionary endeavors, and new ideas of community, benevolence, and motherhood.

Early Americans responded to suffering and change creatively, relying on their religion, their medical knowledge, and their community, while also considering their past, their current situation, and the meaning and implications of their actions for the future. Some early Americans, like the Puritans and Pietists, hoped their participation in medical developments was a natural outpouring from their state of election or grace. Some, like the Methodists, believed their actions to ameliorate suffering contributed to their salvation. Many, from Cotton Mather and Johann Boltzius to Absalom Jones, Richard Allen, and John Redman, thought that their efforts to heal, to promote medicine, or to advocate for political change demonstrated their commitment to God's direction and to spreading the Gospel far and wide. Others, like the civic committee members who responded to the 1793 yellow fever epidemic in Philadelphia or the advocates of male midwifery, were convinced that they were confirming and participating in new social understandings of human goodness and scientific knowledge, provided by God's design or the natural world. Even with more secular language, however, they nonetheless still grounded their hopes in human advancement with an appeal to providential direction.

We cannot time travel to the eighteenth century, but we can encounter sickness and health in the eighteenth century through careful attention to a wide range of sources and voices. In so doing, we not only transform our understanding of religion and medicine, of providence, and of secularization but also engage early Americans and their ideas with respect for the fullness of human life. Eighteenth-century Protestants lived embodied lives; they suffered, they witnessed suffering, and they sought to help people and to improve the world. Insofar as we are able, we must attend to the diversity of their experiences and the ways in which they lived out ideas in their bodies and actions. The doctrine of providence was bound inextricably to early Americans' corporeal lives and experiences. In their writing, medicine, and efforts to respond to suffering, they depended on, doubted, challenged, and celebrated God's providence.

When we perceive the rich and dynamic tradition of providential thought in the intimate human experience of embodiment, we change our understanding of both the intellectual and social history of early America. Faith in particular providence did not disappear with elite ideas about a mechanistic universe, a distant God, or an increased optimism about human nature and actions. Allusions to God's providential wrath were not, furthermore, merely a tool of those in power to control social change. Far from disappearing in the shift to a more secular political world, providential thought continued to inform and shape early Americans' responses to suffering and health. It promoted Christian action in the spiritual and often personal work of writing and repentance as well as in broader social efforts of medicine and benevolence. And it shaped views of women, civilization, and political belonging.

Eighteenth-century Protestants turned to providence because of its essential place in Christian tradition and narrative; it was a doctrine that had long offered consolation. Yet they also found in providence a way to understand and respond to their modern world and to engage actively the medical knowledge and developments that were transforming their physical lives. Protestants depended on this activating potential of providential thought, moreover, not only in their encounters with sickness and medicine but also in their experiences of social and political change. One such example is found in the debates over the practice of midwifery and emerging ideals of motherhood, child care, and virtue in the late eighteenth century. While we can be disturbed by and critical of the ways providential thought, in conversation with medicine, informed political notions of womanhood and civilization—fraught with problematic colonial ideas of gender, class, and race—we must nonetheless acknowledge its power and significance.

Personal stories of sickness and health challenge our understanding of what providence meant for an eighteenth-century Christian. Made confident by medical developments of recent centuries, we have often assumed that our present response to suffering is more effective, more courageous, more active, more *secular* than that of previous eras. By attending to sickness and health in history, however, we are challenged to see both the people of the past and ourselves differently. They were not passive. Providence did not limit them. They were shaped by discourses, norms, and institutions in important ways, but, like us, they lived, suffered, experienced change, and worked actively to do the best they could with the medicine, knowledge, and religious convictions they found in both themselves and their communities.

In *Doomsday Book*, Kivrin's recovery was, in the end, twofold: she survived her sickness, and she returned to her own time with intimate stories of past suffering, stories too often lost to history's ledgers. Sometimes when we encounter the past, we are so determined to highlight the change, transformation, and progress that define our present moment that we fail truly to see those who went before and to recognize our shared humanity. In suffering, in health, and in providence, we find continuities in the midst of change. We find humans who, faced with an uncertain future, persisted in turning to the past, seeking meaning in their faith, in their God, and in their actions.

ACKNOWLEDGMENTS

In the development, research, and writing of this book, I received substantial support from many individuals and institutions, whom I am pleased to acknowledge here.

Catherine Brekus, W. Clark Gilpin, and Richard Rosengarten were crucial advisors and readers of this project from the start. Their expertise, encouragement, and critical questions have shaped this book and my continuing scholarship. I am grateful for their generous mentorship.

For research and travel support, I thank the John W. Kluge Center at the Library of Congress, the Francke Foundations in Halle, the Graduate College at Missouri State University, the Charlotte W. Newcombe Foundation, the McNeil Center for Early American Studies at the University of Pennsylvania, the Martin Marty Center for the Advanced Study of Religion at the University of Chicago Divinity School, the American Antiquarian Society, the Nicholson Center of British Studies at the University of Chicago, the Virginia Historical Society, and the Divinity Students Association at the University of Chicago Divinity School.

With this financial support came a great many experts, colleagues, and friends. I would like to thank librarians and archivists at the American Antiquarian Society, the Archive of the Francke Foundations, the Bodleian Library of Commonwealth & African Studies at Rhodes House, Oxford, the Historical Society of Pennsylvania, the Lambeth Palace Library, the Library of the College of Physicians of Philadelphia, the Library Company of Philadelphia, the Library of Congress, the Lutheran Archives Center at Philadelphia, and the Virginia Historical Society.

A number of colleagues read and commented on parts of the manuscript. I gratefully acknowledge Catherine Brekus, W. Clark Gilpin, Richard Rosengarten, Dan Richter, Pamela Klassen, John Schmalzbauer, and Amy Artman, as well as audiences at talks and workshops at the Francke Foundations, the University of Chicago Divinity School, Princeton University, Indiana University, Missouri State University, Baylor

University, and the McNeil Center for Early American Studies. I thank, also, my editor, Jennifer Hammer, at New York University Press and the anonymous reviewers. Their comments and critiques have made this a better book.

Through fellowships, talks, conferences, and workshops, I have benefitted from a community of scholars and their rich conversation over the years; in addition to those already named, I thank in particular Noelani Arista, Sara Damiano, Curtis Evans, Jan-Hendrik Evers, Wolfgang Flügel, Claire Gherini, Cooper Harriss, Bruce Hindmarsh, Sarah Imhoff, Don Johnson, Christine Koch, Monica Mercado, Mairin Odle, Seth Perry, and Antje Schloms. My cohort and mentors in the Young Scholars in American Religion Program have been a recent and wonderful community, and I thank Amanda Baugh, Anne Blankenship, Vaughn Booker, Jenny Caplan, Janine Giordano Drake, Rachel McBride Lindsey, Lincoln Mullen, Brad Stoddard, and Daisy Vargas, as well as our mentors Jim Bennett and Laura Levitt, for their support.

I am grateful to my department head, Stephen Berkwitz, and colleagues at Missouri State University for their welcome and for providing a collegial academic environment. I thank my graduate assistants, Kayla Jenkins, Anna Redmond, and Bailey Lape, who have provided invaluable assistance in my scholarship and teaching, and all of my students, who have challenged me and continue to make me a better scholar.

Over the years, family and friends have provided hospitality, good talks, hugs, runs, and kind care packages. To Dieter and Julie Koch, Sarah Harriss, Beth Ross, Molly Hallenberger, Kristine Johanson, and Alissa Wardwell, you have my deep thanks and love. My parents, Margaret and Gary Koch, have supported me with ceaseless optimism and faith, and for those reasons—and others too numerous to list here—I dedicate this work to them.

My greatest gratitude goes to Vince Evener. He has shared the joys and trials of graduate school, research, travel, new languages, perfect games, perilous hikes, teaching, and far too many moves. Above all, he shares Casper, Felix, and Jesse. I cherish the grand adventure of our life together.

NOTES

ABBREVIATIONS

Archival Collections

AAS American Antiquarian Society, Worcester, MA

AFST/M Missionsarchiv der Franckeschen Stiftungen, Halle (Saale), Germany

HSP Historical Society of Pennsylvania, Philadelphia

LAC Lutheran Archives Center at Philadelphia

LCP Library Company of Philadelphia

STAB/F Francke-Nachlaß der Staatsbibliothek zu Berlin

VHS Virginia Historical Society, Richmond, VA

Publications

JMB, *Letters* Johann Martin Boltzius. *The Letters of Johann Martin Boltzius: Lutheran Pastor in Ebenezer, Georgia*. Edited and translated by Russell Kleckley in collaboration with Jürgen Gröschl. Lewiston, NY: Edwin Mellen Press, 2009.

URLSPERGER, DR Samuel Urlsperger, ed. *Detailed Reports on the Salzburger Emigrants Who Settled in America*. Edited and translated by George Fenwick Jones et al. 17 vols. Athens: University of Georgia Press, 1968–1995. (Notes include volume number and year of publication.)

People

FMZ Friedrich Michael Ziegenhagen

GAF Gotthilf August Francke

ICG Israel Christian Gronau

JMB Johann Martin Boltzius

PREFACE

1   Susan Sontag, *Illness as Metaphor* (New York: Farrar, Straus & Giroux, 1978), 58;
    Paul Elie, "(Against) Virus as Metaphor," *New Yorker* (19 Mar. 2020): www.newy-
    orker.com.

2   Bret Stephens, "Covid-19: A Look Back from 2025," *New York Times* (3 Apr. 2020):
    www.nytimes.com; Ryan Broderick, "After the Coronavirus Passes, Your World
    Will Not Go Back to Normal," *BuzzFeedNews* (2 Apr. 2020): www.buzzfeednews.
    com; Jim Geraghty, "Maybe the 'New Normal' after Coronavirus Should Keep
    Some of These Changes," *National Review* (19 Mar. 2020): www.nationalreview.
    com; Claudia Gonzales-Diaz, "IU Archives Asks for Personal Accounts of Pan-
    demic from IU Community, Locals," *Indiana Daily Student* (25 Mar. 2020): www.
    idsnews.com; Oya Y. Rieger, "Documenting the COVID-19 Pandemic," *ITHAKA
    S+R* (6 Apr. 2020): https://sr.ithaka.org.

3   On "the religion of healthy-mindedness," see William James, *The Varieties of Re-
    ligious Experience* (New York: Longmans, Green, 1903), 78–126. On the reception
    of Peale in his own time, see Carol V. R. George, *God's Salesman: Norman Vincent
    Peale and the Power of Positive Thinking* (Oxford: Oxford University Press, 2019),
    136–144. On the continuing relevance of positive thought today, see Kate Bowler,
    Everything Happens for a Reason: And Other Lies I've Loved (New York: Random
    House, 2018), xii–xiv; Mark Mulder and Gerardo Marti, "The President, the
    Pandemic and the Limits of Positive Thinking," *Religion News Service* (30 Mar.
    2020): https://religionnews.com; Michael Kruse, "The Power of Trump's Positive
    Thinking," *Politico Magazine* (13 Oct. 2017): www.politico.com; Simon Lewis and
    Heather Timmons, "Trump Seeks to Shore Up Evangelical Support at 'Prosperity
    Gospel' Church," *Reuters* (3 Jan. 2020): www.reuters.com.

4   Roxanne Khamsi, "If a Coronavirus Vaccine Arrives, Can the World Make
    Enough?," *Nature* (9 Apr. 2020): www.nature.com; Michael D. Shear et al., "The
    Lost Month: How a Failure to Test Blinded the U.S. to Covid-19," *New York Times*
    (28 Mar. 2020): www.nytimes.com.

5   Mona Chalabi, "Coronavirus Is Revealing How Broken America's Economy Re-
    ally Is," *Guardian* (6 Apr. 2020): www.theguardian.com; David Blumenthal and
    Shanoor Seervai, "Coronavirus Is Exposing Deficiencies in U.S. Health Care,"
    Harvard Business Review (10 Mar. 2020): https://hbr.org.

6   Elvia Díaz, "Why Is Coronavirus Killing So Many Black Americans? Because They
    Are Poor," *USA Today* (9 Apr. 2020): www.usatoday.com; Melissa Repko and An-
    nie Palmer, "With Strikes and a 'Sick Out,' Some Grocery and Delivery Workers
    Take Defiant Stance: One-Time Bonuses, Temporary Pay Hikes Aren't Enough,"
    CNBC (31 Mar. 2020): www.cnbc.com; Dan Frosch and Christopher Weaver,
    "Coronavirus Hits Native American Groups Already Struggling with Poor Health
    Care," *Wall Street Journal* (22 Mar. 2020): www.wsj.com.

7   Bess Levin, "Texas Lt. Governor: Old People Should Volunteer to Die to Save the
    Economy," *Vanity Fair* (24 Mar. 2020): www.vanityfair.com; Majlie de Puy Kamp,

Curt Devine, and Drew Griffin, "As Coronavirus Cases Grow, Hospitals to Rank Patients for Treatment," *CNN* (3 Apr. 2020): www.cnn.com. See also, in particular, the remarks of the Rev. Dr. William J. Barber II in the roundtable "Restarting America Means People Will Die. So When Do We Do It? Five Thinkers Weigh Moral Choices in a Crisis," *New York Times Magazine* (10 Apr. 2020): www.nytimes.com.

8 Stephanie Becker, "At Least 70 People Infected with Coronavirus Linked to a Single Church in California, Health Officials Say," *CNN* (4 Apr. 2020): www.cnn.com; Michelle Boorstein, "The Church That Won't Close Its Doors over the Coronavirus," *Washington Post* (20 Mar. 2020): www.washingtonpost.com; Tom Plumbley, "God Doesn't Demand We Ignore Coronavirus Medical Advice. Stay Home for Easter, Passover," *Fort Worth Star-Telegram* (9 Apr. 2020): www.star-telegram.com.

9 Ramtin Arablouei, "The Coronavirus Is Stealing Our Ability to Grieve," *Atlantic* (25 Mar. 2020): www.theatlantic.com.

10 Margaret M. Mitchell, "How Republican Politicians Get Schooled on the Bible," *Sightings* (6 Apr. 2020): https://divinity.uchicago.edu/sightings; N. T. Wright, "Christianity Offers No Answers about the Coronavirus. It's Not Supposed To," *TIME* (29 Mar. 2020): https://time.com; Daniel J. Phillips, "The Bible Gives Buckets of Answers about COVID-19. You May Not Like Them," *PJ Media* (31 Mar. 2020): https://pjmedia.com.

11 See chapter 4.

12 Katherine Stewart, "The Religious Right's Hostility to Science Is Crippling Our Coronavirus Response," *New York Times* (27 Mar. 2020): www.nytimes.com; Zachary Cohen, Alex Marquardt, and Kylie Atwood, "Blame Game Escalates between US and China over Coronavirus Disinformation," *CNN* (25 Mar. 2020): www.cnn.com; "One America News: Democrats Exaggerate Coronavirus Fears to Attack Trump," *RealClear Politics* (27 Feb. 2020): www.realclearpolitics.com.

13 Elizabeth Dias, interview with Kate Bowler, "How to Live in the Face of Fear: Lessons from a Cancer Survivor," *New York Times* (5 Apr. 2020): www.nytimes.com. While Bowler speaks against a dominant cultural force in her critique of positive thinking, she does have a tremendous appeal. At the time of this writing, she has over thirty-two thousand followers on both Twitter and Instagram and her book *Everything Happens for a Reason* is a *New York Times* best seller.

INTRODUCTION

1 Alexandra Walsham, *Providence in Early Modern England* (Oxford: Oxford University Press, 1999), 8–12.

2 Charles Taylor, *Sources of the Self: The Making of the Modern Identity* (Cambridge, MA: Harvard University Press, 1992), 266–272; Charles Taylor, *A Secular Age* (Cambridge, MA: Harvard University Press, 2007), 248; Louis Dupré, *The Enlightenment and the Intellectual Foundations of Modern Culture* (New Haven, CT: Yale University Press, 2004), 243–257; David Fergusson, "Divine Provi-

dence," in *The Oxford Handbook of Theology and Modern European Thought*, ed. Nicholas Adams, George Pattison, and Graham Ward (Oxford: Oxford University Press, 2013), 656–658; Richard Rosengarten, *Henry Fielding and the Narration of Providence: Divine Design and the Incursions of Evil* (New York: Palgrave, 2000), 22–23; Christopher Grasso, *Skepticism and American Faith: From the Revolution to the Civil War* (New York: Oxford University Press, 2018), 26, 30. On providence, the Enlightenment, and secularization in other religious communities, see Karl W. Gilberson, ed., *Abraham's Dice: Chance and Providence in the Monotheistic Traditions* (Oxford: Oxford University Press, 2016); Shmuel Feiner, *The Origins of Jewish Secularization in Eighteenth-Century Europe*, trans. Chaya Naor (Philadelphia: University of Pennsylvania Press, 2010); Micah Gottlieb, *Faith and Freedom: Moses Mendelssohn's Theological Political Thought* (New York: Oxford University Press, 2011).

3 The assumption that Christians were antiscientific or fatalist is especially found in the debates over John Wesley's medical work. See G. S. Rousseau, "John Wesley's *Primitive Physic* (1747)," *Harvard Library Bulletin* 16 (1968): 242–256; J. W. Haas, "John Wesley's View on Science and Christianity: An Examination of the Charge of Antiscience," *Church History* 63 (1994): 378–392; John C. English, "John Wesley and Isaac Newton's 'System of the World,'" *Proceedings of the Wesley Historical Society* 48 (1991): 69–86; Deborah Madden, *"A Cheap, Safe, and Natural Medicine": Religion, Medicine, and Culture in John Wesley's Primitive Physic*, Clio Medica 83 (Amsterdam: Rodopi, 2007), 109–125. But it is evident elsewhere. See, for example, Elaine Forman Crane, "'I Have Suffer'd Much Today': The Defining Force of Pain in Early America," in *Through a Glass Darkly: Reflections on Personal Identity in Early America*, ed. Ronald Hoffman, Mechal Sobel, and Fredrika J. Teute (Chapel Hill: University of North Carolina Press, 1997), 370–403; Anne Hunsaker Hawkins, *Reconstructing Illness: Studies in Pathography* (West Lafayette, IN: Purdue University Press, 1993), 2–3, 27.

4 Recent studies offer excellent examples of the importance of considering sickness and medicine alongside religious beliefs and practices in early America. See, for example, Martha L. Finch, *Dissenting Bodies: Corporealities in Early New England* (New York: Columbia University Press, 2010); Paul Kelton, *Cherokee Medicine, Colonial Germs: An Indigenous Nation's Fight against Smallpox, 1518–1824* (Ithaca, NY: Cornell University Press, 2015); Brett Malcolm Grainger, *Church in the Wild: Evangelicals in Antebellum America* (Cambridge, MA: Harvard University Press, 2019).

5 For more on the topic of predestination in the American context, see Peter Thuesen, *Predestination: The American Career of a Contentious Doctrine* (Oxford: Oxford University Press, 2009). Thuesen defines predestination and providence on pages 2–3.

6 Particularly since Keith Thomas's influential work *Religion and the Decline of Magic*, this misconception has caused scholars to limit providentialism to early English Puritanism. Keith Thomas, *Religion and the Decline of Magic* (New York:

Scribner, 1971). For an example of the enduring legacy of Thomas's work, see
Andrew Wear, "Puritan Perceptions of Illness in Seventeenth Century England,"
in *Patients and Practitioners: Lay Perceptions of Medicine in Pre-industrial Society*,
ed. Roy Porter (Cambridge: Cambridge University Press, 1985), 55–99, particularly
59–60, where Wear writes, "It has to be remembered that this highly providen-
tialist vision was relatively short-lived and limited mainly to Puritans, and many
diaries were written by Puritan ministers who would naturally think in this way."

7 Walsham, *Providence in Early Modern England*, 2–3.

8 For excellent work on German-language communities and their importance in
the Atlantic world, see Katharine Gerbner, *Christian Slavery: Conversion and Race
in the Protestant Atlantic World* (Philadelphia: University of Pennsylvania Press,
2018); Patrick M. Erben, *A Harmony of the Spirits: Translation and the Language
of Community in Early Pennsylvania* (Chapel Hill: University of North Carolina
Press, 2012); Hartmut Lehmann, Hermann Wellenreuther, and Renate Wilson,
eds., *In Search of Peace and Prosperity: New German Settlements in Eighteenth-
Century Europe and America* (University Park: Pennsylvania State University
Press, 2000); Kate Carté Engel, *Religion and Profit: Moravians in Early America*
(Philadelphia: University of Pennsylvania Press, 2009).

9 This scholarly misconception is most apparent in literature on the eighteenth-
century development of and debate over smallpox inoculation. See, for example,
Perry Miller, *The New England Mind: From Colony to Province* (Cambridge, MA:
Harvard University Press, 1953), 343; Maxine Van de Wetering, "A Reconsidera-
tion of the Inoculation Controversy," *New England Quarterly* 58 (1985): 59, 66; cf.
Ernst B. Gilman, *Plague Writing in Early Modern England* (Chicago: University of
Chicago Press, 2009), 247.

10 Nathaniel Hawthorne, *The Scarlet Letter* (1850; New York: Modern Library
Edition, 2000), 181. Hawthorne's negative assessment of Calvinism was shared
by other nineteenth-century authors, including Catharine Maria Sedgwick and
Harriet Beecher Stowe. See Sedgwick's *A New-England Tale* (1822) or Stowe's *Uncle
Tom's Cabin* (1852).

11 Arminianism takes its name from Jacobus Arminius (1559–1609), a Dutch Re-
formed theologian. Arminius's views on predestination and the heated debates
they sparked remind us of the diversity of opinion on predestination, human freedom, and providence within the Calvinist tradition. See Carl Bangs, "Arminius,
Jacobus," in *The Oxford Encyclopedia of the Reformation*, ed. Hans J. Hillebrand
(Oxford: Oxford University Press, 1996), www.oxfordreference.com.

12 There is even a phrase for this parallel, "physical Arminianism," which was first
used by James Whorton. See Heather Curtis, *Faith in the Great Physician: Suffering and Divine Healing in American Culture, 1860–1900* (Baltimore: Johns Hopkins
University Press, 2007), 61–62.

13 For Calvin's writing on human knowledge of science and medicine as a natural
gift from God, see John Calvin, *Institutes of the Christian Religion*, ed. John T.
McNeill, trans. Ford Lewis Battles, Library of Christian Classics (Louisville, KY:

Westminster John Knox Press, 1960), 270–277. The relevant sections are in bk. 2, chap. 2, secs. 12–17.

14 Anita Guerrini, *Obesity and Depression in the Enlightenment: The Life and Times of George Cheyne* (Norman: University of Oklahoma Press, 2000), 99, 105. Studies of the Boston smallpox inoculation controversy are particularly good examples of declension or secularization narratives: Van de Wetering, "Reconsideration of the Inoculation Controversy," 46–67; Robert Tindol, "Getting the Pox off All Their Houses: Cotton Mather and the Rhetoric of Puritan Science," *Early American Literature* 46 (2011): 1; Margot Minardi, "The Boston Inoculation Controversy of 1721–1722: An Incident in the History of Race," *William and Mary Quarterly* 61 (2004): 49; Perry Miller argues that William Cooper, the author of one pro-inoculation tract, did not realize "that he had refashioned Calvinism into an activism more Pelagian than any seventeenth-century Arminianism had ever dreamed of." Miller, *New England Mind*, 345–366.

15 See chapter 1.

16 Martin Riesebrodt, *Promise of Salvation: A Theory of Religion* (Chicago: University of Chicago Press, 2010), 175–181; Thomas Tweed, *Crossing and Dwelling: A Theory of Religions* (Cambridge, MA: Harvard University Press, 2006), 50–52; Fergusson offers an interesting account of providence in modernity, arguing that providence's encounter with Deism did not make it disappear but rather caused its "refraction" in the secular world. He focuses on the "discourse of providence" in imperial expansion and market economies. Fergusson, "Divine Providence," 655–673.

17 W. Clark Gilpin, preface to *The Pilgrim's Progress: From This World to That Which Is to Come* and *Grace Abounding to the Chief of Sinners*, by John Bunyan (New York: Vintage, 2004), ix–xvi; Rosengarten, *Henry Fielding and the Narration of Providence*, 2–4.

18 August Hermann Francke, *An Abstract of the Marvellous Footsteps of Divine Providence. In the Building of a Very Large Hospital, or Rather, a Spacious College, for Charitable and Excellent Use in the Maintaining of Many Orphans and Other Poor People Therein* (London: Downing, 1706); for the German text, see August Hermann Francke, *Segens-volle Fußstapfen des noch lebenden und waltenden liebreichen und getreuen Gottes* (Halle: Verlegung des Wäysen-Hauses, 1709). It was first published in 1701 and was likely translated into English by Anton Böhme, who was the Lutheran court chaplain in London at the time and who translated many Pietists' writings into English. See Arno Sames, *Anton Wilhelm Böhme (1673–1722): Studien zum Ökumenischen Denken und Handeln eines Halleschen Pietisten* (Göttingen: Vandenhoeck & Ruprecht, 1989), 19–22; Peter James Yoder, "Rendered 'Odious' as Pietists: Anton Wilhelm Böhme's Conception of Pietism and the Possibilities of Prototype Theory," in *The Pietist Impulse in Christianity*, ed. Christian T. Collins-Winn, Christopher Gehrz, G. William Carlson, and Eric Holst (Cambridge: James Clark, 2011), 17–28. For references to Francke's work in eighteenth-century writings, see, for example, Catharina Gronau to Samuel

Urlsperger, 8 Jan. 1745, Missionsarchiv der Franckeschen Stiftungen (hereafter AFSt/M) 5 A 11: 28a; Cotton Mather, *Nuncia Bona e Terra Longinqua. A Brief Account of Some Good & Great Things a Doing for the Kingdom of God, in the Midst of Europe* (Boston: Green, 1715); Journal of Sarah Osborn in Newport, Rhode Island, 21 Feb. 1758, Newport Historical Society; George Whitefield, *A Continuation of the Account of the Orphan-House in Georgia, from January 1741 to June 1742. To Which Are Also Subjoin'd Some Extracts from an Account of a Work of a Like Nature, Carried on by the Late Professor Franck in Glaucha Near Hall in Saxony* (Edinburgh: Lumisden and Robertson, 1742). Cf. Wolfgang Splitter, "Reconsiderations: The Fact and Fiction of Cotton Mather's Correspondence with German Pietist August Hermann Francke," *New England Quarterly* 83 (2010): 102–122.

19 Francke refers to such providential occurrences throughout the account. Francke, *Abstract of the Marvellous Footsteps of Divine Providence*, esp. 4–5, 24–25, 27, 32–36; Woodward's words appear on pages 2 and 3 of the preface, which is not paginated.

20 Catherine A. Brekus, "Contested Words: History, America, Religion," *William and Mary Quarterly* 75 (2018): 34–36; Catherine A. Brekus and W. Clark Gilpin, "Introduction," in *American Christianities: A History of Dominance and Diversity*, ed. Catherine A. Brekus and W. Clark Gilpin (Chapel Hill: University of North Carolina Press, 2011), 1–24; Christopher Grasso, *Skepticism and American Faith: From the Revolution to the Civil War* (New York: Oxford University Press, 2018), 10.

21 Riesebrodt, *Promise of Salvation*, 175–178. On the continuing influence of Christianity in American and modern Western politics, see Tracy Fessenden, "Christianity, National Identity, and the Contours of Religious Pluralism," in Brekus and Gilpin, *American Christianities*, 399–426; Winnifred Fallers Sullivan, "Reforming Culture: Law and Religion Today," in *The Cambridge Companion to Religious Studies*, ed. Robert Orsi (Cambridge: Cambridge University Press, 2012), 319–337; Paul Christopher Johnson, Pamela E. Klassen, and Winnifred Sullivan, *Ekklesia: Three Inquiries in Church and State* (Chicago: University of Chicago Press, 2018). For a helpful and brief overview of secularization theories and their place in higher education, see Peter L. Berger, "The Desecularization of the World: A Global Overview," in *The Desecularization of the World: Resurgent Religion and World Politics*, ed. Peter L. Berger (Grand Rapids, MI: William B. Eerdmans, 1999), 1–17.

22 Riesebrodt, *Promise of Salvation*, 178; Jason Ā. Josephson-Storm, *The Myth of Disenchantment: Magic, Modernity, and the Birth of the Human Sciences* (Chicago: University of Chicago Press, 2016), 3–13; Taylor, *Secular Age*, 219–225; Dupré, *Enlightenment*, 243–257; Fergusson, "Divine Providence," 655–673. On the "resiliency" of this narrative, see Simon Grote, "Review-Essay: Religion and Enlightenment," *Journal of the History of Ideas* 75 (2014): 137–160. I am indebted to Simon for a thought-provoking conversation while resident fellows at the Archive of the Francke Foundations.

23 Rosengarten, *Henry Fielding and the Narration of Providence*, 22–23.

24 Colin Jager, *The Book of God: Secularization and Design in the Romantic Era* (Philadelphia: University of Pennsylvania Press, 2006), 2–4, 26–30. Jager is in conversation here with José Casanova, *Public Religions in the Modern World* (Chicago: University of Chicago Press, 1994).

25 See Riesebrodt, *Promise of Salvation*, 178, 181; Josephson-Storm, *Myth of Disenchantment*, 3–13.

26 Although I am sympathetic to Riesebrodt's argument, I think much remains to be explored. Riesebrodt acknowledged the benefits of religion in this sense: religion "not only makes it possible for the inexplicable to be explained; it also maintains people's ability to act in situations in which they run up against their own limits." But he also points to problems when "the institutionalization and internalization of religious ideas . . . prevent people from rationally coping with their fate themselves when they are capable of doing so." The role of the religious institution and its relation to the individual in such situations deserves further study. It seems problematic to me that while critically assessing the failures of modernity—an age characterized by its faith in reason and rationality—Riesebrodt at the same time criticizes religious ideas and institutions for preventing people from "*rationally* coping" (emphasis added). Riesebrodt, *Promise of Salvation*, 169–174. See also Riesebrodt's critique of Charles Taylor's *A Secular Age* in William Schweiker et al., "Grappling with Charles Taylor's *A Secular Age*," *Journal of Religion* 90 (2010): 399–400.

27 Nicholas Guyatt, *Providence and the Invention of the United States, 1607–1876* (Cambridge: Cambridge University Press, 2007); cf. Sara Georgini, *Household Gods: The Religious Lives of the Adams Family* (Oxford: Oxford University Press, 2019), 8–9, 20–21, 34; Grasso, *Skepticism and American Faith*, 10, 17.

28 Kate Bowler, *Everything Happens for a Reason: And Other Lies I've Loved* (New York: Random House, 2018), xiv, 112–113.

29 Ibid., 159–160.

30 Guyatt, *Providence and the Invention of the United States*, chaps. 3, 5, and 6; Emily Conroy-Krutz, *Christian Imperialism: Converting the World in the Early American Republic* (Ithaca, NY: Cornell University Press, 2015), xv–xvi, 35–39; Philippa Koch, "Slavery, Mission, and the Perils of Providence in Eighteenth-Century Christianity: The Writings of Whitefield and the Halle Pietists," *Church History: Studies in Christianity and Culture* 84 (2015): 369–393.

1. WHOLESOME WORDS

1 Cotton Mather, *Wholesome Words: A Visit of Advice, Given unto Families That Are Visited with Sickness* (Boston: Henchman, 1713). Mather mentions the 1702 edition in his diary, but it is not available. Cotton Mather, *Diary of Cotton Mather, 1681–1724* (Boston: Massachusetts Historical Society, 1911), 446. I use the 1713 edition. Although the content is the same, a 1721 edition was published under a different title: Cotton Mather, *A Pastoral Letter, to Families Visited with Sickness* (Boston:

Green, 1721). For context, see Kenneth Silverman, *The Life and Times of Cotton Mather* (New York: Harper & Row, 1984), 179–184, 269–275.

2 Christopher Grasso, *Skepticism and American Faith: From the Revolution to the Civil War* (New York: Oxford University Press, 2018), 16, 30, 482–483.

3 Samuel Urlsperger, *Der Kranken Gesundheit und der Sterbenden Leben* (Stuttgart: Müller, 1723). The 1750 edition, which was sent to the Pietist community in Ebenezer, Georgia, was published under a similar title: *Der Kranken Gesundheit und der Sterbenden Leben; oder Schrifftmässiger Unterricht für Kranke und Sterbende nach göttlicher Heilsordnung* (Augsburg: Brinhaußer, 1750). I consulted the 1750 edition at the Archive of the Francke Foundations, but it is also available digitally through the website of the Sächsische Landesbibliothek—Staats- und Universitätsbibliothek, Dresden. On the reception of Urlsperger's books in Georgia in 1751, see Johann Martin Boltzius's journal entry from late August 1751 in Samuel Urlsperger, ed., *Detailed Reports on the Salzburger Emigrants Who Settled in America*, trans. and ed. George Fenwick Jones et al. (Athens: University of Georgia Press, 1990), 15:122 (hereafter Urlsperger, *DR*). Unless otherwise noted, all translations are my own.

4 The methodological approach of "lived religion" in American religious history emerged from a 1990s conference and volume developing from the work of Danièle Hervieu-Léger. David D. Hall, ed., *Lived Religion in America: Toward a History of Practice* (Princeton: Princeton University Press, 1997). As Hall outlined in the introduction, this method was to avoid the pitfalls of "popular history" approaches by avoiding distinctions between "high and low" and by not "displac[ing] the institutional or normative perspectives on practice" (ix). Many scholars of early American Protestantism have pursued work that highlights thought and practice in their diversity. See, for example, Martha L. Finch, *Dissenting Corporealities in Early New England* (New York: Columbia University Press, 2010); Adrian Chastain Weimer, *Martyrs' Mirror: Persecution and Holiness in Early New England* (Oxford: Oxford University Press, 2011); Kathryn Gin Lum, *Damned Nation: Hell in America from the Revolution to Reconstruction* (Oxford: Oxford University Press, 2014); and Catherine A. Brekus, *Sarah Osborn's World: The Rise of Evangelical Christianity in Early America* (New Haven, CT: Yale University Press, 2013).

5 Elaine Forman Crane, "'I Have Suffer'd Much Today': The Defining Force of Pain in Early America," in *Through a Glass Darkly: Reflections on Personal Identity in Early America*, ed. Ronald Hoffman, Mechal Sobel, and Fredrika J. Teute (Chapel Hill: University of North Carolina Press, 1997), 370–403; Andrew Wear, "Puritan Perceptions of Illness in Seventeenth Century England," in *Patients and Practitioners: Lay Perceptions of Medicine in Pre-industrial Society*, ed. Roy Porter (Cambridge: Cambridge University Press, 1985), 55–99.

6 Foucault's influence on literary criticism and the history of medicine is immense. On power and the body, see particularly *Discipline and Punish: The Birth of the Prison*, trans. Alan Sheridan (New York: Vintage, 1995); on Foucault's effect on

the history of medicine, see Roger Cooter, "After Death/After-'Life': The Social History of Medicine in Post-Postmodernity," *Social History of Medicine* 20 (2007): 448–453. The influence of both Douglas and Gilman stems from their writings on order and control. According to Douglas, "Culture, in the sense of the public, standardized values of a community, mediates the experience of individuals. It provides in advance some basic categories, a positive pattern in which ideas and values are tidily ordered. And above all, it has authority, since each is induced to assent because of the assent of others." Douglas argues that cultures must have "various provisions for dealing with ambiguous or anomalous events" and that "by settling for one or other interpretation, ambiguity is often reduced." Gilman argues that "the image of all disease, the very face of the patient, is a continuous one, and through a study of its continuities comes a sense of the interrelationship of all our projected fears of collapse. This continuity, however, reflects changing functions that the image of disease has within an age's or an individual's overall sense of control. . . . How we see the diseased, the mad, the polluting, is a reflex of our own sense of control and the limits inherent in that sense of control." Mary Douglas, *Purity and Danger: An Analysis of Concepts of Pollution and Taboo* (Baltimore: Penguin, 1966), 52; Sander Gilman, *Disease and Representation: Images of Illness from Madness to AIDS* (Ithaca, NY: Cornell University Press, 1988), 3; cf. David E. Shuttleton, *Smallpox and the Literary Imagination, 1660–1820* (Cambridge: Cambridge University Press, 2007), 3–12; Ann Carmichael, "The Last Past Plague: The Uses of Memory in Renaissance Epidemics," *Journal of the History of Medicine and Allied Sciences* 53 (1998): 133–134, 141–142, 158–159; Margaret Healy, *Fictions of Disease in Early Modern England: Bodies, Plague, and Politics* (New York: Palgrave, 2001), 16; Cristobal Silva, *Miraculous Plagues: An Epidemiology of Early New England Narrative* (Oxford: Oxford University Press, 2011), 17–18; Priscilla Wald, *Contagious: Cultures, Carriers, and the Outbreak Narrative* (Durham, NC: Duke University Press, 2008), 53; Priscilla Wald, "Imagined Immunities," in *Cultural Studies and Political Theory*, ed. Jodi Dean (Ithaca, NY: Cornell University Press, 2000), 189–208. On narratives of Philadelphia's yellow fever epidemic and the blame of African American nurses, see chapter 4.

7 Mary Lindemann, *Medicine and Society in Early Modern Europe* (Cambridge: Cambridge University Press, 1999), 64–65.

8 Anne Hunsaker Hawkins, *Reconstructing Illness: Studies in Pathography* (West Lafayette, IN: Purdue University Press, 1993), 48–49, 59–60. Cf. Arthur W. Frank, *The Wounded Storyteller: Body, Illness and Ethics* (Chicago: University of Chicago Press, 1997); Arthur Kleinman, *The Illness Narratives: Suffering, Healing, and the Human Condition* (New York: Basic Books, 1988). The growing interest in modern pathography represents in part a response to Susan Sontag's work on illness and metaphor and in part a growing interest in the patient within the history of medicine, which has accompanied a criticism of the "dehumanized character of modern medical treatment." Lindemann, *Medicine and Society*, 2; cf. Jürgen Helm, *Krankheit, Bekehrung und Reform. Medizin und Krankenfürsorge im Halleschen*

Pietismus, Hallesche Forschungen 21 (Tübingen: Max Niemeyer Verlag, 2006), 1. Sontag sought to divest the discourse surrounding disease of its metaphorical language, arguing that "nothing is more punitive than to give a disease a meaning— that meaning being invariably a moralistic one. Any important disease whose causality is murky, and for which treatment is ineffectual, tends to be awash in significance." For Sontag, applying meaning to disease—that is, discourse about disease removed from the purely scientific realm—opened possibilities for stigmatizing disease and the diseased. Susan Sontag, *Illness as Metaphor* (New York: Farrar, Straus & Giroux, 1978), 58. Others argue, however, that the effort to give meaning to disease has cultural significance and can be empowering for suffering individuals. Roy Porter and G. S. Rousseau write that "people and cultures always have given meaning to disease. And that is partly because disease categories have helped to articulate the experience of the body itself, and hence the project of the individual person." Porter and Rousseau emphasize this post-Foucauldian point, asking, "Why should the language of sickness *not* be available for staking out claims about the self? Might *not* there be a therapeutic value and possibly even virtual healthiness in owning one's own disorders?" Roy Porter and G. S. Rousseau, *Gout: The Patrician Malady* (New Haven, CT: Yale University Press, 1998), 284–285; cf. Jackie Stacey, *Teratologies: A Cultural Study of Cancer* (London: Routledge, 1997), 13–15; Christina Crosby, *A Body, Undone: Living On after Great Pain* (New York: New York University Press, 2016), 115–116; Elaine Scarry, *The Body in Pain: The Making and Unmaking of the World* (New York: Oxford University Press, 1985), 6–14.

9 Lauren F. Winner, *A Cheerful and Comfortable Faith: Anglican Religious Practice in the Elite Households of Eighteenth-Century Virginia* (New Haven, CT: Yale University Press, 2010), 143.

10 Hawkins, *Reconstructing Illness*, 2–3, 27; Crane, "'I Have Suffer'd Much Today,'" 370–403; Wear, "Puritan Perceptions of Illness in Seventeenth Century England," 55–99.

11 Roger Chartier, Alain Boureau, and Cécile Dauphin, *Correspondence: Models of Letter-Writing from the Middle Ages to the Nineteenth Century*, trans. Christopher Woodall (Princeton: Princeton University Press, 1997), 2–7; David D. Hall, *Ways of Writing: The Practice and Politics of Text-Making in Seventeenth-Century New England* (Philadelphia: University of Pennsylvania Press, 2008), 9–10; Benedict Anderson, *Imagined Communities: Reflections on the Origin and Spread of Nationalism*, 2nd ed. (1983; New York: Verso, 2006), 10–16. See also the highly influential work on religion and social discipline: E. P. Thompson, *The Making of the English Working Class* (London: Penguin, 1963). For a brief discussion of Thompson and scholarship on religion and social discipline in eighteenth-century England, see Deborah Madden, "Medicine and Moral Reform: The Place of Practical Piety in John Wesley's Art of Physic," *Church History* 73 (2004): 751.

12 Mather, *Wholesome Words*, prefatory comments (no pagination). These comments are not included in the 1721 edition, which instead begins, "From several

MINISTERS of BOSTON, At a time of *Epidemical Sickness* Distressing of the Town." Mather, *Pastoral Letter*, 1.

13 One horrified modern response to Mather's imagery is Maxine Van de Wetering, "A Reconsideration of the Inoculation Controversy," *New England Quarterly* 58 (1985): 46–67. Not only does she miss the biblical reference, Van de Wetering also problematically uses the tract to exemplify Mather's unstinting orthodoxy in the early eighteenth century before his shift to a kinder, Enlightenment figure by the 1720s, overlooking that *Wholesome Words* was republished in the 1720s under a different title. Van de Wetering is part of a long history of scholarship on Mather that focuses on his concern for his own power and corresponding obsession with a harsh theological orthodoxy. See, for example, scholarship related to his role in the inoculation debates in 1720s Boston: Perry Miller, *The New England Mind: From Colony to Province* (Cambridge, MA: Harvard University Press, 1953), 345–366; Robert Middlekauff, *The Mathers: Three Generations of Puritan Intellectuals, 1596–1728* (New York: Oxford University Press, 1971), 354–367. It should be noted that some scholars have looked at inoculation as the first serious contribution to American medicine: Otho T. Beall Jr. and Richard H. Shryock, *Cotton Mather, First Significant Figure in American Medicine* (Baltimore: Johns Hopkins University Press, 1954), and I. Bernard Cohen, ed., *Cotton Mather and American Science and Medicine: With Studies and Documents Concerning the Introduction of Inoculation or Variolation* (New York: Arno, 1980).

14 See, for example, Adrian Chastain Weimer, "From Human Suffering to Divine Friendship: *Meat Out of the Eater* and Devotional Reading in Early New England," *Early American Literature* 54 (2016): 3–39; Harry Stout, *The New England Soul: Preaching and Religious Culture in Colonial New England* (Oxford: Oxford University Press, 1988), 54, 166–167.

15 Mather, *Wholesome Words*, 10, 5.

16 Cotton Mather, *The Angel of Bethesda*, ed. Gordon W. Jones (Barre, MA: American Antiquarian Society, 1972), 6. For a basic introduction and outline of Calvinist understandings of original sin, see John Calvin, *Institutes of the Christian Religion*, ed. John T. McNeill, trans. Ford Lewis Battles, Library of Christian Classics (Louisville, KY: Westminster John Knox Press, 1960), 241–254. The relevant portion is in bk. 2, chap. 1. Elaine Crane points out that contemporary Americans still connect sickness to "moral deficiency." Crane, "'I Have Suffer'd Much Today,'" 402.

17 Unlike other Protestants, Quakers did not believe that infants were born with original sin, but rather thought humans were born with a tendency to sin due to the fall of Adam and Eve. Even so, Quakers appear to have agreed that sickness was a condition associated with the fallenness of human creation, a condition that would be relieved only upon salvation. See, for example, the letter of the Quaker Sarah Rhoads to Samuel W. Fisher during the 1793 yellow fever epidemic in Philadelphia, in which she wrote, "May a Gratefull Sense of Divine Goodness ever live in my Heart, not only During this Awful Dispensation, but may the few remaining Days of my Pilgrimage be spent in a Prepara-

tion, for that Habitation, the Inhabitants of which *never* say I am Sick." Sarah Rhoads to Samuel W. Fisher, 19 Sept. 1793, Samuel W. Fisher Papers, Historical Society of Pennsylvania; cf. Robert Barclay, *An Apology for the True Christian Divinity: Being an Explanation and Vindication of the Principles and Doctrines of the People Called Quakers* (New York: Samuel Wood and Sons, 1827), 94–98.

18 Mather, *Angel of Bethesda* (1972), 6. Note that while *The Angel of Bethesda*, in its entirety, remained unpublished until the twentieth century, part of it did appear in Mather's lifetime: Cotton Mather, *The Angel of Bethesda, Visiting the Invalids of a Miserable World* (New London, CT: Timothy Green, 1722).

19 John Wesley, *Primitive* [*sic*] *Physic; or, An Easy and Natural Method of Curing Most Diseases*, 16th ed. (Trenton, NJ: Quequelle and Wilson, 1788), iii–iv. This book went through twenty-three editions before Wesley's death in 1791 and thirty-seven editions total before 1859. See Deborah Madden, *"A Cheap, Safe, and Natural Medicine": Religion, Medicine, and Culture in John Wesley's Primitive Physic*, Clio Medica 83 (Amsterdam: Rodopi, 2007), 11–12.

20 Katharina Ernst, *Krankheit und Heilung: Die medikale Kultur württembergischer Pietisten im 18. Jahrhundert* (Stuttgart: W. Kohlhammer Verlag, 2003), 71–72; Helm, *Krankheit, Bekehrung und Reform*, 16–22.

21 On the reception of Urlsperger's books in Georgia in 1751, see Johann Martin Boltzius's journal entry from the end of August 1751 in Urlsperger, *DR* (1990), 15:122.

22 Urlsperger, *Der Kranken Gesundheit* (1750), 149. Urlsperger lifted portions from the Nürnberger pastor Bernhard Walter Marperger's *Getreue Anleitung zur wahren Seelen-Cur bei Krancken und Sterbenden* (*Faithful Instruction on the True Soul-Cure for the Sick and the Dying*) (1717) and a posthumous work of Johann Reinhard Hedinger (d. 1704), court preacher in Stuttgart. See Ernst, *Krankheit und Heilung*, 71–72. While the literal translation of *Paradisgärtlein* is "Little Garden of Paradise," it was published in English as Johann Arndt, *The Garden of Paradise* (London: J. Downing, 1716).

23 Urlsperger, *Der Kranken Gesundheit* (1723), pages 2–3 of preface. The 1750 edition has slight changes in the wording. Italics represent bold typeface in the original.

24 Urlsperger, *Der Kranken Gesundheit* (1723), 146–147.

25 Helm, *Krankheit, Bekehrung und Reform*, 16–22; for a discussion of this in the Puritan context, see W. Clark Gilpin, preface to *The Pilgrim's Progress: From This World to That Which Is to Come* and *Grace Abounding to the Chief of Sinners*, by John Bunyan (New York: Vintage, 2004), ix–xvi.

26 Urlsperger, *Der Kranken Gesundheit* (1723), preface pages 3–5. Italicized portions represent bold typeface in the original.

27 Susan Schreiner, "'Why Do the Wicked Live?' Job and David in Calvin's Sermons on Job," in *The Voice from the Whirlwind: Interpreting the Book of Job*, ed. Leo G. Perdue and W. Clark Gilpin (Nashville, TN: Abingdon Press, 1992), 136–143.

28 Mather, *Wholesome Words*, 5, 10.

29 Ronald K. Rittgers, *The Reformation of Suffering: Pastoral Theology and Lay Piety in Late Medieval and Early Modern Germany* (New York: Oxford University Press, 2012), 198.

30 Gilpin, preface to *Pilgrim's Progress*, ix–xvi.

31 George M. Marsden, *Jonathan Edwards: A Life* (New Haven, CT: Yale University Press, 2004), 154.

32 Ralph Waldo Emerson, "Mary Moody Emerson," *Atlantic* (Dec. 1883): www.theatlantic.com.

33 Maxine Van de Wetering, "Reconsideration of the Inoculation Controversy," 46–67; Miller, *New England Mind*, 345–366; Middlekauff, *The Mathers*, 354–367; cf. Beall and Shryock, *Cotton Mather*; Cohen, *Cotton Mather and American Science and Medicine*. There are multiple problems with the reigning characterization of the inoculation controversy, not least that it incorrectly presumes that Calvinist theology prohibits human endeavors in science and benevolence; that is not the topic here, but for John Calvin's discussion on science and medicine, see Calvin, *Institutes of the Christian Religion*, 270–277. The relevant sections are in bk. 2, chap. 2, secs. 12–17.

34 Van de Wetering, "Reconsideration of the Inoculation Controversy," 60–62. I am influenced here by Ludmilla Jordanova's historiographical essay on social constructionist approaches to the history of medicine, in which she writes, "Exponents of a medicalization approach tend to see medical power as gained with relative ease or even simply appropriated. A social constructionist will more likely look for the points of tension, for negotiations and conflicts through which particular kinds of authority may or may not be gained, and specify rather precisely the social groupings involved." Ludmilla Jordanova, "The Social Construction of Medical Knowledge," *Social History of Medicine* 8 (1995): 367–368.

35 Mather, *Wholesome Words*, title page, 2, 6, 8, 10.

36 Ibid., 12–14. See the scriptural gloss and commentary accompanying the Geneva Bible version of Psalm 91.

37 Mather, *Wholesome Words*, 15–16; "cordial, adj. and n.," in *Oxford English Dictionary Online* (Oxford: Oxford University Press, 2016), www.oed.com.

38 Mather, *Wholesome Words*, 17–22.

39 Ibid., title page.

40 For a classic study examining the role of Pietism in the emergence of nationalism, see Koppel F. Pinson, *Pietism as a Factor in the Rise of German Nationalism* (New York: Columbia University Press, 1934). Pinson argued that the "early German nationalist was what I have termed an 'enlightened Pietist,' an individual deeply imbued with emotional enthusiasm and that sense of dependence so strongly emphasized in Pietist religious literature from Spener to Schleiermacher, but one who no longer could find the support which he craved solely in his Christian religion but was forced to seek a secular outlet for his enthusiasm and his feeling of social kinship. This outlet was provided by the national group." Arguments about Pietism, its authoritarianism, and its role in nation building continue.

See Richard L. Gawthrop, *Pietism and the Making of Eighteenth-Century Prussia* (Cambridge: Cambridge University Press, 1993). Gawthrop argues that "Francke and his co-workers . . . regarded themselves as an elite group with the power to direct and control the souls entrusted to them. They legitimized this position, not by birthright or clerical office, but by the knowledge of God's commands made possible by their post-conversion 'experience' of God. They claimed to possess, as many modern ideologues have done, a type of knowledge that was simultaneously empirical and absolute" (152–153). In response to such scholarly characterizations, Jonathan Strom has argued that the emphasis on social discipline within studies of Pietism has been, in part, shaped by scholarship on the early modern era that, particularly since the 1980s, has stressed confessionalization, discipline, and state formation. Strom argues that such statist paradigms are not as useful for understanding Pietist movements, which often emerged in response to or in opposition to confessionalization. Jonathan Strom, "Problems and Promises of Pietism Research," *Church History* 71 (2002): 553–554.

41 Ernst, *Krankheit und Heiligung*, 71–72; Helm, *Krankheit, Bekehrung und Reform*, 16–22; Johann Martin Boltzius's journal entry from late August 1751 in Urlsperger, *DR* (1990), 15:122.

42 Urlsperger reported on a number of social divisions within Augsburg, including factions that were created among community members as displayed in raucous behavior in local beerhouses. "Bericht von Samuel Urlsperger über verschiedene Konferenzen mit dem evangelischen Ministerium Augsburg zu umstrittenen Textstellen aus seiner Schrift 'Der Kranken Gesundheit und den [*sic*] Sterbenden Leben,'" 1723, Francke-Nachlasses der Staatsbibliothek zu Berlin-Preußischer Kulturbesitz (hereafter Stab/F) 21, 2, 1/7: 89. I viewed this item on microfilm at the Archive of the Francke Foundations in Halle.

43 "Veränderungsvorschläge zu verschiedenen Textstellen aus Samuel Urlspergers Schrift 'Der Kranken Gesundheit und der Sterbenden Leben,'" 1723, Stab/F 21, 2, 1/7: 92.

44 Martin Luther, "On the Bondage of the Will," in *Luther and Erasmus: Free Will and Salvation*, ed. and trans. E. Gordon Rupp and Philip S. Watson, Library of Christian Classics (Louisville, KY: Westminster John Knox Press, 2006), 329.

45 Samuel Urlsperger to August Hermann Francke, 28 Oct. 1725, Stab/F 21, 2, 1/7: 11.

46 Alexander Pyrges, *Das Kolonialprojekt EbenEzer* (Stuttgart: Steiner, 2015), 333–334.

47 Rittgers, *Reformation of Suffering*, 198–199.

48 Urlsperger, *Der Kranken Gesundheit* (1723), preface, 3–5.

49 Mather, *Wholesome Words*, 12–14; Urlsperger, *Der Kranken Gesundheit* (1750), 147.

50 Urlsperger, *Der Kranken Gesundheit* (1723), 1–2.

51 Ibid., 1–2.

52 Ibid., 1–2.

53 Ibid., 3–5.

54 Ibid., 3–5. It should be noted that Urlsperger not only skirted close to a language of works righteousness here but also appealed to a mystical notion of surrender.

55 Ibid., 147–148.

56 Ibid., preface page 5.

57 On emotion and mourning practices, see Winner, *Cheerful and Comfortable Faith*, 160. The discussion of intimacy, relationship, and the practice of emotions in this section is informed by the work of Constance Furey and Monique Sheer. Constance M. Furey, "Body, Society, and Subjectivity in Religious Studies," *Journal of the American Academy of Religion* 80 (2012): 7–33; Monique Scheer, "Are Emotions a Kind of Practice (and Is That What Makes Them Have a History)? A Bourdieuian Approach to Understanding Emotion," *History and Theory* 51 (2012): 193–220. On intimacy and relationship, Furey writes, "The focus on intimacy and intimate relationships . . . corrects the tendency in body and society studies to focus on disciplinary practices and discursive control. The study of intimate relationships between people who claim one another as family, friends, parents, children, lovers, or dependents deepens the study of power by showing how power is relationally internalized, enacted, and transformed, and by exploring the multiple ways that the desire manifest in these relational exchanges can elude conscious control and social containment, with destructive and formative consequences for individuals and society alike" (23). Scheer's work on emotions as a practice develops from the work of Pierre Bourdieu. She writes, "Conceiving of emotions as practices or acts also provides a way of counterbalancing the dominant language of emotions as always and essentially *reactions*, or triggered responses. . . . Instead of searching the historical record for the 'trigger' to explain the emotion that followed, the emotions can be viewed as the meaningful cultural activity of ascribing, interpreting, and constructing an event as a trigger." This understanding of emotions as practice rather than simply reaction shapes the way we consider subjectivity. Scheer writes, "As Michel Foucault argued, subjectivity can be achieved only through passivity. We are subjected by and through emotions—the fact that they 'overcome' us and are outside our control is the embodied effect of our ties to other people, as well as to social conventions, to values, to language. Emotions do not pit their agency and autonomy against ours; they emerge from the very fact that subjectivity and autonomy are always bounded by the conditions of their existence, by the fundamental sociability of the human body and self" (206–207).

58 Mather, *Diary*, 446. For context, see Silverman, *Life and Times of Cotton Mather*, 179–184, 269–275.

59 Furey, "Body, Society, and Subjectivity," 23–25. The importance of sympathy and community is discussed at length in Abram Van Engen, *Sympathetic Puritans: Calvinist Fellow Feeling in Early New England* (Oxford: Oxford University Press, 2015).

60 Mather, *Diary*, 425–445.

61 Ibid., 441–442.

62 Ibid., 455–456; Cotton Mather, *Meat Out of the Eater* (Boston: Eliot, 1703), n.p.

63 Following the translation in the Geneva Bible.

64 Weimer, "From Human Suffering to Divine Friendship," 8–11. Weimer details the marginalia and signs of use that appear in the few extant volumes of the various editions of Wigglesworth's work, highlighting the personal significance of the work and its use in colonial devotional practice. Michael Wigglesworth, *Meat Out of the Eater* (Cambridge, MA: Samuel Green and Marmaduke Johnson, 1670).

65 Mather, *Meat Out of the Eater*, 192–193, 211–218.

66 See Mather, *Diary*, 450; Mather, *Meat Out of the Eater*, 221–222, and frontispiece to section on Abigail Mather's funeral.

67 On Calvin's understanding of the church, see Calvin, *Institutes of the Christian Religion*, 1012–1014 (bk. 4, chap. 1, sec. 2).

68 Mather, *Wholesome Words*, 17–22.

69 Ibid., 22–24.

70 Ibid., 22–24.

71 Cf. Furey, "Body, Society, and Subjectivity," 23.

72 Bruce Hindmarsh, "Religious Conversion as Narrative and Autobiography," in *The Oxford Handbook of Religious Conversion*, ed. Lewis R. Rambo and Charles E. Farhadian (Oxford: Oxford University Press, 2014), 347–350, 360; John Bunyan, *The Pilgrim's Progress* (Oxford: Oxford University Press, 1984). Cf. Richard A. Rosengarten, "The Recalcitrant *Distentio* of Ricoeur's *Time and Narrative*," *Literature & Theology* 27 (2013): 174–175. See also Stacey, *Teratologies*. The author, a sociologist, describes the challenges of rewriting the narrative of her body and sickness as she progressed through cancer: "The usual temporal sequencing is both disrupted and reimposed in the search for order, reason and predictability. The past must now be reimagined and rescripted. . . . In the light of the diagnosis, the recent past must be reexamined for clues of this newly revealed deception" (4–5).

73 Bruce Hindmarsh, *The Evangelical Conversion Narrative: Spiritual Autobiography in Early Modern England* (Oxford: Oxford University Press, 2008), 43–46, 51–61, 67–80, 91–95, 131. Hindmarsh is influenced by Jürgen Habermas's understanding of the "bourgeois public sphere" in *The Structural Transformation of the Public Sphere: An Inquiry into a Category of Bourgeois Society*, trans. Thomas Burger (Cambridge, MA: MIT Press, 1991). Hindmarsh argues, however, that although the social transformations of the eighteenth century contributed to revivalism, "the international Protestant awakening of the eighteenth century was constituted chiefly by the repeated experience of evangelical conversion, and that there was an irreducibly religious element in this experience that was in continuity with seventeenth-century Puritanism and related traditions" (80). See also Hindmarsh, "Religious Conversion as Narrative and Autobiography," 343–368; Gilpin, preface to *Pilgrim's Progress*, ix–xvi; Hall, *Ways of Writing*, 9–10.

74 Michael McGiffert, ed., *God's Plot: The Paradoxes of Puritan Piety; Being the Autobiography and Journal of Thomas Shepard* (Amherst: University of Massachusetts Press, 1972), 20, 24–26.

75 Samuel Urlsperger to August Hermann Francke, 18 June 1718, Stab/F 21, 2, 1/7: 33.

76 Urlsperger, *Der Kranken Gesundheit* (1750), 142–145.

77 Ibid., 145–146.

78 Ibid., 148.

79 Mather, *Wholesome Words*, 22–24.

80 It is not entirely clear what this disease was; some scholars have translated it as "the purples." See George F. Jones, *The Georgia Dutch: From the Rhine and Danube to the Savannah, 1733–1783* (Athens: University of Georgia Press, 1992), 235. There were, in the same time period, epidemics of measles and scarlet fever in Ebenezer. See the journal entries in Urlsperger, *DR* (1989), 13:161–207. For Jones's explanation of the Rothe Friesel, see Urlsperger, *DR* (1989), 13:v–vi, 226n24.

81 On the epidemic among the cattle, see Johann Martin Boltzius (hereafter JMB) and Israel Christian Gronau (hereafter ICG) to Gotthilf August Francke (hereafter GAF), Aug. 1743, AFSt/M A 11: 3. The story is from Jones's translation of Boltzius's published journal; see Urlsperger, *DR* (1990), 14:186. The scriptural quotation is from the King James Version.

82 Furey, "Body, Society, and Subjectivity," 25.

83 Hawkins, *Reconstructing Illness*, 2–3, 27.

2. WRITING SICKNESS, WITNESSING PROVIDENCE

1 Eli Forbes to Ebenezer Parkman, 17 Jan. and 2 Mar. 1776, Parkman Family Papers, box 3, folder 3, American Antiquarian Society (hereafter AAS); cf. Lauren F. Winner, *A Cheerful and Comfortable Faith: Anglican Religious Practice in the Elite Households of Eighteenth-Century Virginia* (New Haven, CT: Yale University Press, 2010), 141–143, 147.

2 Cf. Mary Lindemann, *Medicine and Society in Early Modern Europe* (Cambridge: Cambridge University Press, 1999), 64–65.

3 Anne Hunsaker Hawkins, *Reconstructing Illness: Studies in Pathography* (West Lafayette, IN: Purdue University Press, 1993), 2–3, 27; cf. Arthur W. Frank, *The Wounded Storyteller: Body, Illness and Ethics* (Chicago: University of Chicago Press, 1997); Arthur Kleinman, *The Illness Narratives: Suffering, Healing, and the Human Condition* (New York: Basic Books, 1988).

4 Winner, *Cheerful and Comfortable Faith*, 143; Jackie Stacey, *Teratologies: A Cultural Study of Cancer* (London: Routledge, 1997), 4–5, 8–17; Hawkins, *Reconstructing Illness*, 2–3.

5 Bruce Hindmarsh, "Religious Conversion as Narrative and Autobiography," in *The Oxford Handbook of Religious Conversion*, ed. Lewis R. Rambo and Charles E. Farhadian (Oxford: Oxford University Press, 2014), 348; Bruce Hindmarsh, *The Evangelical Conversion Narrative: Spiritual Autobiography in Early Modern England* (Oxford: Oxford University Press, 2008), 131.

6 See Asbury's journal entries for 28 June and 30 June 1774 in Frances Asbury, *An Extract from the Journal of Francis Asbury, Bishop of the Methodist-Episcopal Church in America, from August 7, 1771, to December 29, 1778* (Philadelphia: Crukshank, 1792), 130–134; cf. Hebrews 12:8.

7 *The Arminian Magazine: Consisting of Extracts and Original Treatises on General Redemption* (Philadelphia: Prichard & Hall, 1789). The magazine did not sell as quickly as hoped, and Asbury's journal was spun off into a stand-alone publication beginning in 1792. According to the introduction to the 1792 volume, there had "been no intention for many years, of making [the journal] public." But Asbury's journal, which *"contains the simple exercises of the author's mind and life,"* was well-adapted for *"plain and simple people, who will look for nothing elaborate or refined; but for genuine experience and naked truth."* Asbury, *Extract from the Journal*, preface page A.

8 Hindmarsh, *Evangelical Conversion Narrative*, 102–137; cf. W. R. Ward, *The Protestant Evangelical Awakening* (Cambridge: Cambridge University Press, 1992), 8–9. For examples among German speakers, see the journals of JMB, a Pietist missionary in colonial Georgia. These journals were edited by the Augsburg pastor Samuel Urlsperger and, later, by his son Johann Urlsperger and published in Halle almost annually. The eighteen continuations of the original detailed reports can be found bound together in three volumes: Samuel Urlsperger, ed., *Ausführliche Nachricht von den saltzburgischen Emigranten, die sich in America niedergelassen haben* (Halle/Augsburg, 1735–1753). For the second series, see Samuel Urlsperger and Johann Urlsperger, eds., *Amerikanisches Ackerwerck Gottes* (Augsburg, 1753–1759, 1766). For English translations of the journals, see Samuel Urlsperger, ed., *Detailed Reports on the Salzburger Emigrants Who Settled in America*, trans. and ed. George Fenwick Jones et al. (Athens: University of Georgia Press, 1968–1995). Reports from Ebenezer and other missions, such as Tranquebar, appeared in self-standing editions and were also excerpted in other devotional publications, such as the *Geistliches Magazin* (*Spiritual Magazine*). This German-language magazine featured topics from missions to Native Americans in New England to the conversion of Africans in England and the Danish West Indies. See, for example, "Einige gute Nachrichten aus dem Reiche Gottes: I. Von dem gegenwärtigen Zustande der Saltzburgischen Emigranten in der Americanischen Provintz Georgien," *Geistliches Magazin* 1, no. 1 (1761): 160–175; "Fortsetzung guter Nachrichten aus dem Reiche Gottes, und zwar von den Anstalten zur Bekehrung der armen Negers, auf den Königlich-Dänischen Inseln St. Thomas, St. Croix, und St. Jean," *Geistliches Magazin* 1, no. 4 (1762): 410–430; "Vorläufige Anmerckungen über nachstehende, aus dem Englischen in das Teutsche übersetzte Nachricht, von den Indianischen Armen=Schulen," *Geistliches Magazin* 3, no. 2 (1766): 231–302; "Auszug aus einem Schreiben des Hrn. George Davis, an den Hrn. George Withfield [sic] in London," *Geistliches Magazin* 4, no. 4 (1770): 442–444. There were other, more radical Pietist publications featuring news from around the world as well. See Johann Samuel Carl, ed., *Geistliche Fama* (Berleburg, 1730–1744). This work was sometimes pseudonymously published under "Christianus Democritus" and has been occasionally misattributed to Johann Konrad Dippel, who also used this pseudonym.

9   Ebenezer Parkman, "Memoir of Mrs. Sarah Pierpont," Parkman Family Papers, box 2, folder 4, AAS. Parkman included quotations from Pierpont's journal in his introductory section (there is no pagination in this unpublished memoir). The "motions of the Holy Spirit" is a long-standing theme within Christianity and can be traced within Puritanism to, for example, Richard Sibbes. See Richard Sibbes, *The Complete Works of Richard Sibbes*, vol. 2 (Edinburgh: James Nichol, 1862), 69.

10   Parkman, "Memoir of Mrs. Sarah Pierpont." In a biography of the eighteenth-century Congregationalist Sarah Osborn, Catherine Brekus has argued that writing a memoir allowed Osborn to give "her life a new religious meaning, and whenever she longed for tangible evidence of her salvation she would sit down to reread her story." Catherine A. Brekus, *Sarah Osborn's World: The Rise of Evangelical Christianity in America* (New Haven, CT: Yale University Press, 2013), 133.

11   Suffering could cause a breakdown of language, a phenomenon that the literary scholar Elaine Scarry has well described, but eighteenth-century Protestants made determined efforts to find language and to describe suffering—a moment, Scarry argues, akin to "the birth of language itself," and in which a certain reality is expressed or substantiated. Elaine Scarry, *The Body in Pain: The Making and Unmaking of the World* (New York: Oxford University Press, 1985), 6–14. I find Scarry's work compelling, particularly in its relation to the effects pain has on language in situations of torture and war. I have reservations about the second part of her book—on the "making" of the world—and find it difficult to apply her analysis of the scriptures and Marx to the eighteenth-century manuscript sources with which I am working here. But I think Scarry herself has not settled on a conclusion on the significance of "making" in these narratives: "It may be . . . that no other two texts in western civilization contain such sustained and passionate meditations on the nature of the human imagination. Their shared conviction that the 'problem of suffering' takes place and must be understood with the more expansive frame of the 'problem of creating' may at the very least be taken as an invitation to attend with more commitment, to the subject of making, a subject whose philosophic and ethical import we do not yet fully understand." See 277.

12   John Hargrave to Henry Banks, 1 Sept. 1797, 6 Sept. 1797, 11 Sept. 1797, 20 Sept. 1797, 29 Sept. 1797, 13 Sept. 1798, 16 Sept. 1798, 24 Sept. 1798, 19 Nov. 1798, Henry Banks Papers, sec. 1, folder 8, Virginia Historical Society (hereafter VHS). On tools required for letter writing in this era, see Konstantin Dierks, "Letter Writing, Stationery Supplies, and Consumer Modernity in the Eighteenth-Century Atlantic World," *Early American Literature* 41 (2006): 473–494.

13   John Hargrave to Henry Banks, 11 Dec. 1798, Henry Banks Papers, sec. 1, folder 8, VHS.

14   GAF to JMB and ICG, 15 June 1744, AFSt/M 5 A 11: 12. Unless otherwise noted, all translations are my own.

15   JMB to Samuel Theodor Albinus, 16 May 1754, in JMB, *The Letters of Johann Martin Boltzius: Lutheran Pastor in Ebenezer, Georgia*, ed. and trans. Russell Kleckley

in collaboration with Jürgen Gröschl (Lewiston, NY: Edwin Mellen Press, 2009) (hereafter JMB, *Letters*), 602.

16 JMB to GAF, 27 June 1760, in JMB, *Letters*, 672–684.

17 Parkman, "Memoir of Mrs. Sarah Pierpont." Pierpont wrote a letter with similar reflections on illness and the human body to someone in the Parkman family (the recipient is unclear) on 9 Aug. 1745; it can be found in the Parkman Family Papers, box 3, folder 2, AAS (although note that there Pierpont's name is spelled "Peirpont"). The whole of the passage cited above (from the memoir) reads, "Labouring under great bodily weakness (and knowing Helpe is to be had in God only) I retird this Morning (as I have heretofore practicd, under all my Troubles: and have found it good so to do) The Lord enabled me to pour out my Troubles before him (my Spiritual as well as bodily Maladies) To plead for deliverance if it may consist with his blessed will but above all to give me a will swallowed up in his good pleasure. I was led I trust with all my Heart to bless the Lord for every Affliction that ever he laid upon me even the most bitter of them at the same Time bewailing the wretchedness of Heart & Life that call for so frequent Chastisements and Now blessed Saviour thou great Physician of Soul & Body only speak the word Say Be thou healed be thou cleansed and the Cure shall be effected to the glory of thy great Name Lord let it be so & let me be forever devoted to thee May I live a Life of Holiness be much in the Duties of Selfe Denial & Mortification Patience & every other Christian Grace O that I might be a shining Example before all I shall Converse with that my Life & Conversation may be a Continual & powerful Sermon to all about me Dear Saviour this is the Life I long to live and tho I am sensible I can no more live such a Life of my Selfe & hone my own strength than I can create a world yet I know if thou pleases thou canst effect it O blessed Spirit of all Grace & Power grant me thy renewing, quicking & sanctifying Presence and the thing shall be done & the Glory shall be thine O adorable Three amen, amen amen."

18 Scarry, *Body in Pain*, 6–14.

19 Brekus, *Sarah Osborn's World*, 290–291.

20 Greg Dening, "Texts of Self," in *Through a Glass Darkly: Reflections on Personal Identity in Early America*, ed. Ronald Hoffman, Mechal Sobel, and Fredrika J. Teute (Chapel Hill: University of North Carolina Press, 1997), 161–162; Catherine A. Brekus, ed., *Sarah Osborn's Collected Writings* (New Haven, CT: Yale University Press, 2017), 93, 364n21; cf. Mark 7:37; Psalm 118:13; 1 Samuel 7:12.

21 Accounts of final sickness and death were frequently requested. See, for example, the requests recorded in Samuel Stearns to Simon Houghton, 15 May 1784, Samuel Stearns Papers, folder 1, AAS; Elizabeth Stearns to Martha Houghton, 25 Dec. 1810, Samuel Stearns Papers, folder 1, AAS. In the first, Samuel Stearns requests an account of his sister's last days; the second is a response from Elizabeth Stearns to her sister-in-law's request for details of Samuel Stearns's final sickness.

22 Parkman cited Pierpont's earlier journal entries on the illness and deaths of her near relations to add support for the plausibility of his imagined account, and

then he ventured into a scripturally infused narrative of Pierpont as a fearless and faithful martyr. Parkman, "Memoir of Mrs. Sarah Pierpont."

23 As Catherine Brekus has shown, Samuel Hopkins, the pastor of Sarah Osborn, similarly tried to fill in the silences of Osborn's later life with a "happy ending" of spiritual "serenity." Brekus, *Sarah Osborn's World*, 321. Cf. the discussion of women and deathbed scenes in Winner, *Cheerful and Comfortable Faith*, 147: "The choreography of the deathbed scene often provided dying women a powerful opportunity to speak—to have their words listened to attentively, and recorded."

24 Parkman, "Memoir of Mrs. Sarah Pierpont."

25 Bruce Redford, *The Converse of the Pen: Acts of Intimacy in the Eighteenth-Century Familiar Letter* (Chicago: University of Chicago Press, 1986), 7–9.

26 Scholars have demonstrated how eighteenth-century laymen and laywomen engaged the expanding epistemological emphasis on firsthand observation and used familiar genres, like the letter or the conversion narrative, in order to write about a range of topics—from medical cases to religious experience. Sarah Knott, "The Patient's Case: Sentimental Empiricism and Knowledge in the Early American Republic," *William and Mary Quarterly* 67 (2010): 645–676; Sarah Rivett, *The Science of the Soul in Colonial New England* (Chapel Hill: University of North Carolina Press, 2011), 5–17, 29–31; Hindmarsh, *Evangelical Conversion Narrative*, 20–22, 79–80; Brekus, *Sarah Osborn's World*, 9–10, 185. On the *Ars moriendi*, see Brad Gregory, *Salvation at Stake: Christian Martyrdom in Early Modern Europe* (Cambridge, MA: Harvard University Press, 1999), 52–53, 195; Winner, *Cheerful and Comfortable Communion*, 145; Austra Reinis, *Reforming the Art of Dying: The Ars Moriendi in the German Reformation (1519–1528)* (Farnham: Ashgate, 2006). On the use of martyrological narrative in early modern Protestantism, see John N. King, *Foxe's Book of Martyrs and Early Modern Print Culture* (Cambridge: Cambridge University Press, 2006); John R. Knott, "John Foxe and the Joy of Suffering," *Sixteenth-Century Journal* 27 (1996): 721–734; Adrian Chastain Weimer, *Martyrs' Mirror: Persecution and Holiness in Early New England* (Oxford: Oxford University Press, 2011); Philippa Koch, "'God Made This Fire for Our Comfort': Puritan Children's Literature in Context," in *The Study of Children in Religions: A Methods Handbook*, ed. Susan B. Ridgely (New York: New York University Press, 2011), 202–219.

27 Eli Forbes to Ebenezer Parkman, 17 Jan. and 2 Mar. 1776, Parkman Family Papers, box 3, folder 3, AAS; Redford, *Converse of the Pen*, 7–9.

28 Catharina Gronau to Samuel Urlsperger, 18 Jan. 1745, AFSt/M 5 A 11: 28a; Catharina Gronau to Christian Friedrich Gottlob Gronau, 19 Jan. 1745, AFSt/M 5 A 11: 28. A note at the top of the letter to Urlsperger describes it as a copy. I am unsure where the original might be, but I find the language and writing style of the two letters consistent. Without evidence to the contrary, I am treating the copy as faithfully done. Gronau begins each letter with words from the hymns "Jehova ist mein Hirt und Hüter, nun wird kein mangel treffen mich" and "Gott du Tieffe sonder grund!" See Johann Anastasius Freylinghausen, *Geistreiches Gesang-Buch,*

den Kern alter und neuer Lieder in sich haltend, ed. GAF (Halle: Waysenhaus, 1741), 233, 266–267. Hymnals were often included in the shipments of goods to Ebenezer from Halle and were occasionally directly requested by the pastors. See, for example, JMB and ICG to GAF, 7 Jan. 1743, in JMB, *Letters*, 356.

29 Catharina Gronau to Christian Friedrich Gottlob Gronau, 19 Jan. 1745, AFSt/M 5 A 11: 28; cf. Job 1:21.

30 Catharina Gronau to Samuel Urlsperger, 18 Jan. 1745, AFSt/M 5 A 11: 28a; Catharina Gronau to Christian Friedrich Gottlob Gronau, 19 Jan. 1745, AFSt/M 5 A 11: 28.

31 The German Bible to which Boltzius referred has a different numeration of the verses of Tobit than is found in English versions. The original verse in the Luther Bible (1545) reads, "Geheimnisse eines Königs soll man verschweigen; aber Gottes Werke offenbar zu machen und zu preisen bringt Ehre."

32 JMB to GAF, 14 Oct. 1741, in JMB, *Letters*, 338–342 (following Kleckley's translation).

33 These trials included, as the letter enumerates, crop failures, anxieties about relations with the Spanish during the War of Jenkins' Ear, increasing animosities with Moravians in nearby Savannah (which, in turn, caused tensions in Ebenezer's relationship with friend and benefactor George Whitefield), and flood damage to the wood mill. On the Moravians, note that Boltzius was especially concerned with the "Herrnhuter Hagen." See JMB to GAF, 13 May 1741, in JMB, *Letters*, 325. Hagen/Haagen—and his ties to George Whitefield—had been an ongoing concern of the Ebenezer ministers and GAF. See ICG to GAF, 20 Sept. 1740, AFSt/M 5 A 9: 15, and GAF to ICG, 27 Jan. 1741, AFSt/M 5 A 9: 22. For another example of Boltzius's citation of Tobit 12:8, see JMB to GAF, 27 June 1760, in JMB, *Letters*, 672–684.

34 John Ballantine Diary, Apr.–Aug. 1743, AAS. For an example of Ballantine's summary charts, see the entry at the end of 1757. This is also the year in which, according to the transcriber and editor, Ballantine ceased to use an interleaved almanac for his journal. I do not have a population estimate for Westfield at this time. Ballantine would occasionally record the number of church members, but not everyone in the community was a member and Ballantine visited, prayed for, and attended the funerals of non-church members, including affiliated adults, children, Africans, and "Separates." For more information on diaries in interleaved almanacs, see Thomas Knoles, "A Tour of the New England Diary, 1650–1900," in *In Our Own Words: New England Diaries, 1600 to the Present*, ed. Peter Benes, Dublin Seminar for New England Folklife Annual Proceedings 1 (Boston: Boston University Press, 2006–2007), 27–41.

35 John Ballantine Diary, 10 and 14 July 1743; 25 and 26 Jan. 1759, AAS.

36 John Ballantine Diary, 29 May, 24 June, 29 June, 31 Aug., 14 Sept. 1759, AAS.

37 John Ballantine Diary, 23 Sept., 10 Nov. 1759, AAS; cf. John 9:4.

38 Thaddeus Maccarty to Mary West and Lucretia Maccarty, 12 Jan. 1784, Maccarty Family Papers, AAS.

39 Thaddeus Maccarty Sermon, 26 Nov. 1779, Maccarty Family Papers, AAS. This particular sermon can be found in the booklet labeled "1. Worcester, June 23d. 1779, No. 457." It is the "second sermon" in the book and is labeled "No. 458." The text is Psalm 30:5. Maccarty paraphrases a commentary on Psalm 30:5 by Matthew Henry (1662–1714), a Presbyterian minister. Matthew Henry, *Commentary on the Whole Bible Volume III (Job to Song of Solomon)* (1708–1710), n.p., see chap. 30: Psalms. Also available online at www.ccel.org.

40 Justus Forward Diary, 1, 12–16, 26 Apr., 20–22 May, 13 June 1766, AAS.

41 Justus Forward Diary, 24–27 May, 13 June 1766, AAS.

42 JMB to GAF, 14 Sept. 1750, in JMB, *Letters*, 571–572. I have followed Kleckley's translation here, but I also consulted the original manuscript: JMB to GAF, 14 Sept. 1750, AFSt/M 5 B 1: 41; cf. John 2:4; Mark 5:36; Luke 8:50.

43 Mary Fleming to Charles Fleming, 16 Apr. 1777, Mss2 F6295 a 1, VHS; cf. 1 Corinthians 2:9.

44 Charles Taylor, *A Secular Age* (Cambridge, MA: Harvard University Press, 2007), 266–274, 649; Brekus, *Sarah Osborn's World*, 83–85; on debates over predestination, see Peter Thuesen, *Predestination: The American Career of a Contentious Doctrine* (Oxford: Oxford University Press, 2009), 75–99.

45 W. Clark Gilpin, preface to *The Pilgrim's Progress: From This World to That Which Is to Come* and *Grace Abounding to the Chief of Sinners*, by John Bunyan (New York: Vintage, 2004), ix–xvi; Brekus, *Sarah Osborn's World*, 318, 322–329.

46 See Jeremy Belknap to Ebenezer Hazard, 12 Dec. 1788, 8 Dec. 1792; Ebenezer Hazard to Jeremy Belknap, 17 Dec. 1788, 13 Jan. 1789, 28 Mar. 1789, 4 Apr. 1789, 14 Nov. 1792, in Jeremy Belknap and Ebenezer Hazard, *The Belknap Papers*, Collections of the Massachusetts Historical Society, 5th series (Boston: Massachusetts Historical Society, 1877), 2:81, 84, 96, 113, 115, 316, 318.

47 Richard Rosengarten, *Henry Fielding and the Narration of Providence: Divine Design and the Incursions of Evil* (New York: Palgrave, 2000), 22–23; Taylor, *Secular Age*, 232–233.

48 John Ballantine Diary, 15 Mar. 1759, 24 June 1759, 14 Sept. 1759, 13 Aug. 1760, AAS.

49 Cotton Mather, *Wholesome Words: A Visit of Advice, Given unto Families That Are Visited with Sickness* (Boston: Henchman, 1713), 22–24.

50 Eli Forbes to Ebenezer Parkman, 17 Jan., 2 Mar. 1776, Parkman Family Papers, box 3, folder 3, AAS; cf. Psalm 46:10.

51 Forbes edited this section of his letter as he struggled with voice and pronouns. I have noted the corrections to the original in the following transcription: "She prayed me to imbrace the first opportunity to acquaint ~~my~~ her Father of ~~my~~ her Death and thank him for his pious Care of ~~my~~ her Youth, tell him [inserted in margin: "So she"] those impressions made on my mind by the grace of God thru his pious care offerd me the greatest Support in Death." Eli Forbes to Ebenezer Parkman, 17 Jan., 2 Mar. 1776, Parkman Family Papers, box 3, folder 3, AAS.

52 Eli Forbes to Ebenezer Parkman, 14 Mar. 1776, Parkman Family Papers, box 3, folder 3, AAS.

53 Samuel West, Memoirs (1807), 5–8, AAS.

54 Ibid., 83–87, AAS.

55 Mather, *Wholesome Words*, 22–24; West, Memoirs, 83–87, AAS. As Christopher Grasso writes, "Death, believers said, was the ultimate test—the existential crisis revealing the pathetic inadequacy of skeptical philosophy." Christopher Grasso, *Skepticism and American Faith: From the Revolution to the Civil War* (New York: Oxford University Press, 2018), 482.

56 West, Memoirs, 150, AAS.

57 Brekus, *Sarah Osborn's World*, 87; E. Brooks Holifield, *Theology in America: Christian Thought from the Age of the Puritans to the Civil War* (New Haven, CT: Yale University Press, 2003), 135–149.

58 West, Memoirs, 150, AAS.

59 Ibid., 324–325.

60 Ibid., 151.

61 Ibid., 36. West might have developed this perspective from his father, who "in old age took great pleasure in recollecting and repeating to his children particular instances of the goodness of God which he had experienced in the course of his life." See 152. For examples of West's various endings and beginnings, see, for example, 202–207 and 308–310.

62 Ibid., 206.

3. EXPERIENCE AND THE SOUL IN EIGHTEENTH-CENTURY MEDICINE

1 JMB to GAF, 21 Apr. 1748, in JMB, *The Letters of Johann Martin Boltzius: Lutheran Pastor in Ebenezer, Georgia*, ed. and trans. Russell Kleckley in collaboration with Jürgen Gröschl, (Lewiston, NY: Edwin Mellen Press, 2009), 495–496 (hereafter JMB, *Letters*).

2 Thilo writes they were eating "*Tabackpfeiffer Stückgen (Stengel wie sie es nannten)*." Christian Ernst Thilo to GAF, Sept. 1747, AFSt/M 5 A 11: 76.

3 GAF to JMB, 9 Sept. 1748, AFSt/M5A11: 87. Outgoing letters from Halle available in the archives were copies or drafts of the letters actually sent. Their composition does not signify their reception at the intended destination.

4 JMB, journal entry, 11 July 1750, in Samuel Urlsperger, ed., *Detailed Reports on the Salzburger Emigrants Who Settled in America*, trans. and ed. George Fenwick Jones et al. (Athens: University of Georgia Press, 1989), 14:89 (hereafter Urlsperger, *DR*). Along with this medical advice, Boltzius also circulated an article he translated regarding a famous cure for the rattlesnake bite, which had been advanced by an enslaved man named Caesar.

5 Romans 7:18–19 (New Revised Standard Version).

6 A version of this chapter previously appeared as Philippa Koch, "Experience and the Soul in Eighteenth-Century Medicine," *Church History: Studies in Christian-*

ity and Culture 85 (2016): 552–586. © *Church History: Studies in Christianity and Culture.* Reprinted with permission.

7 The U.S. National Library of Medicine at the National Institute of Health has a helpful introduction with visuals to the history of the "passions" on its website for the past exhibit "Emotions and Disease." See "The Balance of Passions," *Emotions and Disease* (2000), www.nlm.nih.gov.

8 See the introduction of W. F. Bynum and Roy Porter, eds., *Medical Fringe & Medical Orthodoxy, 1750–1850* (London: Croom Helm, 1987), 1–4; Deborah Madden, *"A Cheap, Safe, and Natural Medicine": Religion, Medicine, and Culture in John Wesley's Primitive Physic,* Clio Medica 83 (Amsterdam: Rodopi, 2007), 99–114. For a fascinating history of medicine written by an eighteenth-century practitioner, see William Smellie, *A Treatise on the Theory and Practice of Midwifery,* 5th ed. (London: Wilson, 1766), i–lxxi. Smellie is a good example of both the "mechanistic" trend in medicine as well as a continuing insistence on empirical "case" studies. He developed a machine to mimic a pregnant woman for his in-person lectures; he also published, in the second volume of his *Treatise,* extensive cases. Toward the end of his history, which makes up the bulk of his introduction, Smellie remarked that he found in "the ancients several valuable jewels" but also presciently noted that every "young practitioner" should know "that almost every system hath been overthrown by that which followed it" (lxviii, lxx). For excellent historiographical overviews on the history of medicine, see Ludmilla Jordanova, "The Social Construction of Medical Knowledge," *Social History of Medicine* 8 (1995): 361–381; Mary E. Fissell, "Making Meaning from the Margins: The New Cultural History of Medicine," in *Locating Medical History: The Stories and Their Meanings,* ed. Frank Huisman and John Harley Warner (Baltimore: Johns Hopkins University Press, 2004), 364–389.

9 This is especially found in the debates over John Wesley's medical work. See G. S. Rousseau, "John Wesley's *Primitive Physic* (1747)," *Harvard Library Bulletin* 16 (1968): 242–256; J. W. Haas, "John Wesley's View on Science and Christianity: An Examination of the Charge of Antiscience," *Church History* 63 (1994): 378–392; John C. English, "John Wesley and Isaac Newton's 'System of the World,'" *Proceedings of the Wesley Historical Society* 48 (1991): 69–86; Madden, *"A Cheap, Safe, and Natural Medicine,"* 109–125.

10 See, for example, Anita Guerrini, *Obesity and Depression in the Enlightenment: The Life and Times of George Cheyne* (Norman: University of Oklahoma Press, 2000), 99, 105. For examples of declension or secularization narratives, see Maxine Van de Wetering, "A Reconsideration of the Inoculation Controversy," *New England Quarterly* 58 (1985): 46–67; Robert Tindol, "Getting the Pox off All Their Houses: Cotton Mather and the Rhetoric of Puritan Science," *Early American Literature* 46 (2011): 1; Margot Minardi, "The Boston Inoculation Controversy of 1721–1722: An Incident in the History of Race," *William and Mary Quarterly* 61 (2004): 49; Perry Miller, *The New England Mind: From Colony to Province* (Cambridge, MA: Harvard University Press, 1953), 345–366. Miller argues that

William Cooper, the author of one pro-inoculation tract, did not realize "that he had refashioned Calvinism into an activism more Pelagian than any seventeenth-century Arminianism had ever dreamed of" (365–366). Calvin's discussion of science and medicine can be found in John Calvin, *Institutes of the Christian Religion*, ed. John T. McNeill, trans. Ford Lewis Battles, Library of Christian Classics (Louisville, KY: Westminster John Knox Press, 1960), 270–277. The relevant sections are in bk. 2, chap. 2, secs. 12–17.

11 Madden, *"A Cheap, Safe, and Natural Medicine,"* 141; Phyllis Mack, "Religious Dissenters in Enlightenment England," *History Workshop Journal* 49 (2000): 16–17. Guerrini's work on Cheyne also fits into this narrative, although Cheyne was not a Methodist. See Guerrini, *Obesity and Depression in the Enlightenment*, 149–152. "Physical Arminianism" is a phrase that has been used to characterize the perceived parallel between Arminian soteriology and nineteenth-century religious health movements. James Whorton first used the phrase. See Heather Curtis, *Faith in the Great Physician: Suffering and Divine Healing in American Culture, 1860–1900* (Baltimore: Johns Hopkins University Press, 2007), 61–62. The perception of Calvinists as "fatalists," passively accepting disease as a scourge sent by providence, seems to have been a common claim or understanding of nineteenth-century health reformers and remains a significant assumption in some scholarship today. See R. Marie Griffith, *Born Again Bodies: Flesh and Spirit in American Christianity* (Berkeley: University of California Press, 2004), 45; Madden, *"A Cheap, Safe, and Natural Medicine,"* 128–129; Andrew Wear, "Puritan Perceptions of Illness in Seventeenth Century England," in *Patients and Practitioners: Lay Perceptions of Medicine in Pre-industrial Society*, ed. Roy Porter (Cambridge: Cambridge University Press, 1985), 55–99. On Methodist expansion in the early United States, see Mark Noll, *America's God: From Jonathan Edwards to Abraham Lincoln* (Oxford: Oxford University Press, 2005), 181.

12 For general overviews of the inoculation controversy, see John Duffy, *Epidemics in Colonial America* (Baton Rouge: Louisiana State University Press, 1953), 16–29; Kenneth Silverman, *The Life and Times of Cotton Mather* (New York: Harper & Row, 1984), 335–363; Van de Wetering, "Reconsideration of the Inoculation Controversy," 46–67.

13 Otho T. Beall Jr. and Richard H. Shryock, *Cotton Mather, First Significant Figure in American Medicine* (Baltimore: Johns Hopkins University Press, 1954); I. Bernard Cohen, ed., *Cotton Mather and American Science and Medicine: With Studies and Documents Concerning the Introduction of Inoculation or Variolation* (New York: Arno, 1980); Van de Wetering, "Reconsideration of the Inoculation Controversy," 46–67; Miller, *New England Mind*, 345–366; Tindol, "Getting the Pox Off," 1–2; Louise A. Breen, "Cotton Mather, the 'Angelical Ministry,' and Inoculation," *Journal of the History of Medicine and Allied Sciences* 46 (1991): 333–357. For general—non-inoculation-focused—discussion of Mather, witchcraft, and the Enlightenment, see Margaret Humphreys Warner, "Vindicating the Minister's Medical Role: Cotton Mather's Concept of the *Nishmath-Chajim* and the

Spiritualization of Medicine," *Journal of the History of Medicine* 36 (1981): 278–295; Richard Lovelace, *The American Pietism of Cotton Mather: Origins of American Evangelicalism* (Grand Rapids, MI: Christian University Press, 1979), 41–51.

14 Mather worked on *Angel of Bethesda* between 1710 and 1724, but except for a small portion of it, most of the work remained unpublished until 1972. Cotton Mather, *The Angel of Bethesda*, ed. Gordon W. Jones (Barre, MA: American Antiquarian Society, 1972), 5–6; for the portion of *Angel of Bethesda* published in Mather's lifetime, see Cotton Mather, *The Angel of Bethesda, Visiting the Invalids of a Miserable World* (New London, CT: Timothy Green, 1722); Silverman, *Life and Times of Cotton Mather*, 406.

15 Breen describes this as the "analogical use of conversion." Breen, "Cotton Mather," 357.

16 Mather, *Angel of Bethesda* (1972), 12–13, 17, 22–23. On Cheyne and his influence, particularly on Wesley, see Guerrini, *Obesity and Depression in the Enlightenment*, 101, 149–152, 161–162. On Cheyne's cultivation of close relationships with his patients, see Stephen Shapin, "Trusting George Cheyne: Scientific Expertise, Common Sense, and Moral Authority in Early Eighteenth-Century Dietetic Medicine," *Bulletin of the History of Medicine* 77 (2003): 263–297.

17 Mather, *Angel of Bethesda* (1722).

18 Mather, *Angel of Bethesda* (1972), 28–38. There has been some scholarly attention to Mather's concept of the "Nishmath-Chajim." See Warner, "Vindicating the Minister's Medical Role." Warner argues that Mather used a "purportedly scientific concept," in order to claim an important and new role for clergy in health matters and thereby "improve his own position as a figure of importance." It is unclear what Warner finds "new" about Mather's claim for the importance of clergy in health matters in New England. There was a long history of ministers, often the most educated members of rural New England communities, working to help the sick and diseased. See Patricia Ann Watson, *Angelical Conjunction: The Preacher-Physicians of Colonial New England* (Knoxville: University of Tennessee Press, 1991). For more recent scholarship on the Nishmath-Chajim, see Brett Malcolm Grainger, "Vital Nature and Vital Piety: Johann Arndt and the Evangelical Vitalism of Cotton Mather," *Church History* 81 (2012): 852–872. Grainger, influenced by the work of W. R. Ward, is especially attuned to Mather's interest in "vitalism" extending from the work of Paracelsus. See W. R. Ward, *Early Evangelicalism: A Global Intellectual History, 1670–1789* (Cambridge: Cambridge University Press, 2006). While Mather was certainly interested in Paracelsus and his followers, it is also important to consider how Mather interacted with contemporary medical ideas and practice. This interaction need not be described in overly simplistic terms, which Grainger seems to think has been the case. Grainger, "Vital Nature and Vital Piety," 853n4.

19 Richard Toellner, "Die Geburt einer sanften Medizin," in *Die Geburt einer sanften Medizin: Die Franckeschen Stiftungen zu Halle als Begegnungsstätte von Medizin und Pietismus im frühen 18. Jahrhundert*, ed. Richard Toellner (Halle: Verlag der

Franckeschen Stiftungen, 2004), 17–21; Jürgen Helm, *Krankheit, Bekehrung und Reform. Medizin und Krankenfürsorge im Halleschen Pietismus*, Hallesche Forschungen 21 (Tübingen: Max Niemeyer Verlag, 2006), 31. Although it is not known whether Mather was familiar with Stahl's work, he did cite Stahl's colleague Friedrich Hoffman. See Gordon W. Jones, introduction to *The Angel of Bethesda* by Cotton Mather (Barre, MA: American Antiquarian Society, 1972), xxiii; Mather, *Angel of Bethesda* (1972), 16. On Hoffman and Stahl, see Almut Lanz, *Arzneimittel in der Therapie Friedrich Hoffmans (1660–1742)* (Braunschweig: Braunschweiger Veroffentlichungen zur Geschichte der Pharmazie und der Naturwissenschaften, 1995), 30–35; Roger French, "Sickness and the Soul: Stahl, Hoffman and Sauvages on Pathology," in *The Medical Enlightenment of the Eighteenth Century*, ed. Andrew Cunningham and Roger French (Cambridge: Cambridge University Press, 1990), 88–110.

20 Mather, *Angel of Bethesda* (1972), 31–32.

21 Ibid., 33; Warner, "Vindicating the Minister's Medical Role"; Guerrini, *Obesity and Depression in the Enlightenment*, 42–43.

22 Mather, *Angel of Bethesda* (1972), 96. For another example of the use of Job in smallpox writing, see Edmund Massey, *A Sermon Against the Dangerous and Sinful Practice of Inoculation* (London: Meadows, 1722), 1; cf. David E. Shuttleton, *Smallpox and the Literary Imagination, 1660–1820* (Cambridge: Cambridge University Press, 2007), 10.

23 Mather, *Angel of Bethesda* (1972), 96–97; cf. Isaiah 1:6; Job 2:7.

24 Disease management was a chief concern of Mather's since at least 1713, when he wrote a tract on measles. He emphasized God's aid in his citation of Psalm 108:12: "Give us aid against the enemy, for human help is worthless." Cotton Mather, *A Letter, about a Good Management under the Distemper of the Measles, at This Time Spreading in the Country. Here Published for the Benefit of the Poor, and Such as May Want the Help of Able Physicians* (1713), 1. Van de Wetering looks at this tract as a sign of Mather's more enlightened thinking because it focuses on remedies rather than repentance. She did not note Mather's scriptural citations. Van de Wetering, "Reconsideration of the Inoculation Controversy," 59.

25 In the pages on smallpox management and treatment written (presumably) before he learned of inoculation, Mather cited Sydenham, Pitcairne, and John Woodward. Mather, *Angel of Bethesda* (1972), 98–107.

26 Ibid., 30, 33, 105.

27 John Woodward, *The State of Physick: and of Diseases: With an inquiry into the Causes of the Late Increase of Them: But More Particularly of the Small-Pox* (London: T. Horne, 1718), 1–5; William Bynum, *The History of Medicine: A Very Short Introduction* (Oxford: Oxford University Press, 2008), 10–18.

28 Mather, *Angel of Bethesda* (1972), 37.

29 Mather's description suggests that he toyed with the idea that smallpox was innate and only awaited a spur to erupt. This idea fully emerged in the 1730s and was a dominant theory of smallpox by the 1750s. Whether or not Mather supported the

idea of innate disease is unclear; he seemed elsewhere to have an (albeit limited) understanding of smallpox as contagious. Sara Stidstone Gronim, "Imagining Inoculation: Smallpox, the Body, and Social Relations of Healing in the Eighteenth Century," *Bulletin of the History of Medicine* 80 (2006): 262.

30 According to the *Oxford English Dictionary*, in Mather's time the word "bowels" could have referred specifically to the intestines or, more generally, to any internal organ, including the stomach. "Bowels" could also refer to the seat of feelings. See "bowel, n.1," *Oxford English Dictionary Online* (Oxford: Oxford University Press, 2019), https://oed.com; Mather, *Angel of Bethesda* (1972), 111–112. William Cooper, another proponent of inoculation, likewise argued, "Why must I *needs* stay till it come in at my *Mouth* or *Nostrils*, or thro' some of the *porous Parts* of my body?" William Cooper, *A Letter to a Friend in the Country, Attempting a Solution of the Scruples and Objections of Conscientious or Religious Nature, Commonly Made Against the New Way of Receiving the Small-Pox* (Boston: Kneeland, 1721), 5.

31 Mather, *Angel of Bethesda* (1972), 111–112.

32 Martha L. Finch, *Dissenting Bodies: Corporealities in Early New England* (New York: Columbia University Press, 2010), 6, 12–14.

33 Benjamin Colman, *Some Observations on the New Method of Receiving the Small-Pox by Ingrafting or Inoculating* (Boston: Green, 1721), 6–8, 12; Mather, *Angel of Bethesda* (1972), 98. John Corrigan has argued that Colman was a part of a "catholick" party that opposed the "Matherian" party. Some of the differences between the two parties are collapsed when attending to their joint efforts in promoting inoculation and their similar understanding of the way smallpox worked within the human body. See John Corrigan, "Catholick Congregational Clergy and Public Piety," *Church History* 60 (1991): 210–222.

34 John Williams, *Several Arguments, Proving That Inoculating the Small Pox Is Not Contained in the Law of Physick, Either Natural or Divine, and Therefore Unlawful*, 2nd ed. (Boston: Franklin, 1721), 5–6.

35 Williams thought that the potential harm of inoculation for neighbors went against the Sermon on the Mount. Though some, like Colman, doubted it, inoculated smallpox was contagious—an enduring problem for smallpox inoculation (which was also limited by its expense) in the eighteenth century. See Williams, *Several Arguments*, 13; Colman, *Some Observations*, 12.

36 Cotton Mather, *Diary of Cotton Mather, Volume II: 1709–1724*, ed. Worthington Chauncey Ford (New York: Frederick Ungar, 1957), 621, 627–628, 633, 637–638. On the grenade episode, see Mather, *Angel of Bethesda* (1972), 113; cf. Psalm 107. Mather began reformatting his journals in 1709: he began each entry with the initials "G.D.," which stood for "Good Devised." This occurred around the same time Mather began corresponding with the Pietist August Hermann Francke. Inspired by Francke's vision to revitalize Christianity and transform society, Mather's reforming impulse grew. Mather, *Angel of Bethesda* (1972), 107; Silverman, *Life and Times of Cotton Mather*, 231–234. Silverman cautions against interpreting Mather's writing as "drift[ing] into secularism. . . . Both he and the Pietists maintained a

delicate synthesis of engagement with the prevailing culture and mortification to life." Cf. Lovelace, *American Pietism*, 49–51. Wolfgang Splitter argues against overstating the influence of the correspondence between Mather and Francke. Wolfgang Splitter, "The Fact and Fiction of Cotton Mather's Correspondence with German Pietist August Hermann Francke," *New England Quarterly* 83 (2010): 102–122. See also Kuno Francke, "Further Documents Concerning Cotton Mather and August Hermann Francke," *Americana Germanica* 1 (1897): 54–66; Kuno Francke, "The Beginning of Cotton Mather's Correspondence with August Hermann Francke," *Philosophical Quarterly* 5 (1926): 193–195.

37 Francke told Ebenezer's ministers that the Georgia Trustees had decided to support Thilo with three years of provisions and the SPCK had given him thirty pounds sterling. Samuel Berein to GAF, 14 Oct. 1737, AFSt/M 5 A 5: 13; Friedrich Michael Ziegenhagen (hereafter FMZ) to GAF, 23 Sept. 1737, AFSt/M 5 A 6: 3; GAF to JMB and ICG, 7 Nov. 1737, AFSt/M 5 A 3: 53. For the official letter indicating the Georgia Trustees' support, see Harman Verelst to FMZ, 3 Oct. 1737, AFSt/M 5 A 5: 14. The Trustees hoped "Thielow" would also "be assistive to all other Settlers in the Neighbourhood of Ebenezer that may want his help." The Francke Foundations had previously supported a physician in Ebenezer, Johann Andreas Zwiffler, who left after controversy regarding reimbursement for his work. According to Boltzius, Zwiffler had been provided with supplies and medicines from the Francke Foundations, with the intention that he would provide the community with cost-free care. Urlsperger, *DR* (1972), 3:117–118, 172–173; and JMB and ICG to Samuel Urlsperger, 6 Oct. 1736, in JMB, *Letters*, 177–179.

38 Renate Wilson briefly touched on Ebenezer and Thilo in *Pious Traders in Medicine: A German Pharmaceutical Network in Eighteenth-Century North America* (University Park: Pennsylvania State University Press, 2000), x, xxiv–xv, 26, 51, 119, 145, 156, 170–172. (Note that Wilson occasionally confuses Thilo's name, calling him variously Georg Ernst Thilo and Ernst Thilo.) See also Joseph Krafka Jr., "Medicine in Colonial Georgia," *Georgia Historical Society* 20 (1936): 335; Renate Wilson, "Halle and Ebenezer: Pietism, Agriculture and Commerce in Colonial Georgia" (PhD diss., University of Maryland, College Park, 1988), 83–84.

39 Samuel Berein to GAF, 14 Oct. 1737, AFSt/M 5 A 5: 13; FMZ to GAF, 23 Sept. 1737, AFSt/M 5 A 6: 3; GAF to JMB and ICG, 7 Nov. 1737, AFSt/M 5 A 3: 53.

40 Unless otherwise noted, all translations are my own. JMB to GAF, 27 Feb. 1738, AFSt/M 5 A 5: 19; JMB to GAF, 17 May 1738, AFSt/M 5 A 5: 23. The latter source appears to be a private journal in which Boltzius recorded details of Thilo's behavior not included in the official journal, which was published. Among many problems, Boltzius was concerned that Thilo sought a "spiritual sister- and brother-hood" with the wives of the orphanage overseer (Kalcher) and the school-teacher (Ortsmann). It is not entirely clear what this meant. Thilo seemed to be interested in forming his own church, but the ministers were concerned about sexual impropriety. There were initially some positive responses to Thilo's arrival; see Achnes Liesabetha Wöllner [Müller] to GAF, 8 Feb. 1738, AFSt/M 5 A 7: 5; cf.

Samuel Urlsperger, ed., *Zweyte Continuation der ausführlichen Nachricht von den saltzburgischen Emigranten, die sich in America niedergelassen haben* (Halle: Waysenhaus, 1738–1741), 2574. The journal sections of the *Ausführliche Nachricht* are available in translation in Urlsperger, *DR*, but letters like Müller's are not always included in the English translations. See also Wilson, "Halle and Ebenezer," 83–84.

41 JMB to Jakob Gottfried Bötticher, 9 May 1734; JMB and ICG to GAF, 12 July 1734; JMB and ICG to Samuel Urlsperger, 6 Oct. 1736, in JMB, *Letters*, 99, 105–106. Urlsperger, *Zweyte Continuation*, 701, 706–707, 710, 721–722; Urlperger, *DR* 3 (1972), 156–172, 186–187. On the move of Ebenezer, see FMZ to James Edward Oglethorpe, 2 June 1736, AFSt/M 5 A 3: 40.

42 George Fenwick Jones, introduction to Urlsperger, *DR* (1972), 3:xix.

43 JMB and ICG to GAF, 29 May 1740, AFSt/M 5 A 9: 6; following the translation in JMB, *Letters*, 298–299.

44 The name of Urlsperger's physician was recorded as "Plohs." JMB and ICG to GAF, 29 May 1740, AFSt/M 5 A 9: 6; following translation in JMB, *Letters*, 298–299.

45 Andreas-Holger Maehle, "Experience, Experiment and Theory: Justifications and Criticisms of Pharmaco-Therapeutic Practices in the Eighteenth Century," in *Medical Theory and Therapeutic Practice in the Eighteenth Century: A Transatlantic Perspective*, ed. Jürgen Helm and Renate Wilson (Stuttgart: Franz Steiner Verlag, 2008), 65; Mary Lindemann, *Medicine and Society in Early Modern Europe* (Cambridge: Cambridge University Press, 1999), 9–10. In England, Sydenham's experience with quinine and recognition that it was a "specific" transformed his understanding of disease and contributed to the modern classification of disease. Bynum, *History of Medicine*, 37–38.

46 On Carl, Juncker, and Thilo, see Wilson, *Pious Traders in Medicine*, 170–171; on Stahl and the organic method, see Maehle, "Experience, Experiment and Theory," 65–66; JMB, *Letters*, 298–299fn. I do not mean to imply here that Stahl, Carl, Juncker, and Thilo were identical in their medical theories; Stahl's stance on Cinchona did, however, influence his students. For a critique of scholars who identify a single "Pietist medicine," see Jürgen Helm, *Krankheit, Bekehrung und Reform. Medizin und Krankenfürsorge im Halleschen Pietismus*, Hallesche Forschungen 21 (Tübingen: Max Niemeyer Verlag, 2006), 11–14.

47 Johann Samuel Carl to GAF, 7 Mar. 1743, AFSt/M 5 A 10: 58; Wilson, *Pious Traders in Medicine*, 171–172; Johann Juncker to GAF, 7 Nov. 1737, AFSt/M 5 A 5: 16; JMB and ICG to FMZ, 26 Aug. 1738, AFSt/M 5 A 7: 22; also in JMB, *Letters*, 248.

48 GAF to JMB and ICG, 15 Nov. 1743, AFSt/M 5 A 10: 55; GAF to JMB, 6 Jan. 1745, AFSt/M 5 A 11: 17.

49 JMB to GAF, 26 Aug. 1738, in JMB, *Letters*, 245; JMB and ICG to FMZ, 26 Aug. 1738, AFSt/M 5 A 7: 22; also in JMB, *Letters*, 248.

50 Wilson, *Pious Traders in Medicine*, 171–172; Wilson writes that the Cinchona bark had been promoted among the Ebenezer community "against the wishes of the pastors and the local physician from Halle since the 1750s by new arrivals from

Augsburg," and that Cinchona bark was, like opium, never included in shipments of medicine from Halle. Ibid., 51, 151n17. As I discuss in this section, however, correspondence suggests this promotion actually extends back to at least the 1740s and that the local pastors were actually part of this promotion. On Gronau and bloodletting, see ICG to GAF, 9 June 1737, AFSt/M 5 A 3: 58.

51 JMB to Henriette Rosine Goetze, 28 July 1749, in JMB, *Letters*, 539–540, or AFSt/M 5 B 1: 19; JMB to GAF, 28 Mar. 1749, and JMB to GAF, 16 Feb. 1755, in JMB, *Letters*, 521, 622; following translation in JMB, *Letters*. In 1749, Gertraud Kroher Boltzius was around thirty years old. She was from Salzburg and had arrived with the first transport to Ebenezer in 1734. She married Boltzius in 1734 and had four children between 1735 and 1749. She was literate and became skilled at silk reeling. Boltzius trusted his wife with the management of the properties and goods he left behind, making her his sole heir. See Catharina Kroher Gronau, Gertraud Kroher Boltzius, and Maria Kroher Gruber to Matthias Rohrmoser, 9 July 1739, in Urlsperger, *Zweyte Continuation*, 2288; JMB to GAF, 1 Sept. 1735, and JMB to Eva Rosina Boltzius, 1 Sept. 1735, in JMB, *Letters*, 144–145, 148; Renate Wilson, "Public Works and Piety in Ebenezer: The Missing Salzburger Diaries of 1744–1745," *Georgia Historical Quarterly* 77 (1993): 360–361; Wilson, *Pious Traders in Medicine*, 154–155; JMB to Samuel Theodor Albinus, 3 Mar. 1755, in JMB, *Letters*, 623–624; JMB, Testament, 1 June 1763, Hauptarchiv der Franckeschen Stiftungen RB 3: 2; Hermann Heinrich Lemke to GAF, Jan. 1766, Stab/F 32/3: 10. On Thilo's early care of Gertraud Boltzius, see JMB to GAF, 17 Mar. and 2, 3, 7 Apr. 1738, AFSt/M 5 A 5: 23.27. Goetze took over household responsibilities for Francke after the death of her daughter in 1743; she eventually moved to Halle from nearby Leipzig after the death of her husband. She had taken great interest in the Salzburger exiles who had traveled through her town in 1732, and it is possible she met Boltzius in Leipzig or Halle. [Henriette Rosine Goetze?] to [Johanna Henriette Francke?], [1732?], AFSt/M 5 C 5: 10. On Goetze, see the database of the Archives of the Francke Foundations; the entry for GAF in *Neue Deutsche Biographie*, ed. der Historischen Kommission der Bayerischen Akademie der Wissenschaften, vol. 5 (Berlin, 1971), 325 (available online: http://daten.digitale-sammlungen.de); Heinrich Melchior Mühlenberg, *Die Korrespondenz Heinrich Melchior Mühlenbergs: 1740–1752*, ed. Kurt Aland, vol. 1 (Berlin: de Gruyter, 1986), 14n5.

52 JMB to Henriette Rosine Goetze, 28 July 1749, AFSt/M 5 B 1: 19; following translation in JMB, *Letters*, 538–542.

53 JMB to Henriette Rosine Goetze, 22 July 1749, in JMB, *Letters*, 532–533, or AFSt/M 5 B 1: 18.

54 Following Kleckley's translation, with slight changes. JMB to Henriette Rosine Goetze, 28 July 1749, AFSt/M 5 B 1: 19; in JMB, *Letters*, 538–541. Although "hysterical" could refer to a disorder of the passions or nerves, in this case the illness seems to have been related to the uterus and/or general damage to Gertraud Boltzius's reproductive organs.

55 JMB to GAF, 21 Apr. 1750, AFSt/M 5 B 1: 28, and in JMB, *Letters*, 558–559; JMB
    to GAF, 14 Sept. 1750, in JMB, *Letters*, 572–573; Daniel Samuel v. Madai, "Stel-
    lungnahme zur Diagnose und Behandlung der Erkrankung Gertraud Boltzius," 16
    Oct. 1750, AFSt/M 5 B 1: 32. The doctor J. H. Schomburg also offered a diagnosis
    of Gertraud Boltzius's illness, but the letter is extremely difficult to read. It is
    interesting that he addressed the letter to a noble woman and unclear how they
    became involved in the case. See J. H. Schomburg to [Charlotte Christiane Alber-
    tine Henckel v. Donnersmarck?], 27 Dec. 1749, AFSt/M 5 B 1: 31.

56 Urlsperger, *DR* (1989), 13–14:178. For Jones's explanation of the Rothe Friesel, see
    his comments on v–vi, and 226n24.

57 Urlsperger, *DR* (1989), 13–14:204–205. Following Jones's translations.

58 Helm, *Krankheit, Bekehrung und Reform*, 28.

59 GAF to JMB, 27 Mar. 1743, AFSt/M 5 A 10: 34; cf. Wilson, "Halle and Ebenezer,"
    19.

60 The first transport to Ebenezer included approximately fifty immigrants. Wilson,
    "Halle and Ebenezer," 86; JMB, *Letters*, 35n79. The first transport was supple-
    mented by transports in 1735, 1737, and 1741, bringing the population to 249 adults
    and children by the end of 1742. This number did not significantly change until
    the early 1750s, when new transports of immigrants and increasing childhood
    survival rates finally brought the population to approximately 650 people by 1754.
    Although small, this number nonetheless represented, according to Wilson, 12
    percent of the population of the entire colony of Georgia at this time. Wilson,
    "Halle and Ebenezer," 99–100.

61 See especially Boltzius's journal entries from 28 Jan., 12, 21 Oct., 3, 6, 9, 17, 18, 24,
    26, 28 Nov., 6, 8, 9, 13 Dec. 1750, in Urlsperger, *DR* (1990), 15:161–207. Instead of
    offering a direct translation of the German scripture Boltzius cited, I use the John
    13:7 translation from the King James Version, the contemporary English-language
    Protestant Bible.

62 See Boltzius's journal entry from 13 Dec. 1750, in Urlsperger, *DR* (1990), 15:206–
    207.

63 John Wesley, *Primitive Physic: Or an Easy and Natural Method of Curing Most
    Diseases*, 21st ed. (Philadelphia: Prichard & Hall, 1789), xxvii–xxviii. I consulted
    the 1789 editions located at the American Antiquarian Society and the Library
    Company of Philadelphia. On the publication history of *Primitive Physic*, see
    Madden, "A Cheap, Safe, and Natural Medicine," 11–12; Rousseau, "John Wesley's
    Primitive Physic," 253–256.

64 The most extensive study of Wesley and medicine is Madden, "A Cheap, Safe, and
    Natural Medicine." See also Rousseau, "John Wesley's *Primitive Physic*"; English,
    "John Wesley"; Philip W. Ott, "John Wesley on Health as Wholeness," *Journal of
    Religion and Health* 30 (1991): 43–57; Haas, "John Wesley's View"; Deborah Mad-
    den, "Medicine and Moral Reform: The Place of Practical Piety in John Wesley's
    Art of Physic," *Church History* 73 (2004): 741–758; Randy L. Maddox, "John Wes-
    ley on Holistic Health and Healing," *Methodist History* 46 (2007): 4–33. Finally,

Guerrini and Mack both include discussions of the topic within their larger work: Guerrini, *Obesity and Depression in the Enlightenment*, 160–162; Mack, "Religious Dissenters," 3; Phyllis Mack, *Heart Religion in the British Enlightenment: Gender and Emotion in Early Methodism* (Cambridge: Cambridge University Press, 2008), 174–182.

65 Rousseau, "John Wesley's *Primitive Physic*," 242. The 1789 edition of the Library Company of Philadelphia, for example, has at least three different owners listed on the first two pages; the names are difficult to make out because they have been obscured by a bookplate of the Historical Society of Pennsylvania, but the third name begins with "Margaret." The 1788 edition at the Library Company appears to have been re-bound with extra pages interspersed throughout, so that the owner could take his or her own notes. There is only one place in which such a note was added, after St. Anthony's Fire (pp. 23–24): "St. Anthony's Fire. Strong liquors should be avoided as poison. This disease raged severely in the year 1093 in the 11th Century under Urban the 2d. The Religious Order of St Anthony was formed for the relief of persons afflicted with this dreadfull disorder. NB. Scorbutic people are most subject to it." John Wesley, *Primative [sic] Physic; or, An Easy and Natural Method of Curing Most Diseases*, 16th ed. (Trenton, NJ: Quequelle and Wilson, 1788).

66 Although the theological views of early Methodism are often overlooked in favor of emphasizing its "practical" theology or piety, the Methodists' practical interest in medicine and health demonstrates deeply theological commitments, including a strong belief in providence. Noll, *America's God*, 331–331; E. Brooks Holifield, *Theology in America: Christian Thought from the Age of the Puritans to the Civil War* (New Haven, CT: Yale University Press, 2003), 256–257.

67 Madden uses the phrase "Christian enlightened thinking" without offering an exact definition. Madden, "Medicine and Moral Reform," 742, 745. Two scholars briefly mention Wesley's understanding of providence: English, "John Wesley," 74–75; Haas, "John Wesley's View," 392.

68 Wesley's great-grandfather, Bartholomew Wesley, worked as both a minister and a physician until the 1662 Act of Uniformity, after which he supported himself solely through medical work. Maddox, "John Wesley," 5, 26–27, 99; Ott, "John Wesley on Health," 43–50; Rousseau, "John Wesley's *Primitive Physic*," 243; Madden, "Medicine and Moral Reform," 744; Guerrini, *Obesity and Depression in the Enlightenment*, 49–50, 67, 160. On clergy practicing medicine in other contexts, see Watson, *Angelical Conjunction*.

69 Wesley, *Primative Physic*, iv–v. While the preface remained the same throughout the various editions, the citations here are to the 1788 edition I consulted at the American Antiquarian Society (unless otherwise noted). On Cheyne and regimen, see Guerrini, *Obesity and Depression in the Enlightenment*, 139–140.

70 Wesley, *Primative Physic*, v–vi.

71 Ibid., vi.

72 Ibid., vi–x; Madden, "*A Cheap, Safe, and Natural Medicine*," 101, 142–144.

73 Wesley, *Primative Physic*, viii, x–xi; Madden, "A Cheap, Safe, and Natural Medicine," 108–111; Maddox, "John Wesley," 23. On Wesley's efforts to make Cheyne's
advice—directed to the middle and upper classes—available to the lower class, see
Maddox, "John Wesley," 19. On Wesley's conception of the limitations of human
knowledge, see especially Haas, "John Wesley's View," 384–386.

74 Mack, *Heart Religion*, 178; Madden, "A Cheap, Safe, and Natural Medicine," 113–115;
Rousseau, "John Wesley's *Primitive Physic*," 247–250; Haas, "John Wesley's View,"
381–382; Wesley, *Primative Physic*, xi, xvii.

75 Wesley, *Primative Physic*, xiv. This passage is misattributed to Wesley by Ott,
"John Wesley," 51, and Mack, *Heart Religion*, 175, who quotes it from E. Brooks
Holifield, *Health and Medicine in the Methodist Tradition: Journey toward Whole-
ness* (New York: Crossroad, 1986), 21.

76 Guerrini notes that "it is not known whether Cheyne read Stahl." Guerrini,
Obesity and Depression in the Enlightenment, 124–125; cf. Mack, *Heart Religion*,
176–177. Guerrini's analysis of the religious dimensions of Cheyne's work questions Roy Porter's description of Cheyne's later work, *The English Malady* (1733),
as "a highly secularized work." Guerrini argues instead that "a pervasive sense
of sin underlies Cheyne's discussion, culminating in his autobiography," which
appears at the end of the book. Guerrini finds this to be an important continuity
with Cheyne's earlier work and subsequent development. Guerrini, *Obesity and
Depression in the Enlightenment*, 149; cf. Maddox, "John Wesley," 13–16.

77 Wesley, *Primitive Physic* (1789), xxvii–xxviii. The sixteenth edition, cited throughout this section, was published in Trenton in 1788, and the twelfth edition was
published in Philadelphia (by Steuart) in 1764. I have also viewed the 1764 edition
at the Library Company of Philadelphia. It has the standard early prefaces and
quotations from Cheyne, but predates Wesley's insertion of asterisks to indicate
cures he had himself tried. John Wesley, *Primitive Physic*, 12th ed. (Philadelphia:
Steuart, 1764).

78 *The Arminian Magazine: Consisting of Extracts and Original Treatises on General
Redemption*, vol. 1 (Philadelphia: Prichard & Hall, 1789), iii–v. I consulted the edi-
tion at the Library Company, which was owned by John Dickinson. On the Book
Concern, see Noll, *America's God*, 336; Holifield, *Theology in America*, 257; Nathan
Bangs, *History of the Methodist Episcopal Church*, vol. 4 (New York: Mason and
Lane, 1839), chap. 16, available online at www.ccel.org; on *Imitation of Christ* and
holistic care, see Maddox, "John Wesley," 8; on Methodist membership, see Noll,
America's God, 181.

79 Noll, *America's God*, 331–336; Haas, "John Wesley's View," 382–383; on early Methodist involvement in the founding of voluntary hospitals, see Madden, "Medicine
and Moral Reform," 746.

4. PROVIDENCE AND BENEVOLENCE IN PHILADELPHIA'S YELLOW FEVER EPIDEMIC

1 Justus Heinrich Christian Helmuth, journal, 13 Sept. 1793, Lutheran Archives Center at Philadelphia (hereafter Helmuth journal, LAC). Unless otherwise noted, all translations are my own.

2 See, for example, the letters of Elizabeth Rhoads Fisher to her husband Samuel W. Fisher, dated between 11 Sept. and 17 Oct. 1793. She had fled Philadelphia to Woodfield. Samuel W. Fisher Papers, Historical Society of Pennsylvania (HSP). During the 1798 yellow fever epidemic, Peter Grotjan fled Philadelphia to Reading. Peter Adolph Grotjan, memoirs, 2:93–97, HSP. Edward Garrigues stayed in Philadelphia during the 1798 epidemic, but his diary nonetheless has extensive discussion of those who fled. See his entries from August through November 1798 in Edward Garrigues, diary, HSP.

3 Helmuth journal, 12–23 Sept. 1793, LAC.

4 J. Worth Estes and Billy G. Smith, eds., *A Melancholy Scene of Devastation: The Public Response to the 1793 Philadelphia Yellow Fever Epidemic* (Canton, MA: Science History Publications/USA, for the College of Physicians of Philadelphia and the Library Company of Philadelphia, 1997); J. H. Powell, *Bring Out Your Dead: The Great Plague of Yellow Fever in Philadelphia in 1793* (Philadelphia: University of Pennsylvania Press, 1949); Simon Finger, *The Contagious City: The Politics of Public Health in Early Philadelphia* (Ithaca, NY: Cornell University Press, 2012); Billy G. Smith, *Ship of Death: A Voyage That Changed the Atlantic World* (New Haven, CT: Yale University Press, 2013). For one study that investigates the importance of religious beliefs for scientific views, see Thomas Apel, *Feverish Bodies, Enlightened Minds: Science and the Yellow Fever Controversy in the Early American Republic* (Stanford, CA: Stanford University Press, 2016). On race and religion, see Richard S. Newman, *Freedom's Prophet: Bishop Richard Allen, the AME Church, and the Black Founding Fathers* (New York: New York University Press, 2008), chaps. 3 and 4; Joanna Brooks, *American Lazarus: Religion and the Rise of African American and Native American Literatures* (Chicago: University of Chicago Press, 2003), 151–178.

5 Charles Taylor, *A Secular Age* (Cambridge, MA: Harvard University Press, 2007), 15–16, 257–262. The idea that privatized charitable action is secular has played out in several studies. Kathleen D. McCarthy argues, for example, that Benjamin Franklin "fastened on [Cotton Mather's] ideas, secularized them, and made them his own." Kathleen D. McCarthy, *American Creed: Philanthropy and the Rise of Civil Society, 1700–1865* (Chicago: University of Chicago Press, 2005), 15. Susan M. Ryan has described nineteenth-century benevolence as emerging from two separate genealogies: one religious and one secular. Susan M. Ryan, *The Grammar of Good Intentions: Race and the Antebellum Culture of Benevolence* (Ithaca, NY: Cornell University Press, 2003). In a study focused on Helmuth in Philadelphia, A. G. Roeber argues that the privatization of charity "ended any chance that Pennsylvania,

or any state, could legitimately be described as a 'Christian Republic.'" A. G. Roeber, "J. H. C. Helmuth, Evangelical Charity, and the Public Sphere in Pennsylvania, 1793–1800," *Pennsylvania Magazine of History and Biography* 121 (1997): 77–78; cf. Jessica Roney's study on the tradition of voluntary societies in eighteenth-century Philadelphia and the ways in which they provided care when the civic government failed and religious institutions were still growing, and Bruce Dorsey's work on benevolence and reform in antebellum Philadelphia, which addresses the lack of historical studies of religion in antebellum Philadelphia: Jessica Roney, *Governed by a Spirit of Opposition: The Origins of American Political Practice in Colonial Philadelphia* (Baltimore: Johns Hopkins University Press, 2014), 60–61; Bruce Dorsey, *Reforming Men and Women: Gender in the Antebellum City* (Ithaca, NY: Cornell University Press, 2002), 2–3, 10, 21, 27–28, 46–47.

6 On connections between Christian and Enlightenment thought in eighteenth-century understandings of benevolence, see Norman S. Fiering, "Irresistible Compassion: An Aspect of Eighteenth-Century Sympathy and Humanitarianism," in *Race, Gender, and Rank: Early Modern Ideas of Humanity*, ed. Maryanne Cline Horowitz (Rochester, NY: University of Rochester Press, 1992), 378–401 (originally published under the same title in *Journal of the History of Ideas* 37 [1976]: 197–218); Catherine A. Brekus, *Sarah Osborn's World: The Rise of Evangelical Christianity in Early America* (New Haven, CT: Yale University Press, 2013), 217–247.

7 There are some studies on the connections between Pietism and Puritanism in early America, but they mostly focus on the early eighteenth century, even though Pietism continued to shape the experience of German and Scandinavian Protestant immigrants in America into the nineteenth century. On earlier connections, see F. Ernest Stoeffler, ed., *Continental Pietism and Early American Christianity* (Grand Rapids, MI: Eerdmans, 1976); W. R. Ward, *The Protestant Evangelical Awakening* (Cambridge: Cambridge University Press, 1992); W. R. Ward, *Early Evangelicalism: A Global Intellectual History, 1670–1789* (Cambridge: Cambridge University Press, 2006); Mark Noll, *The Rise of Evangelicalism: The Age of Edwards, Whitefield, and the Wesleys* (Leicester: Intervarsity Press, 2004), 58–59; Jonathan Strom, Hartmut Lehmann, and James Van Horn Melton, eds., *Pietism in Germany and North America, 1680–1820* (Farnham: Ashgate, 2009); Hartmut Lehmann, Hermann Wellenreuther, and Renate Wilson, eds., *In Search of Peace and Prosperity: New German Settlements in Eighteenth-Century Europe and America* (University Park: Pennsylvania State University Press, 2000). There has been some scholarly attention to Helmuth and his influence in late eighteenth-century Philadelphia. See, for example, Roeber, "J. H. C. Helmuth"; Wolfgang Flügel, "Selbstbildnis mit Amerika—Hallenser Pastoren in Pennsylvania in der Ära nach Mühlenberg," in *Freiheit, Fortschritt und Verheißung. Blickwechsel zwischen Europa und Nordamerika seit der frühen Neuzeit*, ed. Claus Veltmann, Jürgen Gröschl, and Thomas Müller-Bahlke (Halle: Franckeschen Stiftungen, 2011), 117–129.

8 African American ministers Richard Allen and Absalom Jones have been recognized as important early black leaders, but less attention has been given to their

description of their actions and experiences during the epidemic as the result of human sympathy and an earnest faith in God's guidance. See Newman, *Freedom's Prophet*, 78–127; Phillip Lapsansky, "'Abigail, a Negress': The Role and the Legacy of African Americans in the Yellow Fever Epidemic," in Estes and Smith, *Melancholy Scene of Devastation*, 61–65; Brooks, *American Lazarus*, 162–178.

9 The physician John Redman, who was one of the first American practitioners to train in Europe, was a devout Presbyterian whose medical practice was based on his strong conviction that doctors have a duty to serve their fellow humans to the glory of God. He has been only briefly acknowledged as a teacher of the more famous Benjamin Rush and as a founder of the College of Physicians. George H. Ingram, "Biographies of the Alumni of the Log College: 10. John Redman," *Journal of the Presbyterian Historical Society* 13 (1929): 356–362.

10 See, for example, Ryan, *Grammar of Good Intentions*, 14–15; Fiering, "Irresistible Compassion," 381–396; Karen Halttunen, "Humanitarianism and the Pornography of Pain in Anglo-American Culture," *American Historical Review* 100 (1995): 303–307.

11 The Committee, for example, was made up of middling white men who remained in the city while the federal and civic governments fled; although their actions have been explained in terms of their political significance, their work has also been described with ample reference to compassion, affection, and providence. Sally Griffith, "'A Total Dissolution of the Bonds of Society': Community Death and Regeneration in Mathew Carey's *Short Account of the Malignant Fever*," in Estes and Smith, *Melancholy Scene of Devastation*, 55–56.

12 Numerous studies have addressed arguments that religious benevolence and reform were rooted in a desire to exert social control. See, for example, Natalie Zemon Davis, "Poor Relief, Humanism, and Heresy," in *Society and Culture in Early Modern France* (Stanford, CA: Stanford University Press, 1975), 17–64 (originally published in *Studies in Medieval and Renaissance History* 5 [1968]); Lee Palmer Wandel, *Always among Us: Images of the Poor in Zwingli's Zurich* (Cambridge: Cambridge University Press, 2003); Cornelia H. Dayton and Sharon V. Salinger, *Robert Love's Warnings: Searching for Strangers in Colonial Boston* (Philadelphia: University of Pennsylvania Press, 2014); Deborah Madden, "Medicine and Moral Reform: The Place of Practical Piety in John Wesley's Art of Physic," *Church History* 73 (2004): 741–758; Conrad Edick Wright, *The Transformation of Charity in Postrevolutionary New England* (Boston: Northeastern University Press, 1992), 10–11; Lois W. Banner, "Religious Benevolence as Social Control: A Critique of an Interpretation," *Journal of American History* 60 (1973): 23–41.

13 Brekus, *Sarah Osborn's World*, 226–227; Paul Langford, *A Polite and Commercial People: England 1727–1783* (1989; Oxford: Clarendon, 1998), 461–487; Carolyn D. Williams, "'The Luxury of Doing Good': Benevolence, Sensibility, and the Royal Humane Society," in *Pleasure in the Eighteenth Century*, ed. Roy Porter and Marie Mulvey Roberts (New York: New York University Press, 1996), 77–108. For contemporary discussions of sensibility and benevolence, see Hugh Blair, an ordained

Anglican and professor at Edinburgh, whose popular *Sermons* were published
in several editions in the early republic. Hugh Blair, *Sermons* (New York: Hodge,
Allen, and Campbell, 1790), 23–24; cf. Samuel Davies, *Religion and Public Spirit: A
Valedictory Address to the Senior Class* (Portsmouth, NH: Fowle, 1762), 11.

14 Helmuth journal, 19 Sept. 1793, LAC.

15 J. Heinrich C. Helmuth, *Nachricht von dem sogenannten Gelben Fieber in Philadelphia für den nachdenkenden Christen* (Philadelphia: Steiner & Kämmerer, 1793);
J. Henry C. Helmuth, *A Short Account of the Yellow Fever in Philadelphia, for the
Reflecting Christian*, trans. Charles Erdmann (Philadelphia: Jones, Hoff & Derrick,
1794), 10–21. I have compared the two editions; the English translation is, overall,
satisfactory, and I provide quotations from it throughout but reference also the
pages from the German edition (the pagination is not consistent between the two
versions). It should be noted, however, that the German edition does have several
paratexts that the English lacks, including a list of the number of dead organized
by date and congregation, a record of weather conditions, and a poem about the
dead in the graveyard. Helmuth's reference to Jesus's lament (Luke 13:34; Matthew
23:37) occurs on page 17 of the English tract and page 31 of the German.

16 *Die Gesellschaft zur Unterstützung der redlichen Hülfsbedürftigen Haus=Armen,
in der Deutsch=Evangelisch= Lutherischen Gemeinde in Philadelphia, in dem Staat
Pennsylvanien, in Nord=America* (1790), 5–6. This tract can be found at LAC, H10
P5G3 1790. On the founding of the society, see Roeber, "J. H. C. Helmuth," 85; on
Philadelphia's tradition of mutual aid and voluntary societies, see Roney, *Gov-
erned by a Spirit*. For Helmuth's biography, see C. R. Demme, *Die letzte Ehre des
Christlichen Predigers in einer christlichen Gemeine. Eine Predigt gehalten vor der
St. Michaelis=und Zions=Gemeine in Philadelphia, am 13. Febr. 1825, als an dem
Tage der Gedächtnissfeier Ihres verewigten Lehrers, des Hochw. J. H. C. Hellmuth,
Doktors der h. Schrift und Seniors des Lutherischen Ministeriums von Pennsyl-
vanien* (Philadelphia: Joh. Georg Ritter, 1825), 14–15. In a letter to the Francke
Foundations, Helmuth reported that his published account of the yellow fever
had brought in over two hundred pounds for the Poor Society. Justus Heinrich
Christian Helmuth to Johann Ludwig Schulze, 7 May 1794, Missionsarchiv der
Franckeshen Stiftungen (hereafter AFSt/M 4) D 3: 31. I am indebted to Wolfgang
Flügel and Jan-Hendrik Evers for sharing their knowledge of Helmuth materials
at the Archives of the Francke Foundations and the Lutheran Archives Center.

17 Fiering, "Irresistible Compassion," 383–392; on the influence of Hutcheson in
America, see Mark A. Noll, *America's God: From Jonathan Edwards to Abraham
Lincoln* (Oxford: Oxford University Press, 2002), 106–111. For an excellent study of
transatlantic humanitarianism, see Amanda B. Moniz, *From Empire to Humanity:
The American Revolution and the Origins of Humanitarianism* (Oxford: Oxford
University Press, 2016).

18 *Die Gesellschaft*, 8. Translation mine. I have found the same hymn in several
nineteenth-century hymnals, but I am not sure when or where it originated. See,
for example, hymn no. 324 in *Eine Sammlung evangelischer Lieder, zum Gebrauch*

der Hochdeutsch Reformirten Kirche in den Der Staaten von Nord Amerika (Chambersburg, PA: Kieffer, 1853), 382.

19 Johann Friedrich Schmidt to Gottlieb Friedrich Stoppelberg, 2 June 1794, AFSt/M 4 D 3: 29; Justus Heinrich Christian Helmuth to Gottlieb Friedrich Stoppelberg, 17 Feb. 1797, AFSt/M 4 D 4: 71; Johann Friedrich Schmidt and Justus Heinrich Christian Helmuth to Johann Ludwig Schulze, 13 Sept. 1796, AFST/M 4 G 10; Justus Heinrich Christian Helmuth to Georg Christian Knapp, 28 July 1800, AFSt/M 4 D 5: 80. Joseph Priestley ended up moving to what is now Northumberland, Pennsylvania. The Library Company of Philadelphia holds part of his library collection. For an example of his writings on Christ's divinity and the human soul, see Joseph Priestly, *Disquisitions Relating to Matter and Spirit: To Which Is Added, the History of the Philosophical Doctrine Concerning the Origin of the Soul, and Nature of Matter; with Its Influence on Christianity, Especially with Respect to the Doctrine of the Pre-existence of Christ* (London: Johnson, 1777).

20 Helmuth, *Short Account*, 32; cf. Helmuth, *Nachricht*, 60; Helmuth journal, 17 Sept. 1793, LAC; cf. Isaiah 55.

21 Helmuth journal, 19 Sept. 1793, LAC; Helmuth, *Short Account*, 28; cf. Helmuth, *Nachricht*, 52.

22 Helmuth, *Short Account*, 28–29; cf. Helmuth, *Nachricht*, 52–55. Helmuth journal, 12 Sept. 1793, LAC. Helmuth mentioned medicine and physicians throughout his journals; he described, for example, Rush and Rush's medicines in entries from 14 Sept. and 18 Sept. 1793.

23 Thomas Reid, *Essays on the Intellectual and Active Powers of Man* (Philadelphia: Young, 1793), 2:227–236. These volumes were first published in the 1780s in Scotland. Mark Noll offers a helpful overview of the influence of Scottish Common Sense philosophy as it was received in revolutionary America, focusing particularly on Frances Hutcheson and John Witherspoon. Reid, although different, was part of this tradition, and his writings were known and published in the United States. See Noll, *America's God*, 93–113.

24 Helmuth journal, 17 Sept. 1793, LAC.

25 Helmuth journal, 14–15 Sept. 1793, LAC.

26 Helmuth, *Short Account*, 46; cf. Helmuth, *Nachricht*, 87. For an example of criticism, see Mathew Carey, *A Short Account of the Malignant Fever, Lately Prevalent in Philadelphia*, 3rd ed. (Philadelphia: Carey, 1793), 105–107.

27 Demme, *Die letzte Ehre*, 16–22. Cf. Roeber, "J. H. C. Helmuth," 77.

28 Helmuth, *Short Account*, 55; cf. Helmuth, *Nachricht*, 103–104.

29 Helmuth, *Short Account*, 30; cf. Helmuth, *Nachricht*, 56; Helmuth journal, 18 Sept. 1793, LAC; cf. Luke 8:27.

30 Helmuth, *Short Account*, 35–36; cf. Helmuth, *Nachricht*, 67.

31 See Williams, "'Luxury of Doing Good,'" 85–86.

32 Committee to Attend to and Alleviate the Sufferings of the Afflicted with the Malignant Fever, minutes, 1793–1794, Library Company of Philadelphia (hereafter the Committee, Minutes, LCP), 1, 3. The quotations and page numbers I use are

from the manuscript minutes, but the Minutes of the Committee were published shortly after the epidemic subsided in 1794. See *Minutes of the Proceedings of the Committee* . . . (Philadelphia: R. Aitken & Son, 1794). For a brief discussion of the political context and the leaders who had left, see Griffith, "'Total Dissolution of the Bonds of Society,'" 55–56.

33 The Committee, Minutes, LCP, 6–7, 14, 25, 28, 39.

34 Ibid., 24, 34, 38–41, 43, 53.

35 Ibid., 21–22, 24, 25, 40, 100, 113–114.

36 See Davis, "Poor Relief, Humanism, and Heresy," 36; Dayton and Salinger, *Robert Love's Warnings*, 5; Wandel, *Always among Us*, 14–16; Wright, *Transformation of Charity*, 10–11; Banner, "Religious Benevolence," 23–41; cf. Dorsey, *Reforming Men and Women*, 2–3; Ryan, *Grammar of Good Intentions*, 1–24.

37 The argument about using religious charity toward social control has an especially long shadow in scholarship on Methodism, due to the influence of E. P. Thompson. For a good overview of scholarship in this area, see Madden, "Medicine and Moral Reform," 749–755. For an interesting study of the influence of Methodism on E. P. Thompson, see David Hempton and John Walsh, "E. P. Thompson and Methodism," in *God and Mammon: Protestants, Money, and the Market, 1790–1860*, ed. Mark A. Noll (Oxford: Oxford University Press, 2002), 99–120.

38 Griffith, "'Total Dissolution of the Bonds of Society,'" 55. As Natalie Zemon Davis, Cornelia Dayton, and Sharon Salinger have shown in earlier eras, those who responded to suffering often had complex and interconnecting reasons, including Christian faith, humanist teachings, and economic and political interests. Davis, "Poor Relief, Humanism, and Heresy," 17–20, 29, 35–37, 41, 57, 61; Dayton and Salinger, *Robert Love's Warnings*, 4–5, 21, 41, 43–45, 49.

39 The Committee, Minutes, LCP, 77–79.

40 Ibid., 77–79.

41 Ibid., 83–84. See Jeremiah 8:22. For an additional example, see the letter from the citizens of Bucks County, ibid., 106–109.

42 Griffith, "'Total Dissolution of the Bonds of Society,'" 45, 47.

43 The Committee Minutes, LCP, 83–84.

44 Ibid., 111, 234.

45 Brooks, *American Lazarus*, 163.

46 Carey, *Short Account*, 37–38.

47 Ibid., 107–108. Helmuth's Lutheran congregation was likely one of the targets of Carey's critique. Helmuth, however, defended his church's continued meetings and worship. He argued that the high interment rates at the Lutheran cemetery were due to the cemetery's openness to outsiders. He also tried to quantify the proportional rate of death compared to other congregations. He argued that more of his congregants stayed in the city and lived in the most highly infected neighborhoods. In this light, the Lutherans actually fared better than what the raw numbers suggest. Helmuth, *Nachricht*, 89–95, 105–116; cf. Helmuth, *Short Account*, 47–50.

48 Carey, *Short Account*, 39.

49 This was the fifth letter in a series of autobiographical letters by Carey. Mathew Carey, "Original Papers: Autobiography of Mathew Carey. Letter V," *New-England Magazine* 6 (1834): 93–94.

50 Carey, *Short Account*, 96–97; Carey, "Original Papers," 93–94; in her study, Griffith took up Carey's invitation and offered a modern psychological assessment of Carey's emotions. She suggested that Carey might have experienced something like what the "psychologist Mihaly Csikszentmihalyi has recently described as a state of 'flow,' in which a person becomes so absorbed in a complex task—that he or she loses all senses of time and self-consciousness, yet experiences the greatest enjoyment." Griffith, "'Total Dissolution of the Bonds of Society,'" 53. Another reading of Carey's experience could be offered by current scholarship on religion and the emotions. Suffering on the scale of an epidemic provokes wonder, an emotion that, one scholar has argued, opens humans to seek meaning beyond the human realm and to "religious sensibility." See Robert Fuller, "Wonder and the Religious Sensibility: A Study in Religion and Emotion," *Journal of Religion* 86 (2006): 364–384.

51 Griffith, "'Total Dissolution of the Bonds of Society,'" 54–56.

52 A[bsalom] J[ones] and R[ichard] A[llen], *A Narrative of the Proceedings of the Black People, during the Late Awful Calamity in Philadelphia, in the Year 1793: And a Refutation of Some Censures, Thrown upon Them in Some Late Publications* (Philadelphia: Woodward, 1794).

53 Carey, *Short Account*, 78; Newman, *Freedom's Prophet*, 87–93.

54 Jones and Allen, *Narrative*; Newman, *Freedom's Prophet*, 78–79, 94–95, 105–127; Lapsansky, "'Abigail, a Negress,'" 61–65; Brooks, *American Lazarus*, 166–170.

55 Lapsansky, "'Abigail, a Negress,'" 61; it is important to keep in mind, as Newman compellingly argues in relation to discourse, that Jones and Allen framed their account to appeal to their audience, and then (per Newman) "in a classical writer's manner revers[ed] sensibilities at key moments to confront a disarmed audience." Newman, *Freedom's Prophet*, 126. My analysis is influenced by the work of Susan Ryan and Bruce Dorsey. In her study of nineteenth-century benevolence, Ryan argues that benevolent actions became associated with citizenship with important implications for black Americans. Although the context is different, Ryan's argument is helpful for analyzing the actions of free blacks during the yellow fever. Ryan, *Grammar of Good Intentions*, 7–8. Dorsey's focus is also the antebellum era, but he begins with early national Philadelphia and argues that Philadelphia's free black community "discovered that voluntary associations, intimately tied to the African Church, were the best hope for creating an independent and self-reliant black community in Philadelphia." Dorsey, *Reforming Men and Women*, 27. Similar reasoning is briefly suggested in Gary Nash, *Forging Freedom: The Formation of Philadelphia's Black Community, 1720–1840* (Cambridge, MA: Harvard University Press, 1991), 123.

56 Lapsansky, "'Abigail, a Negress,'" 70–73; see also Brooks, *American Lazarus*, 151–152; Newman, *Freedom's Prophet*, 106. On Allen's later embrace of colonization, see Newman, *Freedom's Prophet*, chap. 7.

57 Lapsansky, "'Abigail, a Negress,'" 70–73; Newman, *Freedom's Prophet*, 58–73; see also Brooks, *American Lazarus*, 151–152. For a fascinating treatment of this church community after the epidemic years, see Sarah Barringer Gordon, "The African Supplement: Religion, Race, and Corporate Law in Early National America," *William and Mary Quarterly* 72 (2015): 385–422.

58 Jones and Allen, *Narrative*, 3; Newman, *Freedom's Prophet*, 121–126; cf. Daniel 3.

59 Jones and Allen, *Narrative*, 3–4.

60 Ibid., 4–5, 12, 15; cf. Newman, *Freedom's Prophet*, 84–91. On Methodist understandings of free will, see Noll, *America's God*, 335.

61 Jones and Allen, *Narrative*, 18.

62 [Benjamin Rush], "Memoirs of the Life and Character of John Redman, M.D.," *Philadelphia Medical Museum* 5 (1808): 50. I read this article as a Photostat in the second volume of a collection at the College of Physicians of Philadelphia Historical Library. See *John Redman, M.D., 1722–1808: First President of the College of Physicians of Philadelphia*, compiled and edited by William N. Bradley (Philadelphia, 1948), Library of the College of Physicians of Philadelphia. Bradley attributes authorship to Rush based on a letter Benjamin Rush wrote to John Adams on 5 Apr. 1808. The account had previously been attributed to John Redman Coxe, Redman's grandson and a later editor of the *Pennsylvania Medical Museum*; cf. John Redman, *An Account of the Yellow Fever as It Prevailed in Philadelphia in the Autumn of 1762; A Paper Presented to the College of Physicians of Philadelphia at Its Stated Meeting, September 7, 1793* (Philadelphia, 1865), 2–8.

63 Jones and Allen, *Narrative*, 5.

64 Ibid., 4.

65 Ibid., 11–12; Brooks, *American Lazarus*, 168–169.

66 Jones and Allen, *Narrative*, 7–8.

67 Ibid., 12–14.

68 Ibid., 19.

69 Ibid., 4, 17–20.

70 Ibid., 3; Joanna Brooks has pointed out the scriptural citation and suggests its importance for the black community's understanding of itself as especially covenanted and as opposed to the consumerism it witnessed in Philadelphia. While the black community might have been skeptical of the consumerism, I doubt it reached the level of opposition. Brooks also does not note the significance of God's presence in the "fiery furnace" with the Babylonian Jews, which was an essential part of the parallel for Jones and Allen. See Brooks, *American Lazarus*, 168–169.

71 Jones and Allen, *Narrative*, 23–28; Newman, *Freedom's Prophet*, 109–126.

72 Jones and Allen, *Narrative*, 26–28.

73 Ibid., 20. These lines originally date from 1770. According to a note appended to the source in the Early American Imprints Collection, the lines were part of a

broadside "posted at noonday in the streets of New York by the soldiers on Friday 19 Jan. 1770." 16th Regiment of Foot, *God and a Soldier All Men Do Adore* (New York, 1770).

74 An early and well-known example is Martin S. Pernick, "Politics, Parties, and Pestilence: Epidemic Yellow Fever in Philadelphia and the Rise of the First Party System," *William and Mary Quarterly* 29 (1972): 559–586; Thomas Apel's work focuses on how the debate sparked greater inquiry into "the construction of natural knowledge." See Apel, *Feverish Bodies, Enlightened Minds*, 5–6.

75 *John Redman, M.D.*, 114–118. Originally published as "The Inaugural Address, Made to the College of Physicians, by the First President Thereof, Dr. John Redman," in *The College of Physicians of Philadelphia*, ed. W. S. W. Ruschenberger (Philadelphia, 1887), 179–183.

76 *John Redman, M.D.*, 114–118; Redman, "Inaugural Address," 179–183.

77 *John Redman, M.D.*, 199–200. The original is located in the Rush Family Papers, LCP, 22:8; for an example of Redman's letters to Rush, see John Redman to Benjamin Rush, 21 Dec. 1782, Rush Family Papers, LCP, 22:21. A Photostat of this letter is also available in *John Redman, M.D.*, 97. Redman writes, "We may hope to glide safely through the darksome valley of death, and having his rod & staff to direct & support us, to perceive only the shadows of evil terminating in substantial Joys, & bliss everlasting."

78 Rush, "Memoirs," 52; Redman, *Account*, 6; John Redman to Benjamin Rush, 21 Dec. 1782, Rush Family Papers, LCP, 22:21.

79 Redman, *Account*, 29–31.

80 John Redman to Ashbel Green, 20 Sept. 1797. Original in possession of the Historical Society of Pennsylvania; I viewed the Photostat in *John Redman, M.D.*, 171–172a.

81 Ibid. See Psalm 91:2–6; Redman paraphrased the quote with many partial phrases and etceteras. For the sake of clarity, I quote it in full from the King James Version.

82 John Redman to Ashbel Green, 14 Sept. 1798; I viewed the Photostat copy in *John Redman, M.D.*, 177–178; notes on the Photostat indicate that the original is in the possession of the College of Physicians, but I could not locate it.

83 Ingram, "Biographies of the Alumni," 356–362; Archibald Alexander, *Biographical Sketches of the Founder and Principal Alumni of the Log College. Together with an Account of the Revivals of Religion under Their Ministry* (Philadelphia: Presbyterian Board of Publication, 1851). Tennent went on to become minister of the Second Presbyterian Church of Philadelphia, where Redman worshiped.

84 Ingram, "Biographies of the Alumni," 362.

85 See discussion in Ryan, *Grammar of Good Intentions*, 14–15; Roeber, "J. H. C. Helmuth," 77–78; McCarthy, *American Creed*, 15.

86 Ryan, *Grammar of Good Intentions*, 4–5.

87 See Taylor, *Secular Age*, 15–16, 37–41, 257–263. Max Weber responded to such narratives by arguing that the fundamental shift occurred in how Protestants

interpreted earthly rewards. Whereas early Protestants considered earthly rewards as evidence of God's providence and grace, later Protestants ceased viewing earthly rewards providentially but rather as ends in themselves. See Max Weber, *The Protestant Ethic and the Spirit of Capitalism*, trans. Talcott Parsons (New York: Scribner's Sons, 1958).

5. MEDICINE, PROVIDENCE, AND NATURE IN EIGHTEENTH-CENTURY MATERNITY

1 Samuel W. Fisher, "Biographical Sketch of His Wife Elizabeth Rhoads Fisher (1770–1796)," 1796, Eliza Rhoads Fisher folder 2, Samuel W. Fisher Collection, HSP. Although we have only Samuel's account of the matter and cannot know if it accurately reflects Elizabeth's feelings, it does seem that many early American women found great joy in nursing. See Mary Beth Norton, *Liberty's Daughters: The Revolutionary Experience of American Women, 1750–1800* (Ithaca, NY: Cornell University Press, 1980), 90.

2 Cotton Mather, *Elizabeth in Her Holy Retirement* (Boston: Green, 1710), 6, 9, 13.

3 See the discussion of design, Christianity, and science in Colin Jager, *The Book of God: Secularization and Design in the Romantic Era* (Philadelphia: University of Pennsylvania Press, 2006), 2–4, 12–14; see also Pamela Klassen, *Blessed Events: Religion and Home Birth in America* (Princeton: Princeton University Press, 2001), 137, 170–171. Although studying childbirth in a very different era and context, Klassen's argument regarding the social construction of the "natural" is important here, particularly in her discussion of how people make an effort to claim, through the human body, the authority of certain actions and ideas. She is here invoking Pierre Bourdieu's concept of *habitus* ("society written into the body, into the biological individual"), which "works to structure actions and beliefs while making them appear natural."

4 There are many excellent studies of fertility, maternity, and women's bodies that highlight how important such evidence is for understanding broader society and norms in this era. On motherhood and Enlightenment thought, see, for example, Matthew Garrett, "The Self-Made Son: Social Competition and the Vanishing Mother in Franklin's *Autobiography*," *ELH* 80 (2013): 519–532; Jean-Jacques Rousseau, *Emile, or On Education*, trans. and ed. Christopher Kelly and Allan Bloom, vol. 13 (Hanover, NH: Dartmouth College Press, 2010), 11–18; Ruth Bloch, *Gender and Morality in Anglo-American Culture, 1650–1800* (Berkeley: University of California Press, 2003), 57–77; Linda K. Kerber, *Women of the Republic: Intellect and Ideology in Revolutionary America* (Chapel Hill: University of North Carolina Press, 1980), 7–32; Nicole Fermon, "Domesticating Women, Civilizing Men: Rousseau's Political Program," *Sociological Quarterly* 35 (1994): 431–442. On motherhood, economics, and colonialism, see Ruth Perry, "Colonizing the Breast: Sexuality and Maternity in Eighteenth-Century England," *Journal of the History of Sexuality* 2 (1991): 204–234; Susan Klepp, "Revolutionary Bodies: Women and the Fertility Transition in the Mid-Atlantic Region, 1760–1820," *Journal of American*

History 85 (Dec. 1998): 910–945; Nora Doyle, *Maternal Bodies: Redefining Mother-hood in Early America* (Chapel Hill: University of North Carolina Press, 2018); Jennifer L. Morgan, *Laboring Women: Reproduction and Gender in New World Slavery* (Philadelphia: University of Pennsylvania Press, 2004). On medicine and maternity, see Mary Fissell, *Vernacular Bodies: The Politics of Reproduction in Early Modern England* (Oxford: Oxford University Press, 2004), 1–13; and the ex-cellent collection of essays and articles in Philip K. Wilson, ed., *Midwifery Theory and Practice* (New York: Garland, 1996). There is less scholarship on religion and maternity in the Atlantic world; for one important example, which uses the topic of maternity to refute claims for a widespread disenchantment during the En-lightenment, see Susan Juster, "Mystical Pregnancy and Holy Bleeding: Visionary Experience in Early Modern Britain and America," *William and Mary Quarterly* 57 (Apr. 2000): 252–253.

5 Protestant views of Mary were complex in early modern Europe and in colonial America and could be shaped by rabid anti-Catholicism. See, for example, Laura M. Stevens, "Mary's Magnificat in Eighteenth-Century Britain and New Eng-land," in *Early Modern Prayer*, ed. William Gibson, Laura Stevens, and Sabine Volk-Birke (Cardiff: University of Wales Press, 2017), 91–107. In her study of early modern England, Mary Fissell argues that with the Protestant Reformation came a corresponding effort to strip Marian devotion and religious rituals from practices surrounding childbirth, leading ultimately to a disenchantment of the "female reproductive body," although some practices continued despite these ef-forts. Indeed, the present chapter suggests that—perhaps with more chronological distance from the Reformation—some Protestants were willing to reflect on Mary and the story of the nativity once again in connection to contemporary childbear-ing, albeit with a distinctly Protestant emphasis on dependence. Fissell, *Vernacu-lar Bodies*, 14–52. For an excellent study of Catholic and Protestant celebration of the Virgin Mary alongside issues of anti-Catholicism in the nineteenth century, see Elizabeth Hayes-Alvarez, *The Valiant Woman: The Virgin Mary in Nineteenth-Century American Culture* (Chapel Hill: University of North Carolina Press, 2016).

6 Mather, *Elizabeth in Her Holy Retirement*, 4–7, 16, 19–20; Johann Arndt, *Paradis-gärtlein, voller Christlicher Tugenden, Wie dieselbigen durch andächtige, lehrhafte und Trostreiche Gebete in die Seele zu pflantzen* (Halle: Wäysenhause, 1746), 10–11. This edition was bound together with *Wahres Christentum*.

7 Caroline Walker Bynum, *Jesus as Mother: Studies in the Spirituality of the High Middle Ages* (Berkeley: University of California Press, 1982), 131–134; cf. Juster, "Mystical Pregnancy and Holy Bleeding," 257.

8 Jules David Prown, *Art as Evidence: Writings on Art and Material Culture* (New Haven, CT: Yale University Press, 2001), 127–128; Jane Kamensky, *A Revolution in Color: The World of John Singleton Copley* (New York: Norton, 2016), 270–274; Cassandra Albinson, "Curatorial Comment on Benjamin West, *The Artist and His Family*" (Yale Center for British Art, Jan. 2007), http://collections.britishart.

yale.edu. On religious themes in Copley's art, see Irma B. Jaffe, "John Singleton Copley's 'Watson and the Shark,'" *American Art Journal* 9 (1977): 15–25.

9 Jeremy Taylor, *The Great Exemplar of Sanctity and Holy Life according to the Christian Institution. Described in the History of the Life and Death of the Ever Blessed Jesus Christ the Saviour of the World* (London: Francis Ash, 1649); Adams described Taylor as "a sensual man by nature," in his ability to write "upon subjects which cold men cannot make themselves eloquent upon." Charles Francis Adams, diary entry, 20 Dec. 1829, in *Diary of Charles Francis Adams*, vol. 3, in *Adams Papers Digital Edition* (Massachusetts Historical Society), www.masshist. org. I consulted several examples of North American imprints of Taylor's writings at the Library of Congress. See Jeremy Taylor, *Life of Our Blessed Saviour Jesus Christ* (Greenfield, MA: Dickman, 1796); Jeremy Taylor, *Rule and Exercises of Holy Dying* (Philadelphia: Woodard, 1811); Jeremy Taylor, *Life of Our Blessed Saviour Jesus Christ* (Somerset, PA: Patton, 1818). On Taylor and his historical context, see J. Sears McGee, "Conversion and the Imitation of Christ in Anglican and Puritan Writing," *Journal of British Studies* 15 (1976): 21–39.

10 Jeremy Taylor, *Great Exemplar*, see the epistle dedicatory (n.p.), 14–15.

11 Ibid., 14–15. Even in the much-abridged editions that were printed in the late eighteenth- and early nineteenth-century United States, there is an emphasis on this theme of humility and a God who drank "a little breastmilk" at "Mary's knees thy table." See Jeremy Taylor, *The Life of Our Blessed Saviour Jesus Christ* (1796), 22–23; Jeremy Taylor, *The Life of Our Blessed Saviour Jesus Christ* (1818), 28–30.

12 Arndt, *Paradisgärtlein*, 10–11. On the reception of Mary in early Protestantism, see Beth Kreitzer, *Reforming Mary: Changing Images of the Virgin Mary in Lutheran Sermons of the Sixteenth Century* (Oxford: Oxford University Press, 2005); Christine Peters, *Patterns of Piety: Women, Gender, and Religion in Late Medieval and Reformation England* (Cambridge: Cambridge University Press, 2003), 224.

13 Mather, *Elizabeth in Her Holy Retirement*, 4–7, 16, 19–20.

14 John Cotton, *Milk for Babes: Drawn Out of the Breasts of Both Testaments* (London: Coe, 1646); Paul Royster, "A Note on the Text," *Milk for Babes* (Electronic Texts in American Studies, Paper 18, http://digitalcommons.unl.edu, DigitalCommons@University of Nebraska, Lincoln). Note: Cotton's catechism also appeared under the title *Spiritual Milk for Boston Babes*.

15 Philipp Adolph von Münchhausen, *Geistliche Kinder-Milch, Oder Einfältiger Christen Hauß-Apotheck, Daraus das himmlische Manna und die heilsame Artzney der Seelen fürgetragen wird* (Franckfurt am Mayn: Gensch, 1710); the earliest version of this tract that I have found dates to 1676, although it has similarities to Münchhausen's *HaussBuch* from 1652. Parts of this tract were republished in *Geistliches Magazin*, a popular Pietist periodical that published reports from renewal movements around the world. See Philipp Adolph von Münchhausen, "Zwo Betrachtungen über 1 Tim. 1, 5. und über Joh. 16 gezogen aus des Wohlseligen Herrn Geheimen-Rath von Münchhausen erbaulichen Wercke: Geistliche Kinder-Milch," *Geistliches Magazin* 2 (1764): 116–187.

16 John Cotton, *Milk for Babes* (1646).

17 Münchhausen, *Geistliche Kinder-Milch*, 1.

18 Mather, *Elizabeth in Her Holy Retirement*, 4–7, 16, 19–20.

19 Arndt, *Paradisgärtlein*, 57–58; following translation in the 1716 English edition: John Arndt, *The Garden of Paradise: Or Holy Prayers and Exercise* (London: J. Downing, 1716), 70–71.

20 Mather, *Elizabeth in Her Holy Retirement*, 9, 13.

21 Arndt, *Paradisgärtlein*, 57–58.

22 Ibid., 57–58; following English translation in Arndt, *Garden of Paradise*, 69; Mather, *Elizabeth in Her Holy Retirement*, 16, 21–22; cf. 1 Timothy 2:15. Cf. William Smellie, *A Treatise on the Theory and Practice of Midwifery*, 5th ed. (London: Wilson, 1766), 396; Valentine Seaman, *The Midwives Monitor, and Mothers Mirror: Being Three Concluding Lectures of a Course of Instruction on Midwifery* (New York: Collins, 1800), 76; James McClurg, "Notes on Young's Course on Midwifery, University of Edinburgh" (1769), manuscript notes, Joseph Lyon Miller Papers, 1610–1964, sec. 3, Virginia Historical Society.

23 Arndt, *Paradisgärtlein*, 57–58; cf. Arndt, *Garden of Paradise*, 70–71; on intimacy and the study of religion, see Constance M. Furey, "Body, Society, and Subjectivity in Religious Studies," *Journal of the American Academy of Religion* 80 (2012): 7–33.

24 Sarah Rhoads, "Some Account of My Beloved Daughters," Samuel W. Fisher Collection, HSP. For a helpful introduction to the commonplace book in revolutionary America and its significance among Quaker women, see the editors' preface and introductions in Catherine La Courreye Blecki and Karin A. Wulf, eds., *Milcah Martha Moore's Book: A Commonplace Book from Revolutionary America* (University Park: Pennsylvania State University Press, 2007).

25 Rhoads, "Some Account of My Beloved Daughters."

26 Ibid.

27 Sarah Logan Fisher Diaries, vol. 10, 10 Sept. 1780–31 Dec. 1781, HSP; cf. Norton, *Liberty's Daughters*, 80–83; Klepp, "Revolutionary Bodies," 923.

28 Abigail Adams to John Adams, 9 July 1777, 10 July 1777, 16 July 1777, and 23 July 1777; John Adams to Abigail Adams, 28 July 1777; Adams Family Correspondence, vol. 2, *Adams Papers Digital Edition* (Massachusetts Historical Society): www.masshist.org. See also the discussion of Abigail Adams and providence in Sara Georgini, *Household Gods: The Religious Lives of the Adams Family* (Oxford: Oxford University Press, 2019), 24–25.

29 Ebenezer Parkman, "Memoir of Mrs. Sarah Pierpont," Parkman Family Papers, box 2, folder 4, AAS. This memoir contains fragments of Pierpont's journals. Abigail Adams to John Adams, 9 Oct. 1775, in *Familiar Letters of John Adams and Abigail Adams during the Revolution*, ed. Charles Francis Adams (New York: Hurd & Houghton, 1876), 105–107. As Constance Furey has argued, "The study of religion necessarily involves understanding how people configure themselves in intimate relationships such as friendship, marriage, kinship alliances, or erotic unions." Furey, "Body, Society, and Subjectivity," 24.

30 Phyllis Mack, *Heart Religion in the British Enlightenment: Gender and Emotion in Early Methodism* (Cambridge: Cambridge University Press, 2008), 205–218; cf. Phyllis Mack, "Religious Dissenters in Enlightenment England," *History Workshop Journal* 49 (2000): 1–24. Wesley's letter to Clarke is quoted in Mack, *Heart Religion*, 209.

31 Mack, *Heart Religion*, 205–218.

32 Catherine A. Brekus, *Sarah Osborn's World: The Rise of Evangelical Christianity in Early America* (New Haven, CT: Yale University Press, 2013), 152–167.

33 Jager, *Book of God*, 2–4, 12–13. Jager argues that in the eighteenth century, "for the great majority of British intellectuals, science and theology were mutually informing means of investigating God's world" (2).

34 Jeremy Taylor, *Great Exemplar*, 33–40.

35 Ibid., 33–40.

36 On Galen and "provident nature," see Rebecca Flemming, "The Pathology of Pregnancy in Galen's Commentaries on the 'Epidemics,'" *Bulletin of the Institute of Classical Studies* 77 (2002): 101–112.

37 James E. Force, "Hume and the Relation of Science to Religion among Certain Members of the Royal Society," *Journal of the History of Ideas* 45 (1984): 517–536. For an example of this work of relating providence and mechanism—and its relationship to maternity—see John Arbuthnott, "An Argument for Divine Providence, Taken from the Constant Regularity Observ'd in the Births of Both Sexes," *Philosophical Transactions (1683–1775)* 27 (1710–1712): 186–190. For a wonderful discussion of the variety of Christian discourse on female piety and nursing among sixteenth- and seventeenth-century Catholics and Protestants, see Caroline McManus, "The 'Carefull Nourse': Female Piety in Spenser's Legend of Holiness," *Huntington Library Quarterly* 60 (1997): 381–406. On the diffuse ways in which the word "Nature" or phrases like "laws of nature" were meant and interpreted in seventeenth- and eighteenth-century England, see J. C. D. Clark, "Providence, Predestination and Progress: or, Did the Enlightenment Fail?," *Albion* 35 (2003): 569.

38 Bloch, *Gender and Morality in Anglo-American Culture*, 66; Clark, "Providence, Predestination and Progress," 567–569; cf. Lorraine Daston, "Marvelous Facts and Miraculous Evidence in Early Modern Europe," *Critical Inquiry* 18 (1991): 112–113.

39 Hendrik van Deventer, *The Art of Midwifery Improv'd* (London: Bettesworth, Innys, & Pemberton, 1728), preface. Note that Deventer is misspelled (Daventer) on the title page.

40 John Allen, *Synopsis Medicinæ: or, A Summary View of the Whole Practice of Physick*, 3rd ed. (London: Innys, Meadows Manby, and Cox, 1749), 1:259–260.

41 Smellie, *Treatise on the Theory and Practice of Midwifery*, preface, ii–lxii; on cases in which Smellie recommended and used instruments, see vol. 3. On the "machine," see Brandy Shillace, "Mother Machine: An 'Uncanny Valley' in the Eighteenth Century," *Appendix*, 15 May 2013, http://theappendix.net. On Smellie and anatomical plates, see Carin Berkowitz, "The Illustrious Anatomist: Authorship, Patronage, and Illustrative Style in Anatomy Folios, 1700–1840," *Bulletin of the History of Medicine* 89 (2015): 171–208.

42 Smellie, *Treatise on the Theory and Practice of Midwifery*, ii–lxii, 184–191, 372–376; on cases in which Smellie recommended and used instruments, see vol. 3. For a contemporary critique of Smellie, see *Man-Midwifery Analysed: And the Tendency of That Practice Detected and Exposed* (London: R. Davis, 1764), 2–3, 10–11.

43 *Man-Midwifery Analysed*, 2–3, 10–11.

44 Ibid., 3–5, 7–12, 17–18.

45 Jean-Louis Baudelocque, *A System of Midwifery*, trans. John Heath (London: Parkinson, 1790), advertisement.

46 Ibid.; on Christian views of medicine in this era, see chapter 3; cf. Philippa Koch, "Experience and the Soul in Eighteenth-Century Medicine," *Church History: Studies in Christianity and Culture* 85 (2016): 552–586.

47 "Preternatural, adj. and n.," *Oxford English Dictionary Online* (Oxford: Oxford University Press, 2019), https://oed.com.

48 Seaman, *Midwives Monitor*, iii–ix.

49 Ibid., ix–x, 13–14, 18–19, 42–43.

50 Ibid., iv–vi, 121–122.

51 Taylor, *Great Exemplar*, 31–33. In an interesting historical twist, the wife of Charles Francis Adams, who had found Taylor's discourse on nursing displeasing, would resort to a puppy when she encountered difficulty nursing. Charles Francis Adams, diary entry, 20 Dec. 1829, in *Diary*, vol. 3; see also the first note accompanying Charles Francis Adams, diary entry, 16 Aug. 1831, in *Diary*, vol. 4.

52 Theodore Mayern, Thomas Chamberlain, and Nicholas Culpeper, *The Compleat Midwife's Practice Enlarged* (London, 1698), 91.

53 Doyle argues that by the eighteenth century women understood the practical benefits of nursing their own children as well as the "symbolic" significance: "Breastfeeding had become perhaps the single most important way to demonstrate maternal virtue and dedication." Doyle, *Maternal Bodies*, 115–116. See also Mary Fissell, who argues that "talking about sex is always talking about gender, in the sense that scientific or medical knowledge is always made in a social context." Fissell, *Vernacular Bodies*, 13.

54 Mayern, Chamberlain, and Culpeper, *Compleat Midwife's Practice*, 93; Baudelocque, *System of Midwifery*, 302–304; Cotton Mather, *Angel of Bethesda* (Barre, MA: American Antiquarian Society, 1972), 32; Mather, *Elizabeth in Her Holy Retirement*, 3–4, 35; William Cadogan, *An Essay upon Nursing, and the Management of Children, from Their Birth to Three Years of Age* (London: J. Roberts, 1748), 23–27.

55 Baudelocque, *System of Midwifery*, 444–449; Smellie, *Treatise on the Theory and Practice of Midwifery*, 420; Seaman, *Midwives Monitor*, 116; Cadogan, *Essay upon Nursing*, 11, 13–15; Howard Horton, *An Improved System of Botanic Medicine*, 3rd ed. (Columbus, OH: Howard, 1836), 28–29. On barrenness and lactation, Horton shares the advice of "Dr. Ewell."

56 Cadogan, *Essay upon Nursing*; Nora Doyle, "'The Highest Pleasure of Which Woman's Nature is Capable': Breast-Feeding and the Sentimental Maternal Ideal

in America, 1750–1860," *Journal of American History* 97 (2011): 958–973; Nora
Doyle, "Bodies at Odds: The Maternal Body as Lived Experience and Cultural Expression in America, 1750–1850" (PhD diss., University of North Carolina, Chapel
Hill, 2013); Doyle, *Maternal Bodies*; Marylynn Salmon, "The Cultural Significance
of Breastfeeding and Infant Care in Early Modern England and America," *Journal
of Social History* 28 (1994): 247–269; John Rendle-Short, "William Cadogan,
Eighteenth-Century Physician," *Medical History* 34 (1960): 288–309; Roy Porter
and G. S. Rousseau, *Gout: The Patrician Malady* (New Haven, CT: Yale University
Press, 1998); Peter M. Dunn, "Dr. William Cadogan of Bristol (1711–1797): Father
of Infant Care in Britain," *West of England Medical Journal* 112 (Sept. 2013): 1–4.

57 Cadogan, *Essay upon Nursing*, 3–4, 11, 13–15. As Jason Josephson-Storm argues, both
religion and science set themselves up against "superstition" in the modern world.
Jason Ā. Josephson-Storm, *The Myth of Disenchantment: Magic, Modernity, and the
Birth of the Human Sciences* (Chicago: University of Chicago Press, 2016), 14–15.

58 Cadogan, *Essay upon Nursing*, 3–4, 7, 23–27; Mather, *Elizabeth in Her Holy
Retirement*, 3–4, 35; cf. Smellie, *Treatise on the Theory and Practice of Midwifery*,
430–431; Baudelocque, *System of Midwifery*, 437–438; Hugh Smith, *Letters to Married Women, On Nursing and the Management of Children*, 6th ed. (Philadelphia:
Carey, 1792), 55–61; Roy Porter, *Flesh in the Age of Reason* (New York: Norton,
2003), 238–243. See also Kerber's discussion of Montesquieu's critique of luxury:
Kerber, *Women of the Republic*, 19.

59 Mather, *Angel of Bethesda* (1972), 32; Mather, *Elizabeth in Her Holy Retirement*,
3–4, 35. Mather's writings imply that there were women in his community who
did not breastfeed. According to Mary Beth Norton, the majority of eighteenth-
century American women did breastfeed their own children. Norton, *Liberty's
Daughters*, 90.

60 Cadogan, *Essay upon Nursing*, 3–4, 7.

61 Morgan, *Laboring Women*, 36–49. Cf. Nora Doyle, *Maternal Bodies*, 131–135.

62 Taylor, *Great Exemplar*, 31.

63 Anne Cannon Palumbo, "Averting 'Present Commotions': History as Politics in
'Penn's Treaty,'" *American Art* 9 (1995): 28–55. On debates over women, motherhood, virtue, and politics in the colonial world, see in particular Linda Kerber's
discussion of Hobbes, Montesquieu, Rousseau, and Kames in Kerber, *Women of
the Republic*, 16–27.

64 Mayern, Chamberlain, and Culpeper, *Compleat Midwife's Practice*, 153–154; Johann
Christian Stark, *Hebammenunterricht in Gesprächen* (Jena, 1782), 202–204; Baudelocque, *System of Midwifery*, 446–453; Smellie, *Treatise on the Theory and Practice
of Midwifery*, 448; Jane Sharpe, *The Midwives Book: Or the Whole Art of Midwifry
Discovered*, ed. Elaine Hobby (Oxford: Oxford University Press, 1999), 266–267;
cf. Matthew 7:16–20.

65 Doyle, *Maternal Bodies*, 137; Fissell, *Vernacular Bodies*, chap. 2. Sharpe's *Midwives Book* borrowed liberally from other sources, and it is not entirely certain
if Sharpe was a pseudonym. See Mary Elizabeth Fissell, "The Midwives Book

or the Whole Art of Midwifery Discovered (review)," *NWSA Journal* 13 (2001): 199–200.

66 See, for example, Elizabeth Rhoads Fisher to Samuel Fisher, 10 Sept. 1793 and 17 Oct. 1793, Samuel W. Fisher Papers, HSP; Mary Smith Cranch to Abigail Adams, 24 Dec. 1797, and Abigail Adams to Esther Duncan Black, 15 Apr. 1798, Adams Family Correspondence, vol. 12, *Adams Papers Digital Edition* (Massachusetts Historical Society): www.masshist.org.

67 Christian Friedrich Pressier to GAF, 5 Dec. 1733, AFSt/M 1 B 18: 1.

68 Ibid.

69 Ibid.

70 Juncker did acknowledge some cases that might "free the mother from the burden of lactation," including a lack of milk, high fever, venereal infection, and breast cancer. He offered options for women suffering from these cases. Johann Juncker, Anmerkungen zu einem Brief von Christian Friedrich Pressier, AFSt/M 1B 18:2. Translation mine.

71 Christian Friedrich Pressier to GAF, 5 Dec. 1733, AFSt/M 1B 18: 1. Johann Juncker, Anmerkungen zu einem Brief von Christian Friedrich Pressier, AFSt/M 1 B 18:2. Translation mine. Cf. A. G. Roeber, *Hopes for Better Spouses: Protestant Marriage and Church Renewal in Early Modern Europe, India, and North America* (Grand Rapids, MI: Eerdmans, 2013), 138–139. On the German-Danish-English network of missionaries, naturalists, and physicians who corresponded extensively about religion and scientific inquiries both among each other and with major European universities and medical schools, see Niklas Thode Jensen, "Making It in Tranquebar: The Circulation of Scientific Knowledge in the Early Danish-Halle Mission," in *Beyond Tranquebar: Grappling across Cultural Borders in South India*, ed. Esther Fihl and A. R. Venkatachalapathy (New Delhi: Orient BlackSwan, 2014), 325–351; Will Sweetman, "Unity and Plurality: Hinduism and the Religions of India in Early European Scholarship," in *Defining Hinduism: A Reader*, ed. J. E. Llewellyn (London: Equinox, 2005), 81–99.

72 See, for example, the description of a small child, found drowned and alone. The missionaries reported that "the Mother of the child stood by without any feeling." *Acht und neunzigste Continuation Des Berichts Der Königlich=Dänischen Missionarien in Ost=Indien* (Halle: in Verlegung des Wäysenhauses, 1765), 165–166.

73 Sharpe, *Midwives Book*, 264–265; Nicholas Culpeper, *A Directory for Midwives* (London, 1693), 146–147; Taylor, *Great Exemplar*, 31–33.

74 Cadogan, *Essay upon Nursing*, 6. For similar attitudes in the German context, see Stark, *Hebammenunterricht in Gesprächen*, 12. Cf. Smith, *Letters to Married Women*, 55–61.

75 Taylor, *Great Exemplar*, 34; Kerber, *Women of the Republic*, 7–12, 31; Georgini, *Household Gods*, 29–30, 34.

EPILOGUE

1 Connie Willis, *Doomsday Book* (New York: Bantam Books, 1992), 451.

INDEX

Adams, Abigail, 168–69
Adams, Charles Francis, 160, 251n51
Adams, John Quincy, 168
Allen, John, 175
Allen, Richard, 122, 139–46, 152, 195, 238n8
Arminianism, 5, 92–93, 112, 205n11
Arndt, Johann, 29, 157, 161, 164–65
Asbury, Francis, 58–60, 110, 117–18
Augsburg, Germany, 37–38, 215n42

Bacon, Francis, 91
Ballantine, John, 70–71, 79–80, 223n34;
    death of Abigail Fowler, 71
Baudelocque, Jean-Louis, 177–78, 183–84
Belknap, Jeremy, 78
benevolence, 17–18; as affection, 129; "be-
    nevolent empire," 151; of black workers,
    142–43; breakdown in, 127, 129; caring
    for orphans, 126, 133–34, 180; Christian,
    95, 101–2, 143; doing good, 123, 152; dis-
    interested, 123; duty of, 124, 126, 129, 141;
    economic self-interest and, 143; Enlight-
    enment story of, 122; as God's will, 95;
    God as, 77, 82, 126; medicine as, 102, 120,
    143; form of mission, 102, 119; motiva-
    tions for, 124; as natural instinct, 124–26;
    philosophical understanding of, 137;
    reward for, 124, 152; salvific significance,
    152; scholarship on, 122, 152; skeptics, 123;
    thwarted by fear, 125; virtue of, 123, 129
Bloch, Ruth, 174
bloodletting, 91, 105, 108
Boerhaave, Herman, 115
Boltzius, Gertraud, 75, 107–8, 233n51,
    233nn54, 55

Boltzius, Johann Martin: children of,
    109; death of children, 52, 109; dis-
    satisfied with Christian Thilo, 93,
    103–5, 107–8, 119; fever in Ebenezer,
    69; healthy body and soul, 90, 109;
    hospital aspirations, 109–10; humoral
    medicine, 108; journal of, 53, 62, 89;
    letters of, 75, 87, 104, 106–8; malaria
    in Ebenezer, 104; medical interven-
    tion, 102, 108, 110; narrating sickness,
    52–53, 69, 76, 107; personal and com-
    munal suffering, 62, 69, 87; "Rothe
    Friesel" epidemic, 52, 108; spiritual
    significance of medicine, 102, 109;
    use of Tobit, 69; use of women's
    knowledge, 106, 108. See also Boltzius,
    Gertraud; pica
Boston: inoculation in, 93, 105, 206n14;
    smallpox epidemic (1702–1721), 26,
    43, 45
Bowler, Kate, 14–15, 203n13
Boylston, Zabdiel, 94
breastfeeding. See nursing
Brekus, Catherine, 63, 77, 170, 220n10,
    222n23
Brown, John, 123
Bunyan, John, 48
Bynum, Caroline Walker, 157

Cadogan, William, 184–86, 190–91
Calvin, John, 3, 30; Calvinism, 4–5, 92;
    distinguishing Methodism from
    Calvinism, 112, 117; election, 3, 46; New
    Divinity Movement, 83; predestination,
    3–5, 27, 93

ABOUT THE AUTHOR

PHILIPPA KOCH is Assistant Professor in the Department of Religious Studies at Missouri State University. She received her PhD from the University of Chicago Divinity School. She researches and teaches in the areas of religion, medicine, and sexuality in American history.